Ya Gotta Know It!

A Conversational Approach to American Slang for the ESL Classroom

Hania Hassan

Optima Books

Berkeley, California

Cover and illustrations: Nobuaki Tasaka

Optima Books
2820 Eighth Street
Berkeley, California 94710

ISBN 1-879440-27-X

First printing 2000

Printed in the United States of America

Acknowledgments

I would like to thank Yoko, Yoshihiro and Hisayoshi Charlie Kinemura for graciously providing me with peaceful and inspiring work spaces; without them I could not have written this book. I would like to thank Nobuaki Tasaka for making the characters and stories come to life on paper. In addition, I would like to thank Hisayoshi for his intercontinental translating of the numerous stories; without this the existing artwork would not have been possible. I would also like to thank Kazumi Ishiwa and Tomomi Chigano for the Friday afternoons spent in Mama's Kitchen in Shinjuku, inspiring me to write more by enthusiastically testing out what I had written. I would like to thank the staff of EF Language School in San Diego, Rich McGuirre, and Anthony Field, for allowing me to use <u>Ya Gotta Know It!</u> as the slang text at the school. Furthermore, I would like to thank all of the EF students for their enthusiasm and good eyes. Lastly, I would like to thank the students at Diversified Language Institute in San Diego for inspiring me to take on the enormous task of writing a book on American slang.

Dedication

This book is for my father and mother, Dr. Ata and Najdah Hassan, whose unconditional support has always been there to catch me when I fall and lift me up to higher places.

Introduction

Many ESL students are under the impression that slang is obscene language or is used only by the young or uneducated. In fact, most slang is inoffensive and is an integral and indispensable part of American English. Ya Gotta Know It! is a fun, new way for advanced and high-intermediate ESL students to tackle this often confusing, but vital part of the American lexicon. The terms and phrases introduced in this book will be seen in newspapers and magazines, and heard in everyday conversations, movies, songs, and TV.

Ya Gotta Know It! uses a series of thirty short dialogues to tell a story about four twenty-something main characters (the typical age group for ESL students). These true-to-life dialogues help illustrate present-day American culture (an invaluable aid when learning American English) and enable the student to deduce the meaning of new vocabulary from context, thus encouraging the development of language learning skills.

ESL students at the advanced and high-intermediate levels know more about English grammar than most Americans do, yet still find communication difficult. Rather than burdening the student with lengthy definitions and tedious grammatical explanations, Ya Gotta Know It! uses successful classroom-tested, spill-your-guts follow-up questions to help students develop speaking familiarity with each new vocabulary term. As comprehension and appreciation for proper context improve, students gain both the confidence needed for participating in daily slang-riddled conversations and overcome some of the shyness inherent in learning a new language. In addition, the developing story serves as a student's reference that aids recall of slang terms and their meanings, and provides usage examples appropriate to a particular social context. After completion of this book, the student will have a firm grasp on American slang.

How To Use This Book

Ya Gotta Know It! is arranged in ten units composed of three lessons each. Each lesson introduces twenty to twenty-five new slang terms and expressions. A crossword puzzle review concludes each unit.

Lessons are divided into five sections:

1. Section one starts with warm-up questions (in Standard English) that are directly related to the dialogue and intended for student discussion, either in pairs or as a group.

2. The second section begins with a short, natural dialogue that introduces twenty to twenty-five new examples of slang, typical of what might be encountered in daily experience. The appropriate section of the optional CD or audiocassette tape can be played at this point. The conversation will be heard at normal speed, with natural rhythm and intonation patterns. If the optional audio is not available, the ESL instructor should read the conversation to the students with the proper intonation and speed. The students then separate into pairs, read the dialogues to each other, and attempt to determine the meaning of the new vocabulary from context. As the story develops, the dialogues become progressively more difficult. Slang from previous lessons is included, along with the occasional unfamiliar term to be covered in a subsequent lesson.

3. In section three, students are presented with a challenging exercise that requires them to match each boldface slang term from the dialogue with its corresponding definition in Standard English. Labels (verb, noun, etc.) are provided with each term, indicating their grammatical function in the dialogue. Students use these clues along with context information from the dialogue to complete the exercise. Those who need more information about a particular term can refer to the dictionary at the back of the book which includes complete definitions, sample sentences, and grammar and usage notes.

4. In the fourth section, students develop a speaking familiarity with the new vocabulary by using it in conversation. A series of questions incorporating the new slang is directed at the students, giving them an opportunity to learn about their classmates, teacher, and other cultures (including American). As students use the slang to relate their personal story, it finds a permanent place in their language database, and recalling new terms becomes easier and more natural.

5. In the fifth and last section, students are asked to use the new slang vocabulary in a variety of writing exercises. These vary from individual story writing with a provided topic, to the writing of comical conversations that follow the theme of the dialogue from the lesson. Students can be given more grammatical guidance at this point, as they are now quite familiar with the meaning of the terms.

<u>Ya</u> <u>Gotta</u> <u>Know</u> <u>It</u>! also features a helpful section that included common examples of the relaxed speech (elision) so characteristic of American speakers, a Verb Tense Chart for all verbs, and a Dictionary that lists all of the slang terms and expressions introduced in the dialogues.

<u>Ya</u> <u>Gotta</u> <u>Know</u> <u>It</u>! takes a lighthearted and informal approach to slang. It may be used on its own as a complete, advanced ESL course in slang or to supplement other teaching materials. Even though there is a story line that runs throughout the book, <u>Ya</u> <u>Gotta</u> <u>Know</u> <u>It</u>! is also a conversational book. Any unit or lesson will stand on its own and can really help to liven up a routine day in the ESL classroom. The book is both student and teacher-friendly and is an indispensable component in the ESL students' backpack and the ESL teachers' library.

Table of Contents

Mona   Vic

Renee   Charlie

"We Go Way Back"

1. What *do people* in your native country usually *do after work or school? What do you usually do?*

2. How *do men and women usually meet each other for the first time in your country? Through friends or relatives? At school? At bars? Clubs?*

3. When *going out with friends in your native country, how is it decided who will pay the bill?*

Two friends, a high-school teacher named Charlie, and Vic, a stockbroker, are meeting at a bar for a drink after work. Charlie sees an old friend, Mona. Vic doesn't realize that Charlie knows Mona...

VIC: Man, I'm **beat**! It was a **zoo** at work today! How about you? How was your day?

CHARLIE: **No sweat**! My day was a **breeze**! The students have exams this week, so I got to **take it easy**. However, this weekend is another story.

WAITRESS: What can I get for you guys?

CHARLIE: I'll have a **brewskie**.

VIC: Make that two. Miss, could you **run a tab** for us?

WAITRESS: No problem. I just need some **plastic**.

VIC: This one's **on me**. You got it last time. Wow! Don't look now, but those two **hot chicks** are **heading** our way!

CHARLIE: Don't **let it go to your head**, I know the one on the right. We **go way back**, so don't go trying to **pick her up**! Besides, I hate to **burst your bubble**, but she's **way out of your league** dude!

VIC: **Get out of town**! You know someone that looks like that and you haven't told me about her? She's a **knockout**! **What's up with that**?

CHARLIE: Nothing. We're just pals from high school. Let me introduce you. Hey Mona, **what's up**? I'd like to introduce you to my friend Vic. Vic, this is Mona.

MONA: Nice to meet you.

RENEE: I'm Renee.

CHARLIE: I see you guys are empty handed, would you care for a drink?

MONA: We're fine. The waitress already got our order. So, **what brings you to this neck of the woods**? You don't work around here, do you?

CHARLIE: Nope. I came by to meet Vic, he works across the street. So Mona, **long time, no see**. What's up?

MONA: Well, I just finished my Masters degree.

Grab yourself a partner and get those brains in gear! Match up each term in the left column with its definition from the right column. If you need a hand, look back at the conversation or ask your teacher for help. (answers on page 141)

1. **beat** adj_____

2. **zoo** noun_____

3. **no sweat** exp_____

4. **breeze** noun_____

5. **take it easy** verb_____

6. **brewskie** noun_____

7. **run a tab** verb_____

8. **plastic** noun_____

9. **on someone** verb_____

10. **hot** adj_____

11. **chick** noun_____

12. **head** verb_____

13. **let something go to one's head** verb_____

14. **go way back** verb_____

15. **pick up** verb_____

16. **burst someone's bubble** verb_____

17. **way** adv_____

18. **out of one's league** adj_____

19. **get out of town** exp_____

20. **knockout** noun_____

21. **what's up with that?** exp_____

22. **what's up?** exp_____

23. **what brings you to this neck of the woods?** exp_____

24. **long time, no see** exp_____

A. a very attractive woman

B. "I don't believe you!"

C. "hello"

D. a beer

E. exhausted

F. anything easily accomplished

G. to be in a superior class or category

H. "why is it that way?"

I. a credit card

J. to bring someone down to reality

K. to make a casual acquaintance with someone in anticipation of sex

L. young woman

M. to relax

N. "I haven't seen you for so long!"

O. "no problem"

P. really, much

Q. attractive

R. "why are you in this area?"

S. to come or go towards

T. to be responsible for the bill

U. to have known someone for a long time

V. a busy or chaotic place

W. to keep a record of expenses to be paid at the end of the evening

X. to become vain or conceited

TALKING TIME!

Hook up with a partner and ask each other the following questions. Use as many of the new terms as you can in your answers. While you may not use slang this much in daily conversation, this is the time to make it stick in your head! Go crazy and yap your heads off!

1. Name a person that you **go way back** with? When did you meet? Tell an interesting story that happened to the two of you a long time ago.

2. What do you do when you want to **take it easy**? When was the last time you did it?

3. In your native country, can you **run a tab**? If yes, is it common? Have you **run a tab** since coming to the US? Where? When? How much did it come out to?

4. Is **plastic** common in your native country? Why or why not?

5. When was the last time you said "The bill is **on me**?" Who were you with? Why did you decide to treat them? How about the last time you were told "The bill is **on me**?" Why did they decide to treat you?

6. Who's a **hot** actress or actor in your native country? Would they be considered **hot** in the US? Why or why not?

7. Guys, have you tried to **pick up** any American **chicks** since you came here? Have any American **chicks** tried to **pick** you **up**? How? OK, girls, now its your turn. Have you tried to **pick up** any American guys, or have any American guys tried to **pick** you **up** since you came here?

8. If the teacher tells you that you are their best student, do you **let it go to your head** and look down on the other students, or do you continue to be your modest self? When you were a kid and something **went to your head**, who was the person who usually **burst your bubble**?

9. What subject was a **breeze** for you in high school? Was Lesson One, "We Go Way Back", a **breeze** for you?

10. Do department stores turn into **zoos** when there's a big sale in your country? How about when there is a big sporting event? Tell your partner about such an experience.

11. Now, answer this question: are you **beat**, or are you ready to stuff your brains with more slang?

WRITING TIME!

Let's see how much you can remember! Hook up with a new partner and jot down what happened in the dialogue for Lesson One, using as much slang as you can remember. Come on, get those pencils out and moving!

"We're Roomies"

1. What is the living situation for young single people in your native country? Do they usually live with their parents until they are married? If they move out of their parents' house, do they live alone or do they have roommates? Ask your teacher about the US.

2. How is schooling paid for in your native country? By the parents? The students? The government? Bank loans? Scholarships? Ask your teacher about the US.

3. What's the highest university degree that one can attain in your native country? What stages must one go through to receive such a degree? Ask your teacher about the US.

Charlie and Mona haven't seen each other in a long time, so they are **catching up on** what they have been up to in their lives…

CHARLIE: So you completed your Master's! **Get out of here**! **Way to go**!

MONA: Thanks, but I've still got a long way to go. Now comes the tough part, the PhD.

CHARLIE: Still the **brain** you were in high school! This calls for a celebration!

VIC: **What do you say** we have some **bubbly**?

MONA: That's really nice of you, but I'll have to **pass**. I've got to be up **at the crack of dawn** tomorrow. How about a rain check?

VIC: You tell me when and I'll be there – **scouts honor**.

CHARLIE: Don't mind him. He's a little **toasted**, so he comes on a bit strong. So, how do you guys know each other?

RENEE: Mona and I are **roomies**.

CHARLIE: Really? I didn't know you had a roomie!

MONA: Well, I was getting **in over my head** with student loans. It seemed I was always **broke** and could barely afford my rent. I figured the only way to **make ends meet** was to cut my living expenses and find someone to **chip in on** rent and bills. I was lucky to **end up with** a roomie like Renee.

VIC: I hate to **butt in**, but do you guys think I could get a word in edgewise with this beautiful lady? I mean, you're killing me here!

MONA: Well, you don't **beat around the bush**, do you?

CHARLIE: He's **had his eye on** you since you **came up to** us. He **was all like** "What? You know someone who looks like that and you never told me?" Go for it Vic. I'm heading to the **john**.

Time to rack your brains! Find yourself a partner and match each term in the left column with its definition in the right column. (answers on page 141)

1. **catch up on** verb_____

2. **get out of here** exp_____

3. **way to go** exp_____

4. **brain** noun_____

5. **what do you say?** exp_____

6. **bubbly** noun_____

7. **pass** verb_____

8. **at the crack of dawn** adv _____

9. **scouts honor** exp_____

10. **toasted** adj_____

11. **roomie** noun_____

12. **in over one's head** adj_____

13. **broke** adj_____

14. **make ends meet** verb_____

15. **chip in on** verb_____

16. **end up with** verb_____

17. **butt in** verb_____

18. **beat around the bush** verb_____

19. **have one's eye on** verb_____

20. **come up to** verb_____

21. **be all like** verb_____

22. **john** noun_____

A. to have no money

B. to have enough money to cover expenses

C. "I promise"

D. champagne

E. a roommate

F. to get up-to-date

G. the restroom

H. to interrupt

I. very early in the morning

J. to share the cost

K. "would you consider?" , "how about?"

L. to approach

M. to watch with great interest

N. to say something indirectly

O. "good job!"

P. to decline an offer

Q. overwhelmed by obligations

R. to say

S. "I don't believe you!"

T. drunk, intoxicated

U. an intelligent person

V. to reach an outcome

TALK IT OUT!

Time to flap your lips and get them moving. The best way to remember the slang terms is to associate them with your own experiences. First, hook up with a partner, then talk, talk, talk your heads off! Don't space on using the new slang in your answers.

1. Who was the **brain** in your high school class? Your family? Tell your partner how brainy that person was and what he or she is up to now.

2. When you go back to your native country what's the first thing you'll **catch up on** with your friends? Their school life? Love life? Have you been keeping up with international current events while you've been living in the US or do you feel like you'll have to **catch up on** them when you go back home? How about new music in your country?

3. When you were a student in your country, were you usually **broke**, as most American students are? How about now? Are you having a hard time **making ends meet**? Why or why not?

4. If you wanted to break up with your boyfriend/girlfriend, would you **beat around the bush** or come straight out with it?

5. Is there anyone or anything you **have your eye on**? Is there something you really want that you may not be able to have?

6. Have you ever **butt in** on a conversation? Is it OK to **butt in** on a conversation in your native culture? A line? A dance? What is the reaction if someone **butts in**? Ask your teacher about the US.

7. Listen to what the person next to you is saying. Now tell your partner about it using "He/ She **was all like**..."

8. Do you have a **roomie**? Were you lucky or unlucky to **end up with** this person?

9. Have you gotten **toasted** in the US yet, or do you usually **pass** on alcohol? Who were you hanging out with? How did you get home? Do you get **toasted** often?

10. Who was the last person to **come up to** you and ask you something in English? What did they ask? How did you reply? Use both **be all like** and **come up to** in your answer.

11. Have you ever been in a situation (at work or school, with your family or your boyfriend/ girlfriend) where you felt you were **in over your head**? Are you getting **in over your head** with slang? Not yet? Well hang on to your hats! There's a lot more in store!

WRITE IT UP!

Find yourself a new partner. One of you is the guy, and the other is the hot chick! The guy wants to find out more about this hot chick. Write down a conversation between them that will make your classmates crack up! When you finish, perform it for the class. Remember to use as much slang as possible in your conversation.

"What Line Of Work Are You In?"

1. Which would you choose; a high paying but stressful job, or an average-paying job with no stress?

2. What are some professions in your native country that are underpaid but highly respected? Well-paid but not highly respected? Well-paid and highly respected?

3. In you native country, is it acceptable to ask a person of the opposite sex for their phone number immediately after first meeting them, or is it unheard of?

Now that Vic's buddy Charlie is in the john, Vic can finally get a word in edgewise with Mona...

MONA: So Vic, what line of work are you in?

VIC: Me? I'm a stockbroker.

MONA: Oh, a **suit**! Well you must be **raking in the dough**! As for me, I'm not **into** taking home a big paycheck. I couldn't **put up with** all of the stress **headaches** that come with it.

VIC: Getting your PhD is no **piece of cake**! I've got to **take my hat off to you**. I'm not exactly **rolling in dough**, though. I'm still just **getting my feet wet**. What's your field?

MONA: Psychiatry.

VIC: A **shrink**! You're going to be **hanging out with** the **nutcases** and raking in the dough!

MONA: We prefer the term "mentally unstable."

RENEE: Look, I hate to butt in and break up the party, but I've got to **hit the road**. Are you coming Mona?

MONA: That's my **ride**. I've got to go. Nice meeting you.

VIC: Why don't you stay a little longer. I can give you a **lift**.

MONA: Sorry, I've really got to go home and **crash**. Like I said, I've got to be up at the crack of dawn tomorrow.

VIC: Then, can I get your number? I'll give you a **ring**. Maybe we could go out for a **bite**.

MONA: Sure. It's 555-2323. **Catch you later**. Say 'bye to Charlie.

RENEE: Nice meeting you.

VIC: Same here.

Charlie returns from the john...

CHARLIE: Hey, what's up? Where did they go? Give me the **scoop**!

VIC: Well, I'm in. I got her number! She is **out of this world**!

CHARLIE: Way to go dude! She's a **tough cookie**. She never gives her number out. I can't believe you **pulled that off**!

This is no time to space out, so come back down to earth! Let's get cracking and match each slang term in the left column with its meaning in the right column. (answers on page 141)

1. **suit** noun_____

A. to enjoy, be interested

2. **rake in the dough** verb_____

B. a mentally unstable person

3. **be into** verb_____

C. transportation to one's destination

4. **put up with** verb_____

D. a telephone call

5. **headache** noun_____

E. something easily accomplished

6. **piece of cake** noun_____

F. to tolerate

7. **take one's hat off to** verb_____

G. "goodbye"

8. **rolling in dough** adj_____

H. a small, quick meal

9. **get one's feet wet** verb_____

I. to spend time with

10. **shrink** noun_____

J. to succeed at something difficult

11. **hang out with** verb_____

K. a psychiatrist

12. **nutcase** noun_____

L. to go to sleep

13. **hit the road** verb_____

M. a person with a strong character

14. **ride** noun_____

N. a businessperson

15. **lift** noun_____

O. to make a lot of money

16. **crash** verb_____

P. to leave

17. **ring** noun_____

Q. to begin to get experience

18. **bite** noun_____

R. wealthy

19. **catch you later** exp_____

S. a problem

20. **scoop** noun_____

T. exceptional, marvelous

21. **out of this world** adj_____

U. to express one's respect

22. **tough cookie** noun_____

V. gossip, current information, late breaking news

23. **pull off** verb_____

W. one's means of transportation

TALK IT UP!

Let's get this show on the road! Time to get your mouth moving and your lips flapping. If you and your partner were paying attention to the dialogue, this will be a breeze. Don't forget to use the new slang in your answers!

1. At what time do you usually **crash** on weekdays? How about on weekends? What time did you **crash** last night? How about your teacher?

2. Who do you **hang out with** on week nights? Do you **hang out with** the same people on weekends too? Where do you usually **hang out**?

3. Who was the last person you gave a **ring**? Who will give you a **ring** tonight? Tell your partner you'll call them tonight. Start by saying; "I'll give you a…"

4. Who was the last person you went out with for a **bite**? Was the food **out of this world**, or nothing to write home about?

5. What activity have you **been into** lately? Have you been doing it for a long time or are you just **getting your feet wet**?

6. What if your roomie smokes like a chimney? Would you **put up with** smoking? If not, how would you get rid of this **headache**?

7. Is it common for people to go to a **shrink** in your native country? Explain your answer. Get the **scoop** on **shrinks** in the US from your teacher.

8. Time warp ~ It's ten years from now! Is it important for you to be **rolling in dough**? Why or why not?

9. When class is over do you usually **hit the road** or **hang out** and talk with your pals from class?

10. Do you consider yourself to be a **tough cookie**? Do your friends think you are a **tough cookie**? Which one of your friends would you place in the **tough cookie** category? Why?

11. When you were in high school, what subject was a **piece of cake** for you? Was <u>Lesson</u> <u>Three</u> a **piece of cake**? Would it be a **piece of cake** to **pull off** cheating in your English class? Have you ever cheated on a test? Did you **pull** it **off** or did you get caught?

WRITE IT OUT!

What do you say you try some creative writing by yourself? Let's see what you can come up with. You can write about anything that pops into your head, or ask your teacher for a topic. Just be sure to use the slang from this lesson in your story or conversation.

CROSSWORD REVIEW

Way to go! You've survived <u>Unit One</u>, so let's see how much of a brain you really are. Try to complete the crossword from the clues on the following page without looking back at the lessons. If you're really thrown for a loop, go ahead and sneak a peek. Remember to pay attention to the correct verb tense and form. Good luck! (solution on page 141)

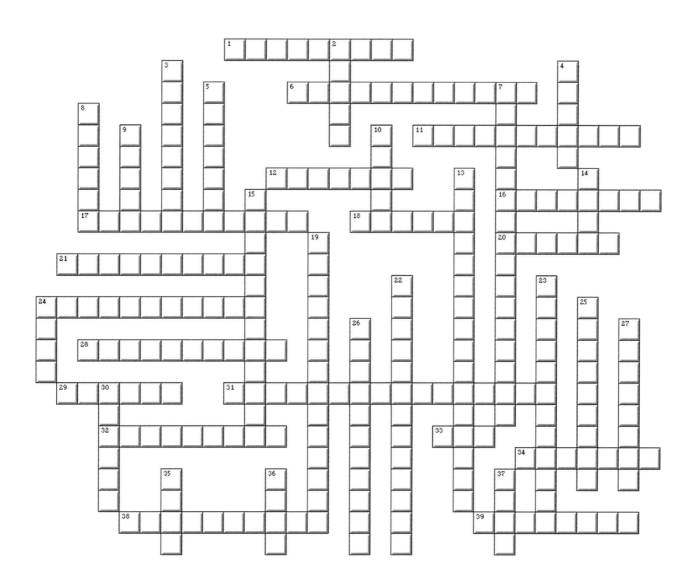

Across

1   Donna and I have known each other since high school. We __ ___ ____.

6   ____ __ ___ ___ we grab a bite to eat? How does pizza sound?

11 Trust me, I never lie! _____ ____!

12 Steve needed a lift home and his place is on my way so I said "Sure, __ _____."

16 Would you like to ____ __ __ a going-away present for our receptionist?

17 This puzzle is so easy! It's a _____ __ ____!

18 Paul has been a little depressed and confused lately so he's been going to see a _____.

20 I love going to the movies. I __ really ____ Sci-Fi flicks.

21 I told Bill to come over and he ___ ___ ____ "now? It's past midnight!"

24 That guy over there keeps looking at you! He really ___ ___ ___ ___ you!

28 After a really tough day at work Mark just wants to go home and ____ __ ____.

29 We got a case of _____ for the New Years party.

31 I've only been doing this job for a month. I'm just _____ __ ___ ___.

32 Mona was really lucky to ___ __ ____ a great roomie like Renee.

33 The parking lot at the mall is always a ___ around Christmas time.

34 Hey Mickey, long time, no see! _____ __?

38 It's getting late and we really should go. It's time to ___ __ ___.

39 That guy just ____ __ __ me and asked me to dance!

Down

2   Mary is really smart. She's a real _____.

3   Trying to think of good ideas for dinner every night is a real _____!

4   What's going on with Kim and Bob? Give me the _____!

5   We tried to convince Jack to believe our story, but we just couldn't ____ it ___.

7   I've got an early meeting tomorrow. I've got to be up __ ___ ___ __ ____.

8   Leslie went out last night wearing a strapless mini dress. All of the guys were trying to ____ her __!

9   I can't go to the movies with you because I don't have any money. I'm flat _____!

10 They go to bed early. They usually _____ about 9:00.

13 Jack's new job pays twice what he used to get. He's really _____ __ ___ ____!

14 Her car died so she needed a ____ home.

15 My job doesn't pay very well so I'm having a hard time trying to ____ ____ ____.

19 That apple cake was fantastic! It was ___ __ ____ ____!

22 Time for me to hit the road. I'll _____ ___ ____!

23 Khalid told me he won the lotto and I was all like "___ ___ __ ____!"

24 The kids look really beat. Let's ____ home.

25 I can't tolerate his smoking. I won't ___ __ ____ it anymore!

26 On the weekends I like to visit my friends, and ____ ___ ____ my pals.

27 Did you see that gorgeous chick that just walked by? What a _____!

30 I heard that the test is really easy. It'll be a _____.

35 I'm starving! What do you say we grab a ____ to eat before the movie?

36 Order whatever you like from the menu. Dinner is going to __ __ me.

37 After two hours at the gym, Joe was really ____.

"Give Me The Lowdown On Mona!"

Many high school students in the US have more on their minds than just their grades. American teenagers often succumb to peer pressure and use alcohol or drugs, or become sexually active before they are ready. In addition, many teenagers find themselves burdened with adult responsibilities because both parents work, or are separated or divorced. Do such problems exist in your country? Why do you think they have become such widespread problems in the US? What do you think would be a good way to tackle these problems? How are such problems dealt with in your country?

Charlie and Vic are still hanging at the bar after Mona and Renee have left. Vic wants to know more about Mona before he calls her up to go out on a date…

VIC: Man that chick, Mona, is hot! Did you check out the **bod** on her? OK dude, give me the **lowdown**!

CHARLIE: As I said, we go way back. I've known her since junior high school, and we've been **through thick and thin** together. When I first met her, her family was **loaded**, I mean really rolling in it! They lived in a ten-bedroom house and had five cars! **I'm talking** some serious **dough**!

VIC: What do you mean, was loaded?

CHARLIE: Well, her **folks** were in the car business. During our junior year in high school, her father got involved with some **shady** business partners. The business went **sour** and the family lost everything. They were pretty **down-and-out**. It was too much for the family to **take** and her folks finally **split up**. Mona really lost it. She started hanging out with the **wrong crowd** and got into drugs pretty heavily. She was doing drugs **left and right** and it got so bad she almost **dropped out of** school. It was a real low point in her life.

VIC: Oh, come on. I don't **buy** that for a minute! You're trying to **pull a fast one** on me, aren't you? She seems so **together**.

CHARLIE: Now, hear me out, I'm **on the up-and-up** here. So, like I was saying, she was at a real low point in her life, but then **boom**, she **snapped out of it** and got herself back together. She finished high school, graduated from college, and completed her Masters degree. Now she's going for a PhD. She really **has her head on right**! But don't tell her I gave you all this dirt, or she'd **freak**!

VIC: Your secret is safe with me, buddy. Not to change the subject, but it's late and I'm beat. What do you say we leave this **joint**? I've had enough **booze** and secrets for one night.

CHARLIE: OK, let's hit the road.

If you're in a trance, you'd better snap out of it! Grab a partner and match up each slang term in the left column with its definition in the right column. Use the dialogue if you need help figuring out the meanings. (answers on page 142)

1. **bod** noun_____

2. **lowdown** noun_____

3. **through thick and thin** adv_____

4. **loaded** adj_____

5. **I'm talking…** exp_____

6. **dough** noun_____

7. **folks** noun_____

8. **shady** adj_____

9. **sour** adj_____

10. **down-and-out** adj_____

11. **take** verb_____

12. **split up** verb_____

13. **wrong crowd** noun_____

14. **left and right** adv_____

15. **drop out of** verb_____

16. **buy** verb_____

17. **pull a fast one** verb_____

18. **together** adj_____

19. **on the up-and-up** adj_____

20. **boom** adv_____

21. **snap out of it** verb_____

22. **have one's head on right** verb_____

23. **freak** verb_____

24. **joint** noun_____

25. **booze** noun_____

A. to tolerate

B. to believe

C. money

D. a lot, frequently

E. wealthy

F. any strong alcoholic beverage

G. one's parents

H. to play a trick

I. frank, genuine, truthful

J. to withdraw from, to quit

K. to become distressed or upset

L. restaurant or similar establishment

M. bad

N. through good and bad times

O. person's body

P. suddenly

Q. dishonest, sneaky

R. information, gossip

S. rebellious young troublemakers

T. to return to one's normal state of mind

U. penniless with no hope for the future

V. to divorce

W. "I'm emphasizing…"

X. to have clear objectives

Y. to be well organized

1. Get the **lowdown** on your partner's best buddy back home. Have the two of them been **through thick and thin** together? Have your partner tell an interesting story that has happened to him. Does this best buddy have his **head on right** or is he still floating through life with no direction? Would he **freak** if he heard your partner's answer to that question?

2. What do your **folks** do? Is this a common line of work in your native country?

3. Is it common in your country for kid's **folks** to **split up**? Do you know anyone whose **folks** have **split up**? Do you know why their relationship went **sour**? Were you a good friend who **hung out with them through thick and thin**, or just an acquaintance?

4. When you were in high school was there a **wrong crowd**? Why were they considered to be the **wrong crowd**? Would your parents have **freaked** if you hung out with them, or were you actually in the **wrong crowd**? Come on now; be **on the up-and-up** with your partner!

5. Your teacher is all like "OK class, if you pass the test with flying colors, tomorrow we can catch a flick." Do you **buy** it or think the teacher is trying to **pull a fast one** on you? Why? When was the last time you **bought** something, but discovered that the person had **pulled a fast one** on you? Who was it? What did you **buy**? Why did you **buy** it? When was the last time you **pulled a fast one** on someone?

6. What American actor do you think has a hot **bod**? How about actress? How about in your class, does anyone have a hot **bod**?

7. Are you the silent type or do you like to talk **left and right**? When you were a kid did your **folks** yell at you **left and right**? How do you think you'll be with your own kids? Be **on the up-and-up**!

8. Think of something that **boom**, suddenly happened to you. Tell your partner what it was.

9. Who's the most **together** person you know? Do you think that if they lost all of their **dough** they would be able to **take** being **down-and-out**? How about you? If for some reason, you lost all of your **dough**, could you **take** being **down-and-out**? Now, instead, suppose you just won a ton of **dough**! **We're talking** serious bread! Can you **take** rolling in it? What's the first thing you would do? Why?

A Ring, A Bite, A Flick

1. Is dating common in your country? Why or why not? If it is, what's the usual activity on a first date?

2. With your partner, write down five questions to ask your teacher about dating customs in the US.

After getting Mona's number, Vic waits the required few days before giving her a ring to ask her out on a date…

RENEE: Hello?

VIC: Hello, Mona ? This is Vic, Charlie's **pal** from the other night.

RENEE: Sorry, wrong girl! This is Renee. Hold on, I'll get Mona for you. Oh, Mona, it's Vic on the phone.

MONA: Thanks Renee, I've got it. Hi Vic!

VIC: Mona, nice to hear your voice again! How have you been?

MONA: Pretty good. What's up?

VIC: Mona, how about **taking** me **up on** my offer of the other night? Are you free this Friday?

MONA: This Friday? No, I'm sorry, I'm already **tied up**.

VIC: Well then, how about Saturday?

MONA: Saturday is **cool**.

VIC: What do you say we go out for a bite then **catch** a **flick**? What's playing at the new multiplex?

MONA: I don't know, but I'm **dying** to see that one movie with that new actor, **what's his face**, the guy who wrote and directed his first film.

VIC: **You've got me**!

MONA: I remember now, Mark Darmon. You know who I mean.

VIC: The name **rings a bell**, but I'm **drawing a blank** on his face. Whatever you want to see is cool with me. I'll **swing by** your **place** around seven?

MONA: OK. See you then. Bye.

VIC: Bye.

Mona hangs up the phone…

RENEE: Mona, you haven't been tied up on a Friday since I don't know when! What gives?

MONA: This guy seems like a good catch! I've got to **play my cards right** and **play** a little **hard to get**. Besides, a little **white lie** never hurt anyone, and he'd think I was a **loser** if I were free on Friday!

RENEE: But, of course you're not a loser! You are tied up on Friday: with me, the **tube**, and a **ton** of popcorn! Let's see what's on! Whoops, **scratch** that! What's up with the TV? It's **on the blink**!

MONA: Let me see. Oh, it's not **busted**, you **dimwit**. It's just unplugged!

20

OK folks, what do you say we get the lowdown on the new slang? With a partner, hook up each term in the left column with its meaning in the right column. Check out the conversation if you need a hand. (answers on page 142)

1. **pal** noun____
2. **take up on** verb____
3. **tied up** adj____
4. **cool** adj____
5. **catch** verb____
6. **flick** noun____
7. **die** verb____
8. **what's his face** exp____
9. **you've got me** exp____
10. **ring a bell** verb____
11. **draw a blank** verb____
12. **swing by** verb____
13. **place** noun____
14. **play one's cards right** verb____
15. **play hard to get** verb____
16. **white lie** noun____
17. **loser** noun____
18. **tube** noun____
19. **ton** noun____
20. **scratch** verb____
21. **on the blink** adj____
22. **busted** adj____
23. **dimwit** noun____

A. "I don't know"
B. one's apartment or living quarters
C. the television
D. a harmless lie
E. a term for a person whose name has been forgotten
F. to have a previous engagement
G. broken, inoperative
H. to accept an offer
I. a movie
J. inoperative, usually said of electrical appliances or equipment
K. one who is unable to succeed
L. a large amount
M. to watch a movie or TV program
N. stupid or foolish person
O. a close friend
P. OK or acceptable
Q. to have a strong desire
R. to stop somewhere briefly
S. to cancel
T. to fail to remember
U. to make good use of one's resources
V. to sound familiar
W. to act coyly, pretend to be uninterested

TALK TURKEY!

Grab a partner or two and answer the questions. This is no time to take it easy! Go wild, let your hair down, and don't be a stick-in-the-mud! Remember to use the new slang in your answers.

1. Who's your best **pal** back home in your native country? How about in the US? What did you usually *do* when you hung out with your **pals** in your country? How about with your new **pals** in the US?

2. What kind of **flicks** do you like? What was the last **flick** you **caught**? How was it? What **flick** are you **dying** to see? See if your partner will **take you up on** an offer to **catch** it with you!

3. You are asked a simple question like "What's the capital of the US?" and for some reason you **draw a blank**. How do you answer? When was the last time you **drew a blank**? What did you **draw a blank** on? A test question? Your address? Your phone number?

4. What shows do you like to **catch** on the **tube** in your native country? Why? What's your favorite show to **catch** on the **tube** in the US? Why? Which program does your teacher think is the hottest show on the **tube** in the US? What makes it so hot?

5. Where is your **place**? Who was the last person to **swing by** your **place**? What does your **place** look like? What do you wish it looked like? If you **play your cards right**, do you think your **place** will look a lot better in the future?

6. Did you tell a **ton** of **white lies** when you were younger? If yes, why? If no, why not? When was the last time you told someone you were **tied up** when you were really as free as a bird? Were you trying to **play hard to get** or was the person just a **loser** that you didn't want to spend time with?

7. What was your last possession that was **on the blink**? When something of yours is **on the blink** do you have it repaired or just buy a new one?

8. Just about everyone has **busted** something that didn't belong to them. How about you – have you ever **busted** something that didn't belong to you? What was it? Did you make up a **white lie** to tell the owner or did you tell the truth? Was the owner **cool** about it?

WRITE UP A STORM!

On your own, write a story about telling a white lie. (The story can be true or made-up) Use at least twelve pieces of new slang in your story. Come on, get those pencils moving!

Hitting It Off

1. Every country has a different concept of what it means to be on time. In your native country, is it customary to be exactly on time, a little late, a little early, or very late? What do you think the custom is in the US? Check with your teacher to see if your thoughts were correct.

2. What kind of movie (romance, drama, sci-fi, action, suspense, comedy, foreign) is your favorite? Why? How about your least favorite? Why?

3. What country's cuisine do you like the most? How often do you eat this kind of food? Do you ever prepare it at home?

It's 6:55 Saturday evening, and as Mona is getting all **dolled up** for her night on the town with Vic, she hears the doorbell ring...

MONA: Renee? Could you see who's at the door? I hope it's not Vic. I've still got to **put my face on**.

RENEE: It's him, so you'd better get a move on! I'll get the door. Oh hi. It's Vic, right?

VIC: **Bingo**, you've got a good memory. Is Mona ready?

RENEE: She'll be ready in just a **sec**. Can I get you something to drink while you're waiting?

VIC: Nah, I'm cool. Wow, Mona! You **look like a million bucks**!

MONA: Thanks. You don't look so bad yourself. So, what's the plan for tonight?

VIC: Well, first we can catch that flick you wanted to see, and after that we can just **play it by ear**.

MONA: Sounds like a plan, but I heard that new Mark Darmon flick I wanted to see was a real **flop**!

VIC: We could catch that new Italian film instead. I've heard it won tons of awards.

MONA: OK by me! I love foreign flicks. Renee, we're off.

VIC: Catch you later Renee.

The movie is over and Vic and Mona are looking for a place to **chow down**...

VIC: So, what did you think?

MONA: It was pretty good. The ending really **blew** me **away**! I couldn't believe that sweet little boy, Marco was the one who **knocked off** that **goon** Giuseppe!

VIC: Marco was a **wolf in sheep's clothing**, but on to more pressing issues! I'm so hungry I could eat a horse! How about you?

MONA: I don't know about eating any horses, but I'm pretty hungry too.

VIC: There's this great new sushi place that just opened up. What do you say we **give it a shot**?

MONA: **Shut up**! You like sushi too? This is just too good to be true!

VIC: Well then, let's go. It's just around the corner, so we can walk there.

Vic and Mona arrive at the restaurant...

VIC: Check this place out! It's **packed**! It'll be **forever and a day** before we get a table here. Let's **bail** and go somewhere else.

MONA: I'm pretty **psyched up** for sushi, but there's this great Thai place right around the corner. It's just a **hole in the wall**, but the food is out of this world!

VIC: **You've got my vote**! So what are we waiting for?

Mona is **on cloud nine** when she gets back to her place...

RENEE: Well, how was it?

MONA: He was great! We really **hit it off**!

RENEE: You're home pretty early though! Did he **make a move** on you?

MONA: Well it wasn't like he tried to **jump my bones**, but we did **make out** a little in his car before we said good night. I'm beat. I'll fill you in on the details in the morning.

Ready to give this a shot? Match up each slang term in the left column with its definition in the right column. (answers on page 142)

1. **doll up** verb____

2. **put one's face on** verb____

3. **bingo** exp____

4. **sec** noun____

5. **look like a million bucks** verb____

6. **play it by ear** verb____

7. **flop** noun____

8. **chow down** verb____

9. **blow away** verb____

10. **knock off** verb____

11. **goon** noun____

12. **wolf in sheep's clothing** noun____

13. **give something a shot** verb____

14. **shut up** exp____

15. **packed** adj____

16. **forever and a day** adv____

17. **bail** verb____

18. **psyche up** adj____

19. **hole-in-the-wall** noun____

20. **you've got my vote** exp____

21. **on cloud nine** adj____

22. **hit it off** verb____

23. **make a move** verb____

24. **jump someone's bones** verb____

25. **make out** verb____

A. a failure

B. to kill

C. to leave or give up on

D. to appear attractive

E. to make an attempt or try

F. to engage in passionate kissing

G. to be excited or enthusiastic

H. to apply one's makeup

I. a stupid person or a bodyguard

J. to eat a lot

K. crowded

L. to have sex with someone

M. to surprise or shock

N. "you're kidding!"

O. "I agree with your suggestion"

P. "that's right" or "correct"

Q. a small, out-of-the-way shop, restaurant, or bar

R. to improvise, to go without preplanning

S. a person whose friendly manner conceals a hostile intent

T. a long time

U. to make sexual advances

V. to get along well with someone from the first meeting

W. to dress attractively

X. very happy

Y. a short time

TALK SHOP!

Hello! It's the time you've all been waiting for. Round up a new partner and make it snappy! It's time to yap your heads off, and don't forget to use the new slang in your answers.

1. Who was the first person you **hit it off** with in the US? How and where did you meet? Do you still hang out with this person?

2. Has anyone tried to **make a move** on you since you came to the US? (white lies are cool!) Have you **made a move** on anyone since you came to the US? (white lies are still cool!)

3. Hey, gals! Are you the type of girl who won't go out until she's **put her face on** or are you more into natural beauty? Do you like to get yourself all **dolled up** before you hit the town? Dudes, are you into girls who must **have their faces on** or are you a sucker for natural beauty? Do you like your girlfriend to get all **dolled up** before you take her out on the town?

4. What are you **psyched up** about or **psyched up** to do in the near future? If you **gave it a shot**, would your partner want to join you?

5. The last time you went out and **played it by ear**, what did you end up doing?

6. What was the last movie you saw that was a **flop**? Was the theater **packed**?

7. Where's the last place you **chowed down**? Who did you **chow down** with? What did you **chow down** on? Was the place **packed**? Is there a popular **hole in the wall** that is always **packed** in your city? Find out about local places from your teacher.

8. Can you think of a person you've known who turned out to be a **wolf in sheep's clothing**? What makes you think so?

9. What's the last thing that **blew** you **away**? Why did it **blow** you **away**?

10. When was the last time you were **on cloud nine**? Why were you **on cloud nine**? What would put you **on cloud nine** right now? Would **bailing** on class put you there?

11. Who was the last person that you thought **looked like a million bucks**?

LET'S WRITE!

On your own, write a story about two people going out on their first date. For inspiration, use your own experiences, or that of Mona and Vic. Your couple's date can be a flop, or they can really hit it off, it's up to you. Just be sure to use at least fifteen new slang terms, and as much slang from previous lessons as possible. When you've finished, share your story with your classmates.

CROSSWORD REVIEW

Dudes, you guys have really got it together! You've made it through <u>Unit Two</u>, so you're not a bunch of dimwits! Don't drop out of the game now. See how much you can remember by letting yourself get tied up in doing the crossword review. Don't forget to pay attention to verb tense and word form! (solution on page 142)

Across

5   I think I'll ____ ___ __ __ your offer of a lift home. Normally, I'd walk, but it's raining cats and dogs outside.

10 I was driving down the street when ____, a dog ran right out in front of my car!

11 Let's call a repairman to fix the TV. It's been _____ for over a week now.

12 I can't ___ that story! I don't believe it for a minute!

13 The grand opening of Leon's new restaurant was a real ____. Not a single person showed up.

17 Don't let his pleasant manner and appearance fool you. In reality, he's a ____ __ _____ _____.

19 I wouldn't trust any of his lowlife friends. They're all pretty _____ characters.

20 Davide drank too much _____ last night so he has a terrible hangover today.

21 All you have to do to qualify for the promotion is to take the test. Come on, give it a ____!

22 We've been good ____ ever since we were kids. We go way back.

24 Sometimes it's better to tell a _____ ___ than to tell the truth and hurt someone's feelings.

25 Tomoko's really happy with her new boyfriend. She's been __ _____ ____ ever since they started dating.

26 Line and Lene really ___ __ ___. They were friends from the moment they met.

29 I'm really _____ about the Vegas trip! I can't wait to go!

32 I couldn't remember a single answer to the test this morning. I ____ _ _____ on every question!

Down

1   Liza's boyfriend is going to _____ when he finds out she's going steady with another guy.

2   I'm not particular about restaurants. Anywhere you want to go is ____ with me.

3   Marisa has been feeling blue all week, and it's starting to get on my nerves. I hope she _____ ___ ___ __ soon.

4   Did you hear that Marco _____ ___ __ school? Nobody knows why he quit.

5   Jack and I have been friends through good times and bad. We've been _____ _____ ___ ____.

6   Have you seen Yasmine's new ____? She just rented a cool loft downtown.

7   The cashier was really slow. It took us _____ ___ _ ___ to get through the checkout line!

8   Eric's new restaurant is just a ____ __ __ ___. It's tiny and hard to find, but the food is out of this world!

9   You have to ____ ____ _____ _____ and do what the boss says if you want to get promoted.

14 Did you see the expensive clothes and jewelry the new student is wearing? She must be _____!

15 You'd better watch that Biff doesn't try to ____ ____ ____ tonight. I heard him bragging to his friends that you were all over him last weekend.

16 The name _____ _ ____. I can't recall where I heard it, but it sounds familiar.

18 Because you've lied to me so many times in the past, I don't think you're being __ ___ __ ___ __ with me.

23 Dude, it's time to book because this party is really a drag. Let's ____ and head to a club downtown.

27 What do you say we catch a ____ this weekend? I hear there's a new horror movie opening.

28 Louie and I are starving, so we're going to ____ ____ on some burgers.

30 That stupid clerk ordered the wrong part three times in a row! Why would the store hire a _____ like that?

31 This place is really _____ tonight. I've never seen it so crowded!

"Give It A Rest, He's History!"

1. Do you have any friends who are in, or have been in a bad relationship? Describe the problems with the relationship.

2. Do you and your friends still talk about your past relationships? Do you enjoy discussing them or would you rather forget about your ex's?

It's dinnertime at Mona and Renee's place. Mona, who just had her first date with Vic last night, wants to tell Renee about Vic. Renee, however, steers the conversation in another direction…

RENEE: So, how was your date last night? Come on, give me the **dirt**!

MONA: He was a real gentleman, a rare breed. Like I said last night, we really hit it off.

RENEE: Well, just be careful. Remember what happened the last time you thought someone was a "real gentleman!"

MONA: What are you **going on about**?

RENEE: Now don't **pull** that innocent act with me. Who was there to hear you **pour your heart out** every night when your last "real gentleman" was **walking all over** you and treating you like you were yesterday's newspaper?

MONA: Oh, **give it a rest**! Why did you have to bring him up again?

RENEE: Hold on! **Hear** me **out**! I'm just looking out for you. Remember how he **suckered** you **into** lending him a thousand **bucks**? Then, after you **walked in on** him with another girl, he **walked out on** you and left you with nothing but a **rubber check**!

MONA: Will you **let up** about him? He's **history**!

RENEE: I'm just concerned about you. You were such a **wreck** when he left. He really **screwed you over*** and I don't want to see you **hit rock bottom** like that again. Oh, by the way, I've been looking for my **shades** all day! Do you happen to know where they are?

MONA: **Beats me**. I haven't seen them… uh… have you tried checking on top of your head?

RENEE: Oh, there they are! I'm such a **ditz** sometimes. Thanks for dinner, it was out of this world! I'm **off** for work. Catch you later, and remember what I told you!

MONA: Renee, could you stop by the store on your way home? We **are out of** coffee, and I think we're **running out of** toilet paper too.

* see dictionary for caution regarding use of this expression

Match 'em up! Hook 'em up! Get a partner and connect the slang terms in the left column with the definitions in the right column. (answers on page 143)

1. **dirt** noun_____

2. **go on about** verb_____

3. **pull** verb_____

4. **pour one's heart out** verb_____

5. **walk all over** verb_____

6. **give it a rest** exp_____

7. **hear out** verb_____

8. **sucker into** verb_____

9. **buck** noun_____

10. **walk in on** verb_____

11. **walk out on** verb_____

12. **rubber check** noun_____

13. **let up** verb_____

14. **history** noun_____

15. **wreck** noun_____

16. **screw one over** verb_____

17. **hit rock bottom** verb_____

18. **shades** noun_____

19. **beats me** exp_____

20. **ditz** noun_____

21. **off** verb_____

22. **be out of** verb_____

23. **run out of** verb_____

A.   a person in poor physical or mental health

B.   to let someone finish what they are saying

C.   to surprise someone in an embarrassing situation

D.   to leave a commitment

E.   to use up one's supply

F.   "please stop talking about the subject!"

G.   to fool someone

H.   to treat someone badly

I.   a stupid or silly girl

J.   to stop or cease

K.   to talk to much

L.   gossip

M.   to treat badly or disrespectfully

N.   to have nothing left

O.   sunglasses

P.   over, finished, the past

Q.   to reach the worst point in one's life

R.   one US dollar

S.   "I don't know"

T.   to attempt

U.   to express one's innermost thoughts and feelings

V.   to leave

W.   a check returned for insufficient funds

1. When you have a problem, who do you **pour your heart out** to? Is the listener all ears, or does she say "Do you ever **let up**?" When was the last time you **poured your heart out**?

2. Do you usually lock the door when you use the bathroom? Has anyone **walked in on** you while you were using the john in the US? Have you ever **walked in on** someone while they were in the can? Give your partner the **dirt**!

3. If you **walked in on** your significant other and someone else doing things you'd rather not see, would you **walk out on** him/her, or give him/her a second chance? Why or why not?

4. When you were a kid, what would your mom **go on about**? How long would she have to **go on** until you listened?

5. Have you been **suckered into** doing or buying anything since coming to the US? Give your partner the **dirt**! Is it common in your country for the natives to try and **sucker** people **into** buying or doing things? Have you ever done it?

6. Are your ex's really **history**, or do you still pick up the phone and give them a ring from time to time?

7. How many **bucks** do you have in your wallet? How much is your rent?

8. When someone asks you a question you don't know the answer to, what new piece of slang do you use to reply?

9. Do you think you have gotten **screwed over** since coming to the US? Who **screwed** you **over**? Does your partner agree that you were **screwed over**? How about your teacher?

10. Is your place spic and span right now, or is it a **wreck**? How about you personally? When was the last time you were physically a **wreck**? Mentally? Did you end up **pouring your heart out** to someone, or did you keep a lid on it?

11. What time are you usually **off** for school in the morning? What new term can you now use when leaving?

12. What are you **running out of** at home? What **are** you **out of** at home? You've been working very hard learning slang! Are you **running out of** energy?

"I've Had It Up To Here With That Job!"

1. After having a hard day at school or work, what do you do to relax? Did you do the same thing in your native country? Why or why not? What does your teacher do to relax after work?

2. Has an American ever done or said something that because of your culture, you found rude or offensive? What did this person do? How did you handle the situation? What other things do you find rude or offensive about American culture? What do you think Americans might find rude or offensive about your culture?

Renee has just gotten back home after a long day at work…

RENEE: My feet are **killing** me. I've been on them all day. Waiting tables really **sucks**!*

MONA: Wow, you're sure in a **crappy*** mood! You do look **worn out**, though.

RENEE: **I've** just **had it up to here** with rude customers treating me like I was their personal slave.

MONA: Sounds like you need a little **pick-me-up**. Why don't you **jump in the shower** while I **run** to the store and pick up some stuff for dinner.

RENEE: I'm up for that.

MONA: Anything special you feel like eating?

RENEE: I've been **dying** for mousaka's all week. Oh, and could you pick up some **munchies** while you're at the store? We're almost out of sugar, too.

Mona comes back from the store…

MONA: Hey Renee, are you out of the shower? Get a load of what happened to me at the store!

RENEE: Tell me, I'm all ears.

MONA: Well, while I was waiting in the express checkout I noticed this **old bag** in front of me counting the number of items I had in my basket. I didn't realize I had one more than I was supposed to, when suddenly this **wacko** starts bitching to the cashier about people bringing in too many items.

RENEE: What did you do?

MONA: I didn't want to **make a stink** about it, so I just **turned the other cheek**. But she didn't stop there! She kept going on, bitching about young people these days and how they think they can get away with anything. You could **tell** the cashier was getting all pissed off and was ready to **blow a fuse**, but she kept her cool.

RENEE: That's all? So what's the big deal?

MONA: Hold on! Here's where the good part starts! So the old bag leaves the store and I start **trashing** her to the cashier, calling her an old whiny **windbag**. Suddenly, **out of the blue**, the cashier **jumps down my throat** and is all like "You'd better watch your mouth! That old bag is my mom!"

RENEE: Oops! **You put your foot in your mouth**, big-time!

MONA: I know! I could feel my face turning **beet red** and I **clammed up**. I couldn't even manage to get an "I'm sorry" to come out of my mouth. I just paid for the stuff and **hauled out of** there! I think I even saw the cashier **giving me the finger*** as I left the store.

RENEE: Well, I guess that means I'll be doing the shopping for the next few months!

           * see dictionary for caution regarding this term

Are you dying to know the meaning of the new terms? Hook up with a partner and match 'em up. But don't wear yourselves out because there's a lot more to come! (answers on page 143)

1. kill verb_____
2. suck verb_____
3. crappy adj_____
4. worn out adj_____
5. I've had it up to here exp_____
6. pick-me-up noun_____
7. jump in the shower verb_____
8. run verb_____
9. die verb_____
10. munchies noun_____
11. old bag noun_____
12. wacko noun_____
13. make a stink verb_____
14. turn the other cheek verb_____
15. tell verb_____
16. blow a fuse verb_____
17. trash verb_____
18. windbag noun_____
19. out of the blue adv_____
20. jump down someone's throat verb_____
21. put one's foot in one's mouth verb_____
22. beet red adj_____
23. clam up verb_____
24. haul out of verb_____
25. give someone the finger verb_____

A. crazy or strange person
B. without warning
C. to hurt
D. to leave a place quickly
E. to complain loudly
F. unattractive elderly woman
G. bad, foul
H. to speak badly about someone
I. to have a strong desire for something
J. to refuse to retaliate to insult
K. to angrily yell at someone
L. to make an obscene gesture using one's middle finger
M. physically tired, exhausted
N. to become silent, often from embarrassment
O. snack foods
P. to lose one's temper
Q. "my patience has been exhausted" or "I won't tolerate anymore"
R. to go somewhere quickly
S. to recognize or realize by observing
T. to inadvertently say something embarrassing
U. to take a quick shower
V. to be objectionable
W. flushed and red from embarrassment
X. something that refreshes or stimulates
Y. a person who talks too much

TALK IT OUT!

Did you wear yourself out? Feeling a little tired? Have you "had it up to here" with using so much brain power? Then what you need is a little pick-me-up. Find a buddy and start exercising those lips. Come on, now, get 'em moving!

1. What is something in your life that really **sucks**? What's the last flick you saw that really **sucked**? Have you ever had a job that really **sucked**? Why did it **suck** so badly?

2. What was the last thing that was **killing** you? Was it your head, back, tooth, or maybe your feet? Did it put you in a **crappy** mood? Is it easy for your friends to **tell** when you are in a **crappy** mood or do you hide it well? What did you use as a **pick-me-up**?

3. What kind of food are you **dying** for? If you're a smoker, do you ever find yourself **dying** for a cigarette? Do you like American **munchies**, or do you think they **suck**? What kind of **munchies** are you **dying** for from your native country?

4. When you were in high school, who did you and your friends like to **trash**? Is there anyone in your life now that you **trash**? Why? Is it for their way of dressing, speaking, or behaving? What famous person do you get a kick out of **trashing**? If you heard someone **trashing** you, would you **make a stink** about it, or just **turn the other cheek**?

5. Just about everyone has **put their foot in their mouth** at some point in their life. What is your "**put my foot in my mouth**" story? Did you turn **beet red** and end up **hauling out of** there?

6. Who was the last person you saw **blow a fuse** and **jump down someone's throat**?

7. Has anyone **given** you **the finger** since you came to the US? Why? Did you **blow a fuse** and call them a **wacko** or just **turn the other cheek**? Have you **given someone the finger** or felt like doing so since you came to the US? Why? What obscene gestures exist in your native country?

8. Are you usually **worn out** by Friday?

9. Name something that you **have had it up to here** with about the US? How is it different in your native country?

10. If you don't understand a question in English, do you **clam up**, or try to answer the question? Do you usually **clam up** when Americans you don't know start to talk to you?

11. In the morning, do you **jump in the shower**, or take forever and a day?

12. Which of these three categories do you fall into: A. You **run** to the store whenever you need something to eat; B. You do all of your food shopping once a week; C. Food shopping? What's that? Can you **tell** which category your teacher falls into? Find out if you were correct!

WRITE IT UP!

Scout out a partner and write a conversation between two people in which one of the characters winds up putting his foot in his mouth. After you've wrapped it up, practice the conversation and then read it out loud for your classmates.

Getting Stuck With Babysitting

1. Do waiters and waitresses work for tips in your native country? What is a normal tip? A good tip? A bad tip? Ask your teacher about the tipping customs in the US. How do you feel about them?

2. In your native country, is it common for parents to go out without their children? If yes, who usually takes care of the kids? If no, why isn't it common?

3. Have you ever babysat? How did it work out?

4. When you were a kid, did you get along with your brothers and sisters?

Mona is supposed to baby sit her sister's kids tonight, but she would rather go out with her new boyfriend, Vic…

RENEE: Hey Mona, do you have a few bucks I can **sponge off of** you?

MONA: Again? Why are you always so **strapped for cash**?

RENEE: Things aren't going too well at the restaurant. I keep **getting stuck with** the bad shifts. Then, get this! Last night two tables **stiffed** me!

MONA: I'll tell you what. I'm **in a jam** myself. I'm supposed to baby sit my sister's brats, I mean, kids, but Vic just called and was all like "I just won two tickets for tonight's performance of "Les Mis". He knows I've been dying to see it! Maybe you could help me **get out of** babysitting.

RENEE: Hmm… Let's **cut to the chase**. How much are you offering?

MONA: How does twenty bucks sound?

At Mona's sisters' place, the kids, Kareem and Jasmine, are **having a field day** as they **bug** each other, and their new babysitter, Renee…

KAREEM: Stop poking me!

JASMINE: You stop pulling my hair first!

KAREEM: If you'd quit **hogging** the entire couch, I'd quit poking you!

RENEE: OK, That's enough! **Pipe down**! Both of you… **knock it off**!

JASMINE: You're still pulling my hair!

KAREEM: Well you're still poking me!

RENEE: I said knock it off! Stop **picking on** each other!

KAREEM: Hey, let's get the babysitter instead!

Jasmine whispers something in Kareem's ear…

RENEE: I can't believe you threw water on me! This situation is **out of hand**. You're not going to **get away with** this. Go brush your teeth. It's time to **hit the sack**.

JASMINE: What do you mean? It's not bedtime yet!

RENEE: You're **dead wrong**! I'm the **head honcho** here. Now stop **dragging your feet** and move, and don't give me any **lip**!

RENEE: (to herself) These kids are **driving me up the wall**! What a **handful**! This is definitely worth more than twenty bucks! I'm gonna **give Mona a piece of my mind** when I get home!

What do you say we get the lowdown on this new slang! Time to get it in gear! Match up the new slang terms with their meanings. (answers on page 143)

1. **sponge off of** verb_____
2. **strapped for cash** adj_____
3. **get stuck with** verb_____
4. **stiff** verb_____
5. **in a jam** adj_____
6. **get out of** verb_____
7. **cut to the chase** verb_____
8. **have a field day** verb_____
9. **bug** verb_____
10. **hog** verb_____
11. **pipe down** exp_____
12. **knock it off** exp_____
13. **pick on** verb_____
14. **out of hand** adj_____
15. **get away with** verb_____
16. **hit the sack** verb_____
17. **dead wrong** adj_____
18. **head honcho** noun_____
19. **drag one's feet** verb_____
20. **lip** noun_____
21. **drive someone up the wall** verb_____
22. **handful** noun_____
23. **give someone a piece of one's mind** verb_____

A.   make someone crazy
B.   to tell someone what's bothering you
C.   to go to bed
D.   to pester or bother
E.   to be left with an undesirable situation
F.   insolent replies, back talk
G.   to refuse to leave a tip for a waiter
H.   "stop it!"
I.   short of money
J.   the person in charge
K.   to get to the main point
L.   "be quiet!"
M.   difficult to control
N.   to move slowly
O.   to borrow
P.   having a problem or difficulty
Q.   out of control
R.   to avoid a responsibility
S.   to take more than one's share
T.   completely wrong
U.   to avoid punishment
V.   to have a great time
W.   to bully or tease

Let's get this show on the road! Find a partner or two and make sure that nobody gets away with not using the new slang in their answers!

1. What was the last thing you were supposed to do, but didn't? How did you **get out of** doing it? Is there anything in the near future that you want to **get out of** doing? See if your partner can help you **get out of** doing it!

2. Who was the last person who **sponged** money **off of** you? How much did they **sponge**? Have they paid you back yet? When someone takes their time paying you back, do you say "No biggy" or do you **give them a piece of your mind**?

3. What really **drives you up the wall**? Imagine that someone is tapping his fingers on the desk and it's **driving you up the wall**! What new slang term do you use to tell him to stop?

4. Do you ever feel like telling your neighbors to **pipe down**? Why or why not? Have your neighbors ever had to tell you to **pipe down**? Why or why not? When you were a kid, how many times a day would your mom have to tell you to **pipe down**?

5. What time did you have to **hit the sack** when you were a kid? Did you have to share a bed with your sister or brother? Who always **hogged** the covers or the bed?

6. Suppose your friend is beating around the bush and it's **bugging** you. Since you don't have the time to listen to her ramble on, what do you say to her? Have you been in a situation like this recently? Tell your partner about it. But don't **drag your feet**. **Cut to the chase**!

7. Have you ever **stiffed** a waiter or waitress? Why did you **stiff** him/her?

8. When you were growing up, who was the **head honcho** in your house? Did you ever give them **lip** when they would **bug** you about something, or were you a well-disciplined child? If you used to give your parents **lip**, tell your partner about a memorable **lip**-giving incident.

9. When you're **strapped for cash**, do you **sponge off of** your friends? Do you repay your loans promptly, or do you **drag your feet** about it?

10. Tell your partner about a problem you were **stuck with** that really put you **in a jam**.

11. When you were a child, were you a **handful** that was able to **get away with murder** or did you have very strict parents who wouldn't let you **get away with** anything? What's the scoop on your teacher?

On your own, write a story about the last time that you had a field day. Make sure that you use a ton of slang. When you're done, share your masterpiece with the dude or chick sitting next to you.

CROSSWORD REVIEW

Way to go! You've almost wrapped up <u>Unit Three</u>! Cut to the chase 'cause it's time to rack your brains. See how much of the new slang has stuck to your noodles by doing the crossword review. If you think you can get out of doing it, you're dead wrong! Go ahead, have a field day. Remember to use the correct verb tense and word form. (solution on page 143)

Across

5   Manny treats his girlfriend like dirt. He _____ ___ ____ her.

6   I just heard that your buddy Nathan has been arrested by the police. Seems he's got himself __ _ ___ again.

7   That homeless lady is crazy. She's a real _____, huh?

8   Tell Frank that we're _____ ___ __ toilet paper. We've only got one roll left!

10   Klaus was never disciplined as a child. His parents would let him ___ ____ ___ murder.

12   Tell those guys yapping back there to ____ ____ so we can hear the movie.

14   You paid five G's for that old heap? Dude, you got _____ ____ big time!

19   Please get to the point. I haven't got all day so ___ __ ___ _____ and tell me what you want.

23   Don't let her remarks get to you. It's better to ____ ___ _____ _____ and walk away.

28   I got into a fender bender this morning. I didn't see the other car until it was too late. He came right ___ __ ___ ___!

30   I hope the rain ____ __ soon, or we'll have to cancel the company picnic.

31   It really _____ that Andres has to work and can't go to the party tonight. I was looking forward to seeing him.

32   Christine lost her sunglasses again so she needs to borrow a pair of _____.

Down

1   I'm a little short of cash right now. Do you think you could lend me a few _____?

2   What a _____ week! It's been one piece of bad news after another.

3   I _____ __ __ my roommate and her boyfriend last night. Wow, was I embarrassed!

4   That dripping faucet is really annoying. It's _____ __ __ ___ ___!

9   Celia can't wait for class to end so she can have a cigarette. She's _____ for a smoke.

11   It's past my bedtime so I'm going to ___ ___ ____.

13   I'm too beat to go out this weekend. Working two shifts has left me pretty ____ ___.

15   I hear things got pretty steamy on your date last night. Come on, give me the ____!

16   Walter has _____ some crazy stunts, but this latest one really takes the cake!

17   Crystal constantly criticizes her friends behind their backs. If she keeps _____ everybody, she won't have any friends left.

18   Serena's parents are counting on her to watch her younger brothers and sisters, so there's no way she can ___ ___ __ babysitting tonight.

20   Chloe can be a real _____ once she's had a few drinks. One time she was even kicked out of a club.

21   Sheila refuses to talk about what happened on her date last weekend. Everytime I bring up the subject, she _____ __.

22   Hey, we're all out of _____. Why don't you pick up some snack food while you're at the store?

24   Firefighters have lost control of the fire and it is now ___ __ ____.

25   You've been on the computer all day. Stop _____ it and let me use it for a while.

26   We need to talk to the boss. Who's the ____ _____ around here?

27   "Dude, do you know that chick's name?" "_____ __. I've never seen her before."

29   No one could ____ that Duc was sleeping in class because his eyes were still open!

"Come Over And I'll Whip Something Up"

1. Everyone has a talent that they use when they want to impress someone. What's your talent? Who do you use your talent on? Who was the last person that received first-hand experience of your talent? What's your teacher's talent?

2. What's your favorite food of your mom's or dad's? Is it difficult or expensive to prepare? How often does she/he make it? Besides your mom or dad, who's the best cook you know? What's the most delicious thing they've made? How about you? Are your culinary skills worth talking about? What about your teacher?

Vic and Mona have been **seeing each other** for the past few months. Vic calls Mona up to show off one of his hidden talents…

VIC:	Hey Mona, it's Vic. What's up?
MONA:	Not much, just **unwinding**. I had a rough day today.
VIC:	Well, it sounds like you could do with a little **TLC**. You know, it just **hit** me that you haven't had my famous Mongolian beef! What *do* you say you come over to my place and I'll **whip up** a batch for you.
MONA:	You'll whip some up for me? This is *too* good to be true.
VIC:	Come on, this will be a good excuse to **break in** my new wok.
MONA:	Perfect. Just let me jump in the shower and freshen up a little and I'll head on over.
VIC:	See you soon. Oh, Mona, could you do me a favor?
MONA:	No sweat, what do you need?
VIC:	Could you stop at the market and pick up some Hoisin sauce? I **spaced out on** it when I was at the market earlier.

Later, at Vic's place…

MONA:	I've been hearing about this Mongolian beef of yours left and right. Let's see if it's all it's **cracked up to be**. Do you need a **hand**?
VIC:	Sure, but it's kind of a **pain**. Could you peel some garlic while I **keep an eye on** the food?
MONA:	No problem; **hand over** the garlic.

The famous Mongolian beef is ready!

VIC:	Just wait until you **sink your teeth into** this! It'll **blow away** any you've ever had before!
MONA:	I love a guy who's confident! But it does look and smell **mighty** good! At least you've got a reason for being a **bighead**!
VIC:	Well, what are we waiting for? **Dig in**! Ladies first. Here, let me give you a hand.
MONA:	Could I have a **tad** more?
VIC:	Sure, I love a girl with a healthy appetite! I've had it up to here with those girls that **eat like birds**!
MONA:	Usually **my eyes are bigger than my stomach**. But, this is **yummy**! I think I'll be able to **polish this off** and maybe even **be up for** seconds. I've got to **hand it to you**! This seriously does blow away any other Mongolian beef I've ever had.
VIC:	Thanks, it was a piece of cake. So, how about you, anything you **have up your sleeve** that I should know about?
MONA:	We'll, I've been getting into extreme sports. How about checking out skydiving with me?

What do you say? Are you up for some brainwork? This is a mighty big task, but don't let it blow you away! Find a partner and give each other a hand figuring out the meanings of the new slang. (answers on page 144)

1. **see someone** verb_____
2. **unwind** verb_____
3. **TLC** noun_____
4. **hit** verb_____
5. **whip up** verb_____
6. **break in** verb_____
7. **space out on** verb_____
8. **cracked up to be** adj_____
9. **hand** noun_____
10. **pain** noun_____
11. **keep an eye on** verb_____
12. **hand over** verb_____
13. **sink one's teeth into** verb_____
14. **blow away** verb_____
15. **mighty** adv_____
16. **bighead** noun_____
17. **dig in** exp_____
18. **tad** noun_____
19. **eat like a bird** verb_____
20. **one's eyes are bigger than one's stomach** exp_____
21. **yummy** adj_____
22. **polish off** verb_____
23. **be up for** verb_____
24. **hand it to someone** verb_____
25. **have something up one's sleeve** verb_____

A. to become fully involved
B. to become aware of
C. to give something to someone
D. an annoyance, difficulty, hassle
E. to forget a responsibility or duty
F. reputed or claimed to be
G. a person with an inflated ego
H. help, assistance
I. to congratulate someone
J. small amount
K. to be in a romantic relationship
L. "eat heartily" or "start to eat"
M. to be much better
N. to eat small portions
O. to produce quickly
P. delicious
Q. to be enthusiastic about doing something
R. to finish completely
S. to watch carefully
T. tender loving care
U. to hide a surprise or secret
V. to relax
W. to make something ready for everyday use
X. to take more than one can handle or eat
Y. really, very

1. Is your best friend **seeing** anyone right now? How long have they been **seeing** each other? Do you think **seeing** someone is all it's **cracked up to be**? Why or why not?

2. Have you **spaced out on** anything since coming to the US? What have you **spaced out on**? Do you usually **space out on** things? Have any of your teachers **spaced** on something in class?

3. What's something you have to do in the US that you didn't have to do in your native country? Is it a **pain**? Why or why not? What's the biggest **pain** about English class?

4. If you were the teacher, which student would you trust to **keep an eye on** the class for you? Why? Which student would you not choose to **keep an eye on** the class? Why not? What was the last thing you **kept an eye on** for someone? What wouldn't you want to **keep an eye on** for someone? Why not?

5. Which of your friends would you say had the **biggest head**? Why do you think they have a **bighead**? Do you think they would agree that they have a **bighead**? Why or why not? Have you met anyone in the US who you think has a **bighead**? What makes you think they have a **bighead**?

6. In your family, did you **eat like a bird** or did everyone think of you as a bottomless pit? Any time they couldn't **polish off** some food, would they ask you for a **hand**? How about now? Can you **polish off** more than one helping of dinner? How many can you **polish off**?

7. What's the last book you really **sunk your teeth into**?

8. Have you eaten any food in the US that **blows away** your mom's food that was made with **TLC**? What's the **yummiest** thing you've **sunk your teeth into** since coming to the US? What's the **yummiest** thing that you can **whip up**?

9. Do you have **eyes that are bigger than your stomach**? Do you always end up putting a **tad** more on your plate than you can eat? When you were a kid did your mom make you **polish off** your plate before leaving the table?

10. When you've had a hard day, what do you do to **unwind**? What do you do when you need a little **TLC**?

11. When did it **hit** you that you could understand more than just a **tad** of English? Who else besides your classmates do you use to **break in** the new slang that you've learned?

"I Don't Think I'd Have The Guts"

1. What's the most exciting thing you've done since coming to the US? Why did you do it? What's the most exciting thing you did when you were back home?

2. Have any of your friends ever convinced you to do something you really didn't want to do? What was it? Why did you finally *do* it? Have you ever convinced a friend to do something they really didn't want to do? How did it turn out?

Charlie and Vic are hanging out, when they begin talking about something crazy that Mona and Vic are going to do tomorrow…

CHARLIE: It's getting late so I think I'll hit the road. It's been a rough week and I really need some **shuteye**.

VIC: **I hear you**! I've got to be up at the crack of dawn tomorrow.

CHARLIE: Why, what's up? Tomorrow's Saturday, the day we all get to sleep late.

VIC: Mona's got this **cockamamie** idea. You know, there's no **talking** her **out of** something once she's got it in her head.

CHARLIE: She has been known to come up with some nutty ideas. Once she tried to **talk** me **into** going bungee jumping!

VIC: And?

CHARLIE: Of course I told her it was **out of the question**! I don't have the **guts**. What did she talk you into?

VIC: Skydiving! Actually, I'm pretty **stoked** about it; sixty seconds of pure free-fall, nothing but you and the air.

CHARLIE: Man, that's exactly what worries me! However, watching you skydive definitely **beats** sleeping in! What time is this all **going down**?

VIC: 8:00 am **sharp**.

CHARLIE: Buddy, I'll **be there with bells on**.

It's now 8:30 sharp on Saturday morning and Vic and Mona once again have their feet planted firmly on the ground…

CHARLIE: Dude, you actually jumped out of a plane at 13,000 feet!

VIC: Yup! I can't believe it myself!

CHARLIE: You wouldn't catch me up there! I can see myself now, **chickening out** as they open up the door.

VIC: I was **in the same boat**! But you can't go **backing out** of it once you're up there. Before you can even think about it, the dude's got his foot out the door and you're attached to him! You feel this blast of cold air in your face and the wind howling in your ears.

CHARLIE: Well, I must say I **look up to** you for **going through with** it!

VIC: You should give it a **shot**. The feeling you get when you're up there is out of this world!

CHARLIE: Hey, Mona! What did you think?

VIC: Looks like skydiving has left her speechless, but get a load of that new **do**! Check out her hair!

CHARLIE: It was a **blast** watching you guys! I've got to go, but let's hook up later. A buddy of mine from work is having a huge **bash**. It's out **in the sticks** but I'll give you all a lift. Mona, you can bring your roommate, Renee. We'll have a ball.

VIC: Mona's still **tongue-tied**, but it sounds good to me. Call me later with the details.

Match 'em up. Now is not the time for getting some shuteye! Find a partner and give this a shot! (answers on page 144)

1. **shuteye** noun_____
2. **I hear you** exp_____
3. **cockamamie** adj_____
4. **talk out of** verb_____
5. **talk into** verb_____
6. **out of the question** adj_____
7. **guts** noun_____
8. **stoked** adj_____
9. **beats** verb_____
10. **go down** verb_____
11. **sharp** adv_____
12. **be there with bells on** verb_____
13. **chicken out** verb_____
14. **in the same boat** adj_____
15. **back out** verb_____
16. **look up to** verb_____
17. **go through with** verb_____
18. **shot** noun_____
19. **do** noun_____
20. **blast** noun_____
21. **bash** noun_____
22. **in the sticks** adj_____
23. **tongue-tied** adj_____

A. impossible
B. sleep
C. courage
D. stupid, crazy
E. to happen or occur
F. to advise against doing something
G. excited, enthusiastic
H. to persuade someone
I. exactly
J. hairstyle
K. party
L. in a similar predicament, to have the same problem
M. to withdraw from a situation
N. a good time
O. "I agree with what you are saying."
P. to carry out, to complete
Q. to be unable to speak
R. to respect, admire
S. to lose one's nerve or courage
T. an attempt or try
U. to surpass, to be better than
V. remote, far away from the city
W. eagerly looking forward to something

TALK TURKEY!

Time to get those mouths moving. Don't get some cockamamie idea that you don't have to answer all of the questions. Remember, talking sure beats doing some boring grammar exercise! So come on, let's give it a shot. Get a partner and use the new slang in your answers.

1. How much **shuteye** did you get last night? Have you been getting enough **shuteye** recently? Why or why not?

2. What was the last thing someone tried to **talk** you **into**? Did you say "No way, man, that's **out of the question**!" or did you **go through with it**? What's the last thing you tried to **talk** someone **into**?

3. Who is the person you **look up to** the most in your life? Why? Who does your teacher **look up to**?

4. Imagine that you and your buddies are crossing a high bridge when you see a big commotion up ahead and wonder what's **going down**. As you get closer, you realize that people are bungee jumping! Which of your buddies would **chicken out** of doing it? Would you have the **guts** to **go through with** it, or would you get **tongue-tied** and not even be able to **talk** your way **out of** doing it?

5. What's something that you would **be there with bells on** to see your best friend do? What would you **be there with bells on** to see your teacher do? Is it worth a **shot** to try to **talk** them **into** doing it?

6. Do you have the **guts** to skydive? What's the **gutsiest** thing you've ever done? Did you have to be **talked into** doing it or were your friends trying to **talk** you **out of** doing it?

7. What's the last thing you were **stoked** about? Why were you **stoked** about it? What are you **stoked** about doing in the near future? Why?

8. What's the most **cockamamie** idea you've heard someone come up with recently? Did they end up **going through with** it or **backing out** of it?

9. Does your knowledge of slang put you **in the same boat** as your partner? Why or why not?

10. In your eyes, what **beats** watching baseball? What **beats** going shopping? What **beats** going to an art museum? Lastly, what **beats** being in English class?

11. What's the wackiest **do** you've ever had? Did your parents freak when they saw you? What did your friends think of your new **do**?

12. Where was the most recent **bash** you attended? Was it a **blast**? What usually **goes down** during New Year's in your country? Is it common in your country to have a huge New Year's **bash**?

13. Do you think living in the city **beats** living **in the sticks**? Why or why not? Did you live in the city or out **in the sticks** in your native country? Do you live **in the sticks** now?

WRITE UP A STORM!

Time to get those pencils in motion. Grab a partner and write down a conversation that takes place between a person who is a chicken and a person with tons of guts. One is trying to talk the other into or out of doing something crazy. If you've got the guts, let your classmates in on what went down by acting out the conversation for them.

The "Save The Ocean" Walk

1. Many Americans are involved in fund raising for charitable organizations. Some of the more well known are those that research diseases such as cancer, AIDS, multiple sclerosis, and other incurable illnesses. One way to support these charities is to participate in walks or runs that they sponsor. Are there such events in your native country? If yes what kind? If no, why not? Have you participated in any charitable fund raising events in the US? How about your teacher? Find out from your teacher about some charitable events occurring in your city.

2. Is the majority of the population of your native country concerned about the environment or do they tend to be apathetic about this issue? How about you? Have you ever participated in any charitable event to help save the environment? What was it? Why did you do it? Have you participated in any charitable fund raising events for the environment in the US?

It's Sunday morning at the park. Renee has signed up Mona, Vic, Charlie and herself for a charity walk to help save the ocean…

RENEE: So, is everybody up for this? Do you think you can go the distance? It's a 25 K walk.

CHARLIE: I'm **game**. It'll be a piece of cake!

RENEE: Are you sure you're going to be able to make it in those sneakers? They're pretty **thrashed**!

CHARLIE: You're telling me! I just got a new pair but I still haven't really broken them in yet, so I figured that thrashed was better than blisters. Hey Vic, how much dough did you guys raise?

VIC: Not much. There are a lot of **tightwads** in my office. Plus, they seem to think these small environmental charities are just a **scam**.

MONA: That **stinks**! What a bunch of lowlifes!

VIC: Now, don't give my coworkers a **bum rap**. They're just **wrapped up in** making a buck. Most people in business are not shady loan shark types where you always have to **watch your back**.

MONA: I'm sorry about **blurting out** the lowlife comment, it's just that we all have to chip in and do our share for the environment. Oh look, we'd better **get cracking**! Everyone's going to the starting line.

The gang of four has now walked 11 kilometers and Charlie's disintegrating sneakers are giving him an excuse to **bail out of** the walk…

RENEE: Well, we're not quite halfway through, but we are **making headway**! How are you guys **holding up**?

CHARLIE: I'm beat and these sneakers have seen better days. I'm dropping out.

RENEE: What's up with that? You said 25 K was a piece of cake!

CHARLIE: **I stand corrected**! Besides, my **ticker** is also about to **give out on** me.

RENEE: You men are all the same; all talk, no action!

MONA: Renee, watch out, there's a pothole…

            Renee falls face first in the muddy ditch!

RENEE: Ahh, **shoot**! Did you have to wait until the last minute to say something?! Look at me!

CHARLIE: You really **ate** it Renee, **huh**? Face first!

MONA: I'm **pooped** too! What do you guys say we **throw in the towel**?

RENEE: You too? What a bunch of **lightweights**! I'm **hanging in there**! A little mud never hurt anyone. How about you Vic? Are you with me?

VIC: I'm going the distance! I'll **tag along with** you for the next 14 K. You two really are lightweights.

MONA: I've got to hand it to you guys! I can barely walk another step, let alone another 14K! We'll see you at the finish line. Have fun!

What do you say? Are you game? Work with your partner to connect the new terms with their meanings. Don't throw in the towel, or you'll never make any headway! (answers on page 144)

1. **game** adj____	A. to be deeply involved
2. **thrashed** adj____	B. to make progress
3. **tightwad** noun____	C. a person's heart
4. **scam** noun____	D. to endure
5. **stink** verb____	E. a stingy or miserly person
6. **bum rap** noun____	F. to persevere, to keep trying
7. **wrapped up in** adj____	G. exhausted
8. **watch one's back** verb____	H. "I was wrong"
9. **blurt out** verb____	I. to speak suddenly without thinking
10. **get cracking** verb____	J. to withdraw from a trying or difficult situation
11. **bail out of** verb____	K. a person who is weak
12. **make headway** verb____	L. to give up, to concede defeat
13. **hold up** verb____	M. to be bad or offensive
14. **I stand corrected** exp____	N. ready, willing to proceed
15. **ticker** noun____	O. an expression of surprise or anger
16. **give out on** verb____	P. to fall hard
17. **shoot** exp____	Q. a fraudulent operation
18. **eat** verb____	R. to go along with someone
19. **huh?** exp____	S. worn out, ruined
20. **pooped** adj____	T. "didn't you?" or "right?"
21. **throw in the towel** verb____	U. to be careful, to be wary
22. **lightweight** noun____	V. an undeserved bad reputation
23. **hang in there** verb____	W. to stop functioning
24. **tag along with** verb____	X. to get going, make a start

TALK SHOP!

Don't bail out now! Blurt out the answers to the questions using the new slang. Hang in there until you've completed all of the questions!

1. Is there any profession in your native country that gets a **bum rap**? Why? Get the scoop from your teacher about professions in the US that get a **bum rap**.

2. What's the last book that you were **wrapped up in**? Are you **wrapped up in** learning new slang? Do you feel you are **making headway**? What else have you been **wrapped up in** lately? When you were growing up was your dad always **wrapped up in** his job? What was your mom **wrapped up in**?

3. Most Americans have tried a fad diet at some point in their lives. Have you ever tried a fad diet? Did it turn out to be just a **scam**? Have you ever been the victim of a **scam** in the US? What happened? Have you ever been a victim of a **scam** back home? If a tourist were visiting your native country, what **scams** would you advise them to avoid?

4. Who's the bigger **tightwad**, your mom or your dad? Do you consider yourself a **tightwad**? Imagine that you have tons of money! Are you going to be all like "it's on me" when you go out with your friends or are you going to be a **tightwad**?

5. Tell your partner how many push-ups can you do before your arms **give out on** you. Go ahead, try and see if it's true! Did you pull it off, or do you have to say "**I stand corrected**."

6. Everyone has **eaten** it at least once in their life! Give your partner the lowdown on your most memorable experience of **eating** it! After you **ate** it did you **throw in the towel** or did you **hang in there**? Which term describes your character better? How about your best friend?

7. What was the last thing you did that made you really **pooped**?

8. What's something about life in the US that you think **stinks**? Why do you think it **stinks**?

9. In your native country, is it common for students to **blurt out** the answers to questions the teacher asks? Why or why not? Do you tend to **blurt out** the answers in class now? Why or why not? What's your teacher's opinion on **blurting out** the answers?

10. What's the last thing you **bailed out of**? Why did you end up **bailing out of** it? What kind of excuse did you give for **bailing out**?

11. What kind of shape is your **ticker** in? How far could you run before your **ticker** would **give out on** you?

12. What's the most **thrashed** thing in your closet? How much longer do you think it/they will **hold up** before you have to buy a new one or pair?

13. Get the scoop from your teacher about local area where you have to **watch your back**. If you're in an area where you have to **watch your back**, who would you want to **tag along with** you? Why?

LET'S WRITE!

Imagine that you and your partner are doing a 10K run for your favorite charity and you've completed 6K. Write a story in which one of you is completely pooped and wants to throw in the towel, but the other wants to hang in there. Use ideas from the story and all the slang you can think of as you come up with reasons to either quit or finish the run.

CROSSWORD REVIEW

Get out of here! You're all done with <u>Unit</u> <u>Four</u>! You must be stoked because you're really making headway, but before you move on, here's something to sink your teeth into. See the clues on the next page, and try to solve the puzzle without looking back at the slang lists. If that's too difficult, then sneaking a peek is cool. (solution on page 144)

Across

2 Sherry didn't get any sleep last night so she went home to get some _____ .

3 My mom tried to _____ me ___ __ snowboarding because she's afraid I'll get hurt.

5 Joe is so conceited. He really has a _____.

6 I don't think I can walk another step. My legs are about to ____ ___ __ me!

10 John has a lot of respect for his parents. He really _____ __ __ them.

12 No bar-hopping for me tonight. I've had a rough day and I need to go home and _____ .

14 You need to _____ ____ ____ if you go down to the bad part of town.

16 I can't seem to put this book down. I'm really _____ __ __ it.

17 My roommate and I are both broke. We're __ ___ ____ ____ .

19 Don't give up now, ____ __ _____ !

21 I'm so hungry I could _____ ____ that whole pie!

24 My parents keep trying to _____ me _____ going to the local college, but I really don't want to.

25 Bill is threatening to quit his job. Do you think he'll __ _____ ____ it?

28 You got laid off on Christmas Eve? That really _____ !

29 She keeps her slim figure because she ____ ____ _ ____ .

30 That movie was really a disappointment. It wasn't all it was _____ __ __ __ .

33 Food's on the table! Everybody ___ __ !

34 Kristine is already more than halfway through her English textbook! She's really _____ _____ .

Down

1 If you don't _____ __ your new shoes, you're going to get blisters.

2 Sorry I'm late. I was watching the football game and I _____ ___ __ the time.

3 Jerry's little sister follows him around everywhere. She even wanted to ___ _____ ____ him when he went out on a date!

4 The pie is in the oven and I don't want it to burn, so will you ____ __ ___ __ it while I go to the store?

7 Josh has been having chest pains, so he went in to the hospital to have his _____ checked out.

8 Your delicious home-made chocolate cake really _____ ____ that store-bought cake.

9 Ask your mom if she'll make one of those _____ cherry pies for desert.

11 You have to be here at 2:00 PM _____ . Don't be late!

13 I'm not going to put money into that get-rich-quick scheme of yours. It's nothing but a ____ .

15 Frank asked his teacher if he could turn in his paper late, and she said "No way, it's ___ __ ___ _____ !"

18 Your party was so much fun. We really had a _____!

20 He lives a long way out of town. His place is really out __ ____ _____ .

21 It's such a ____ taking the bus to school. It's never on time, and I have to transfer twice!

22 You told everybody you were going to do this. You can't _____ ____ now!

23 I can't guarantee that I can fix your computer, but I'll give it a ____ .

24 Bill's old shoes are really _____. The soles are completely worn through.

26 I'll ____ __ some dinner for us in no time!

27 I can't wait to go on vacation to Hawaii next month. I'm really _____ about it!

31 Max really ___ it when he fell off his skateboard.

32 Could you give me a ____ with this? I really need some help.

The Boss From Hell

1. Have you ever had a job? What kind of job/jobs have you had? What would be your dream job?

2. What were your bosses like? Did you get along with them? Why or why not? What would your dream boss be like?

3. If you were the boss, would your employees feel comfortable about telling you what's on their minds, or would they feel nervous just seeing you walk down the hall?

Vic is over at Charlie's place after a frustrating few days at work...

CHARLIE: What's up with you? You **don't look so hot**!

VIC: Aww, nothing man. I'm just a little **bummed**.

CHARLIE: Hey, if you need to **get something off your chest**, I'm **all ears**. **Shoot**.

VIC: Well, it's about work. You see, it all started a few days ago when I **screwed up on** some paperwork. **No biggy**, just a small mistake. But my boss! He **flew off the handle**! You'd have thought I'd lost a major account.

CHARLIE: So that's why you **look like you've lost your best friend**!

VIC: Hang on; it gets worse. Yesterday I felt like I had a **bug**, so I called in sick. When I went into the office this morning, he **was all over** me! He **goes** "Unless you're as sick as a dog, which you don't seem to be, you'd better be in this office!" I was **burning up** inside! I'm always **bending over backwards** to keep that guy happy!

CHARLIE: Maybe you need to **lie low** for a week or so until he cools down.

VIC: I plan to, but my boss is way **out of line**. He's so **bullheaded**; he never listens to anyone else's opinion. If this goes on much longer, I'm going to **crack** and **walk**!

CHARLIE: Now, **hold your horses**! You and I both know you're up for a promotion and don't forget that Sangyo deal you've been working on. You'll rake in some serious dough if you land that account. What you need is to get your mind off this. What do you say we **put back** a few cold ones? That'll calm you down. I'll go grab us a couple from the **fridge**.

VIC: Thanks dude, you're the man!

How about giving your brains a little work out? Match up the new terms with their meanings, and make it snappy! (answers on page 145)

1. one doesn't look so hot exp____

2. bummed adj____

3. get something off one's chest verb____

4. all ears adj____

5. shoot exp____

6. screw up on verb____

7. no biggy exp____

8. fly off the handle verb____

9. look like one has lost one's best friend exp____

10. bug noun____

11. be all over verb____

12. go verb____

13. burning up adj____

14. bend over backward verb____

15. lie low verb____

16. out of line adj____

17. bullheaded adj____

18. crack verb____

19. walk verb____

20. hold your horses exp____

21. put back verb____

22. fridge noun____

A. "it's not a big problem"

B. to make a mistake

C. to go to great lengths to please someone

D. a virus, cold or flu

E. to single out a person for angry criticism

F. "begin to speak"

G. extremely angry

H. to appear sad or depressed

I. to drink a beverage

J. to say

K. to quit a job

L. inappropriate, wrong

M. to break down or go crazy

N. to relieve one's mental burden or guilt

O. listening attentively

P. refrigerator

Q. depressed

R. "wait"

S. to appear sick or troubled

T. to lose one's temper and loudly express anger

U. stubborn

V. to hide, attempt to be inconspicuous

TALKING TIME!

Time to get your mouths in motion, so hook up with a partner. Now, if you really aren't up to spilling a lot of dirt about yourself, make up a white lie or two.

1. What was the last thing that got you **bummed**? When you are **bummed**, what do you do to get out of the dumps?

2. Which member of your family **flies off the handle** the most? Who do they **fly off the handle** at? Why?

3. Who do you usually talk to when you need to **get something off your chest**? What was the last thing you **got off your chest**?

4. How about **screwing up**? What was the last thing you **screwed up on**? After you **screwed up on** it, did you **go "no biggy"** or were you **burning up** at yourself?

5. Are you **all ears** when the teacher is talking, or do you tend to space out and daydream?

6. Is there anyone who **bends over backwards** to please you? What do they do for you? Is there anyone you **bend over backwards** to please? Remember, white lies are OK!

7. Have you had a **bug** since coming to the US?

8. When someone **is all over** you, do you **lie low** until they cool down, or do you tell them that they're **out of line**? Who was the last person that **was all over** you? Why?

9. Who is the most **bullheaded** person among your family or friends? Is your teacher **bullheaded** when it comes to tests?

10. Do you relax after a hard week of school or work by **putting back** a few cold ones? If not, what do you do instead?

WRITING TIME!

Fix yourself up with a partner. One of you is the employee who came down with a bug. The other is the head honcho who flies off the handle at the drop of a hat. The employee has to call the boss and tell her that he won't be in the office today. Yikes! Write down the conversation that occurs, and use all of the slang that you can think of.

Suits At War

1. In the US, the majority of women work. While American women have an opportunity to enter most careers, it can be difficult for them to achieve the success that they strive for, particularly in the world of business. The term "glass ceiling" has been coined to describe this. Is it common for women to work outside the home in your native country? If yes, what kind of job do they usually hold? Are they treated fairly in the workplace? Does your mother work? What does she do? How about other female family members? Ask your teacher about his/her family.

2. Do you think that the majority of the people in the field of business in your country tend to be honest and fair, or are they untrustworthy? Have you ever worked in the field of business? If yes, how did you find the people to be? Ask your teacher about his/her opinion of business people in the US.

It's another cutthroat day in the world of suits for Vic. He's about to do battle with a coworker, Joanna…

JOANNA: Hey Vic! I need to talk to you.

VIC: Hi Joanna, **what's up**?

JOANNA: **Come off it** Vic! You know exactly what's up! I've got a serious **bone to pick** with you.

VIC: **For Pete's sake** Joanna! Is this about the Sangyo account again? Will you ever let up?

JOANNA: Why should I let up? You know you **ripped off** that account from right under my nose.

VIC: Listen Joanna, it's a **dog-eat-dog** world out there! Besides, you're **barking up the wrong tree** if you think I stole that account from you.

JOANNA: What world are you living in?

VIC: The world of business. You're just going to have to **swallow** this. Forget all that **crap*** you learned in college and take this as your first lesson in the real world. What went down here is pretty **run-of-the-mill**. Sure, you **got the ball rolling** on the account, **I'll give you that**. But you never really **buckled down** and worked out the details. I **busted my butt** to give them what they wanted and that's why I **nailed** the contract. Go ahead, ask anyone around here; they'll **back** me **up** on what I'm saying 100%!

JOANNA: So you're saying that you **landed** the Sangyo account **fair and square**.

VIC: Come on, Joanna. **Pull yourself together** and stop bitching. Heck, you're just getting your feet wet in this business. I know exactly how you feel.

JOANNA: Oh, really! Is that why you're called the "cutthroat king" around here?

VIC: Look, I've been in the same boat that you're in now. Well, almost.

JOANNA: What do you mean "almost?"

VIC: I lost an account once too, but it was just **small potatoes**. I'm going to **make a killing** on this Sangyo account! I'm talking **ka-ching** baby! Hey, if you can't handle the competition, then you're not **cut out for** the world of business. Maybe you should throw in the towel!

JOANNA: Oh, I'm not going to listen to this. I'm out of here. You'd better watch your back Vic, because I'm going to make you **eat your words.**

            * See dictionary section for caution note regarding use of this term

Come on, this is no time to slack off. Find a partner, buckle down and bust your butts. Let's see how many of the slang meanings you can nail! (answers on page 145)

1. **what's up** exp_____

2. **come off it** exp_____

3. **bone to pick** noun_____

4. **for Pete's sake** exp_____

5. **rip off** verb_____

6. **dog-eat-dog** adj_____

7. **bark up the wrong tree** verb_____

8. **swallow** verb_____

9. **crap** noun_____

10. **run-of-the-mill** adj_____

11. **get the ball rolling** verb_____

12. **I'll give you that** exp_____

13. **buckle down** verb_____

14. **bust one's butt** verb_____

15. **nail** verb_____

16. **back up** verb_____

17. **land** verb_____

18. **fair and square** adv_____

19. **pull one's self together** verb_____

20. **small potatoes** noun_____

21. **make a killing** verb_____

22. **ka-ching** exp_____

23. **cut out for** verb_____

24. **eat one's words** verb_____

A. to waste one's effort by pursuing the wrong path

B. to make a large profit quickly

C. to regain one's composure or self-control

D. stuff, things, junk

E. average, ordinary

F. to steal or swindle

G. "I agree with you on a particular point"

H. to get serious and apply oneself

I. "what's going on?"

J. to support

K. "my patience has been exhausted!"

L. a complaint or grievance that needs discussion

M. to get things started

N. the sound of a cash register recording a profitable sale

O. to complete or perform a job impressively

P. to be suited for a profession

Q. fairly, honestly

R. to gain or secure something

S. to accept something difficult or displeasing without protest

T. to be forced to retract something one has said

U. something of little importance or worth

V. to work very hard

W. "stop acting or speaking pretentiously"

X. ruthless, vicious, mean

TALK IT OUT!

Let's get the ball rolling! Grab a pal and answer the questions using your own experience. If you don't have any related experience, just make something up. Use the new slang in your answers.

1. When was the last time you had to **bust your butt**? Who would you always **bust your butt** for? Why? Who would you never **bust your butt** for? Why?

2. Have you ever had a **bone to pick** with a service person, sales clerk, waiter, etc in the US? If yes, what was it about? Were any of your friends there to **back** you **up**? Who was the last person you **picked a bone** with? Why? Do you tend to have a lot of **bones to pick**, or are you pretty laid back?

3. When you were a kid, did you and your pals ever **rip** something **off** from a store? What did you **rip off**? Was it something that made you say "**ka-ching**" or was it just **small potatoes**?

4. Have you or anyone you know ever played the stock market? If yes, who? Have they ever **made a killing**? Suppose you **make a killing** in the market! What's the first thing you are going to do?

5. When class starts, how does your teacher **get the ball rolling**? If you were the teacher, how would you **get the ball rolling**? How do they get you to **buckle down** and start studying? How do you get yourself to **buckle down** and start studying?

6. What kind of job do you think you are **cut out for**? Why? What kind of job do you think you are not **cut out for**? Why? How about your best friend, what kind of job are they **cut out for** or are they not **cut out for** working at all? Do you think they would **back up** what you are saying?

7. What are **run-of-the-mill** business practices in your native country? Is the business world a **dog-eat-dog** scene, or do people try to treat each other with respect? Is it pretty **run-of-the-mill** to see women **land** jobs in the business world? What sort of positions do they hold?

8. Almost everyone in the US always has a bunch of **crap** to do. What kind of **crap** do you have to do this weekend? Does your teacher have a lot of **crap** to do this weekend? (Careful; don't use the word **crap** when you ask, he or she may not be able to **swallow** it!)

9. Imagine you just **landed** a new job, and your boss has been giving you the eye all day; he/ she seems to think you're hot. The next thing you know you feel a pinch on your behind… Do you **swallow** it and say nothing, give the boss a piece of your mind, or wait until you get home and **bark up the wrong tree**?

10. Suppose you weren't accepted to the university you were dying to go to. How long does it take you to **pull yourself together**? Your boyfriend/ girlfriend of three years breaks up with you. How long does it take you to **pull yourself together**? If a horrible teacher you had in high school told you that you will never amount to anything did you make them **eat their words**? Have you ever made anyone **eat their words**? What **words** did they **eat**?

WRITE IT UP!

Let's see how well you nailed down all of the new terms. Sit down with your partner and write a story about what went down between Joanna and Vic. A piece of cake, huh? Here's the catch; no peeking at the conversation. If that's too tough, then you can sneak a look at the new slang list.   •

Bitching In The Teacher's Lounge

1. Although there are laws in the US to protect citizens from blatant acts of discrimination, prejudice based on race, religion, age, gender or other differences is very common. Because discrimination can be subtle, it is often difficult to prove in a court of law. What forms of discrimination are illegal in your native country? Does prejudice exist? If so, against which groups? Why? How do you feel about this? Ask your teacher about the US.

2. One group of people that has recently begun to fight for equal treatment in the US is the gay community. There are openly gay communities in many larger cities in the US. How about in your native country? Tell your partner about it. Ask your teacher about the city you now live in and the rest of the US.

Charlie is hanging out in the teacher's lounge at work when a frustrated teacher walks in...

CHARLIE: Hey Peter, whoa! Man, would you **get a load of** those shoes! Leopard print Docs. Pretty **snazzy** dude! I don't think I'd have the guts to wear those, at least not here at school.

PETER: **For crying out loud**! Would you **get off my case**?

CHARLIE: Sorry. **Get up on the wrong side of the bed** today?

PETER: Hey man, I'm sorry I **snapped at** you like that. It's not your fault. I shouldn't **take** this **out on** you.

CHARLIE: Take what out on me?

PETER: **Duh**! The problem I've been having since I landed this job, those **dopes** they call students. Something's definitely **out of whack** in their heads. Hasn't anyone ever taught them about respect for others?

CHARLIE: What are you **bitching** about?

PETER: Those idiots keep **zeroing in on** the fact that I'm gay. You should hear some of the names I've been called! And it's always behind my back, of course.

CHARLIE: Peter, I know it must be tough, but let's **put the cards on the table**. You haven't exactly kept your sexual orientation a secret, and a lot of these kids are just too young to understand. You come from a world they're clueless about, so they ridicule it. You should've **seen this coming a mile away**.

PETER: Maybe you're right, but I think they're just downright mean. Authority figures let them get away with derogatory remarks towards homosexuals. I mean, if it were a racial comment, it would never be tolerated.

CHARLIE: Well, you're right about that. So why don't you **take a stand**?

PETER: As a teacher, it wouldn't be appropriate for me to come out and fight for gay rights at school. Besides, this school is so conservative that I've really got to **keep a lid on** this. **My back is to the wall**. If I make a stink about it, I'm sure the administration will find some reason to **can** me.

CHARLIE: Well, I can't say I've been in the same boat, but I do sympathize. Look, I'll have a talk with the kids that are giving you a hard time. In the meantime, let me give you a little advice; first, don't get yourself too **wound up over** this, and second, those boots you're **sporting**; they're a **dead giveaway**!

Bet you could see this coming a mile away! What, you say? Duh, that's right! Grab a partner and blow the lid off the new slang terms. (answers on page 145)

1. **get a load of** exp____
2. **snazzy** adj____
3. **for crying out loud** exp____
4. **get off one's case** verb____
5. **get up on the wrong side of the bed** verb____
6. **snap at** verb____
7. **take out on** verb____
8. **duh** exp____
9. **dope** noun____
10. **out of whack** adj____
11. **bitch** verb____
12. **zero in on** verb____
13. **put one's cards on the table** verb____
14. **see something coming a mile away** verb____
15. **take a stand** verb____
16. **keep a lid on** verb____
17. **one's back is to the wall** verb____
18. **can** verb____
19. **wind up over** verb____
20. **sport** verb____
21. **dead giveaway** noun____

A. stupid person
B. sarcastic response to the obvious
C. to fire someone from a job
D. to maintain secrecy
E. to be in a bad mood for no particular reason
F. to be candid about one's position
G. broken, improperly adjusted
H. said of one who has no options
I. "look at that!"
J. to recognize that something is bound to occur
K. to focus on
L. to stop criticizing or nagging someone
M. to complain
N. to speak irritably to someone
O. to wear in a showy manner
P. "I'm frustrated" or "I'm angry"
Q. to find a release for one's anger or frustration
R. flashily attractive
S. to adopt a firm position about one's opinion
T. to agitate
U. an obvious sign or indication

1. Have you or someone you know ever been **canned**? Why were you/they **canned**? Before you/they were **canned** could you/they **see it coming a mile away** or was it a total surprise? Have you or someone you know ever **canned** someone? How did you do it? Was it a surprise to them or could they **see it coming a mile away**?

2. When you were a kid and a person did something bad to you, did you **snap** at him or her and **take out** your anger **on** them, or did you find an object to **take** it **out on**? What did you **take** it **out on**?

3. What's the last thing you remember **bitching** about? Was it a serious problem or do you think you just **got up on the wrong side of the bed**?

4. Is anyone in the class **sporting** something that's pretty **snazzy**? Ask your teacher to **put her cards on the table** and see if she agrees with you.

5. Many people try to **keep a lid on** certain things about themselves. What would be a **dead giveaway** that someone was lying? What would be a **dead giveaway** that someone had a crush on you? Is there anything in your life that you are trying to **keep a lid on**? (Maybe you shouldn't answer that. It would be a **dead giveaway** that you have a secret!)

6. Have you been in a situation where you really want to help someone or change something but **your back is to the wall**? Do you let yourself get all **wound up over** it and **bitch** about it or just let it slide? Have you ever been in a situation in which **your back was to the wall**? Let your partner in on the story!

7. Let's **put our cards on the table**! Do you know anyone who tends to get **wound up over** small things? Do they end up **snapping** at and **taking** it **out on** the wrong person? Have they ever done it to you? Did you ever end up telling them to **get off your case**?

8. Is there anything about your teacher that the class tends to **zero in on**? What's something good about yourself that you or others tend to **zero in on**? Something bad?

9. Have you ever **taken a stand** on an important issue? What was it? What was the outcome? Tell your partner the last thing, even if it now seems unimportant, that you **took a stand on**. How did it turn out?

CROSSWORD REVIEW

You guys are hot! Go ahead and give yourselves a pat on the back. You've made it halfway through the book! Hold your horses, though! There is one little piece of business you've got to take care of before you go tooting your own horn. It's no biggy, just the crossword review, which should be cake! Don't forget to use the proper verb tense and word form so you can really nail it. (solution on page 145)

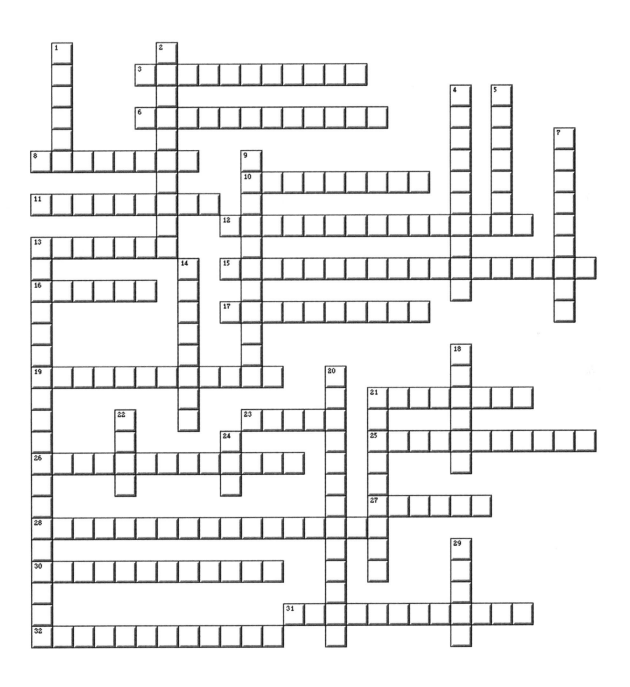

Across

3 You get so ____ __ ____ the silliest things. You've got to learn to relax.

6 Look at how dialated Paul's eyes are! That's a ____ _____ that he's using drugs again.

8 Matt is real good at fixing computers. He can ____ __ __ problems that no one else would find.

10 Wow, look at these blisters on my hands! I don't think I'm ___ ___ ____ physical labor.

11 You had no business criticizing Manny like that. You were really ____ __ ____.

12 I need to talk to you. Something has been bothering me and I need to ___ __ ___ ___ ____.

13 I've got a cold six-pack in the fridge. What do you say we ___ ____ a few?

15 You should be grateful to have an attentive girlfriend like Moira. She always _____ ____ _____ to please you.

16 The boss is really pissed at me for losing our best customer, so I'm going to ___ ___ until he cools down.

17 Craig is so _____ that he'll never change his mind.

19 Bill's stock went up by 200% in just a month. He ____ _ _____ when he sold it.

21 You told me that I could count on your support if I went to the boss with our complaints. Are you still willing to ____ __ __ on this?

23 Marcy's been out of work for a couple of months now, and I'm tired of lending her money. I hope she _____ a job soon.

25 Susan could never afford an expensive blouse like that. She must have _____ __ ___.

26 I didn't cheat on the test. I got that 'A' ____ ___ _____.

27 Jacob got a perfect '10' for his last dive in the springboard competition. He really _____ that dive!

28 I've got to ___ ___ ____ _____ on this term paper, or I'll never get it in on time.

30 I know when my husband has had a bad day at work because he comes home and _____ __ ___ __ me.

31 My dad constantly criticizes me about my clothes and my hair. I wish he would ___ __ __ ____.

32 Nothing much happened at the office today. It was just a ___ __ ___ ____ day.

Down

1 Would you grab me a cold soda from the _____ while you're up?

2 I've got a ____ __ ____ with the manager. She's told me at least three times that she'd repair my heater, but it's still broken.

4 Kevin never sees things as they really are. Something is definitely ___ __ _____ in his head.

5 I'm anxious to hear what happened last night! I'm ___ ____!

7 It can be real competetive when you're in business. It's a ___ ___ ___ world out there.

9 Robert did very badly on his test. He _____ __ __ more that half the questions.

13 I know Sebastian has some personal problems, but he needs to ____ _____ _____ if he wants to get a passing grade this term.

14 Don't tell anyone about what happened at the office today. You've got to ____ _ ___ on it!

18 What a disappointment! I'm really _____ about having to cancel my vacation plans.

20 Nobu worked day and night to make that project a success. He really _____ ___ ____ on it.

21 I've never seen Simone so angry before. She was _____ __!

22 Don't believe any of his stories. They're all a load of ____.

24 Georgia must have picked up a ___ while she was on vacation. She's been complaining of a sore throat and a headache.

29 You're constantly complaining! All you ever do is _____!

Charlie's Missing Student

1. Who usually supports the family in your native country? Was that true in your own family? Ask your teacher about the US.

2. Is it common for high school students to have part-time jobs in your native country? Why or why not? If you had one, what kind of job was it? What did you do with the money you earned? Ask your teacher about the US.

3. Did your parents nag at you a lot when you were a teenager? What did they nag about?

Charlie, a high school teacher, runs into one of his students who hasn't been in class for several weeks! Charlie wants the scoop on the situation…

CHARLIE: Hey, Junior, is that you? I've almost forgotten what your **mug** looks like. What gives? I haven't seen you in class for quite a few weeks.

JUNIOR: Oh, hi Mr. Johnson. Sorry, I've been tied up.

CHARLIE: Tied up doing what? **Cutting** class? Today you couldn't come up with correct answers to even the simplest questions and you need to be **on your toes** to pass this course! In fact, if **my memory serves me right** you weren't looking so hot the last time you were in class either. **Come on** now, **come clean**.

JUNIOR: It's my **old man**, Mr. Johnson. Remember how I told you about him not **pulling his weight** around the house? Well, my mom finally bailed on him about a month ago. She was all like "If you don't get off your lazy butt, get a job, and start **bringing home the bacon,** you're history!" I thought she was just **talking through her nose**, but she was dead serious! It **floored** me when she left him! Since then he's been **on my case** to get a job. I told him I needed to concentrate on studying so I can graduate, but he **put his foot down**. He goes "You need to start **punching the clock** or you're on your own!" The only job I could find was during the day, so I've been going to night school. I'm so **worn out** from working all day that by the time I should start hitting the books my **brain is fried**! My grades have really **taken a nosedive**.

CHARLIE: Sounds like you're in a tight spot. What does your mom have to say about this?

JUNIOR: Well, she's actually not my real mom. Besides she's **shacked up** with her new boyfriend. The guy is **loaded** so she doesn't want me **in her hair**.

CHARLIE: How about if I have a **word** with your father? Maybe I can help straighten the situation out.

JUNIOR: Would you Mr. Johnson? My dad keeps telling me I'll **get the hang of** working and studying, but I don't think so!

CHARLIE: Sure, no problem.

JUNIOR: Thanks. You're **one in a million**. Otherwise, all I can see is my future going **down the drain** fast!

This is no time for fried brains! Make sure you're on your toes, hook yourself up with a partner, and match up the slang terms with their meanings! Make sure you pull your weight, or your partner might get on your case. (answers on page 146)

1. **mug** noun_____

2. **cut** verb_____

3. **on one's toes** adj_____

4. **if one's memory serves one right** exp_____

5. **come on** exp_____

6. **come clean** verb_____

7. **old man** noun_____

8. **pull one's weight** verb_____

9. **bring home the bacon** verb_____

10. **talk through one's nose** verb_____

11. **floor** verb_____

12. **on one's case** adj_____

13. **put one's foot down** verb_____

14. **punch the clock** verb_____

15. **worn out** adj_____

16. **one's brain is fried** exp_____

17. **take a nosedive** verb_____

18. **shack up** verb_____

19. **loaded** adj_____

20. **in someone's hair** adj_____

21. **word** noun_____

22. **get the hang of** verb_____

23. **one in a million** adj_____

24. **down the drain** adj_____

A. to do one's share of the work

B. to be critical of, to nag

C. to intentionally miss

D. wealthy

E. to exaggerate or lie

F. to work at a job that pays hourly wages

G. one's father

H. one is mentally exhausted

I. to live with someone out of wedlock

J. wasted, ruined

K. to become accustomed to

L. "assuming one's memory is correct"

M. physically exhausted

N. to shock

O. to take a firm stand

P. to be a distraction or annoyance

Q. to experience a sudden drop

R. alert, prepared

S. a person's face

T. to tell the truth, to confess

U. a brief but serious conversation

V. an expression used to challenge, or to ask a person to stop

W. earn a salary to support one's family

X. extraordinarily rare

TALK IT OVER!

You'd better be on your toes so you can pull your weight. Slacking off is not allowed! Sit down with your partner and talk through your nose if you need to. Don't forget to use the new slang in your answers.

1. Tell your partner to **come clean**! When was the last time they **cut** class? What did they do instead?

2. Do your roommates **pull their weight** when it comes to housework? If they don't, do you get **on their case** about it? Do you **pull your weight**? If you don't, does your roomie get **on your case** about it? What else do you get **on each other's cases** about?

3. What is something that **floored** you recently? Why did it **floor** you?

4. Who **brings home the bacon** in your house? Have you ever **punched the clock**? What did you do? Were you **on your toes** at work or did your boss have to **put her foot down** about **pulling your weight**?

5. Are you **worn out** by the time your English class is over? When Sunday afternoon rolls around, are you **worn out** from the weekend?

6. How long can you study before you feel like **your brain is fried**?

7. Is it common for unmarried couples to **shack up** before getting married in your native country? Why or why not? Would you **shack up** with your boyfriend/ girlfriend? Why or why not? Find out about the US from your teacher.

8. When you were a kid, did you get **in your mom's hair** when she was trying to prepare dinner or get the house straightened out? Did you ask her tons of annoying questions, want her to hang out and play with you, or…? Are there any kids in your life now? Do they get **in your hair** when you're trying to get something done?

9. Do you have any friends who like to **talk through their noses**? Do they **talk through their noses** about being **loaded**, the number of boyfriends or girlfriends they have, their intelligence…? Do you let them go on or tell them to **come clean**?

10. Who was the last person you had a **word** with? What about?

11. Name a person in your life that you consider to be **one in a million**.

12. Tell your partner about some plans you made that went **down the drain**? Why did they end up going **down the drain**?

WRITE IT DOWN!

Sit down with your partner and write down a conversation that takes place between Charlie and Junior's old man. Go ahead, get on the old man's case for being so hardheaded.

"You've Got Me Stumped!"

1. In your native country, is it acceptable to ask a mutual friend to introduce a person that one is romantically interested in? Why or why not? Have you ever done this for a friend? Has a friend ever done it for you? How did it turn out? Ask your teacher about the US and their experiences.

2. When the teacher gives you a homework assignment do you procrastinate until the last minute and then have to study a lot of material in a short time? Or do you start as soon as you get home? Why? Ask your teacher what his habit was when he was a student.

Mona and Renee are at home shooting the breeze. Renee is worried about her nonexistent love life and Mona is worried about a paper she's got to finish writing…

MONA: Thanks for making dinner Renee, that angel hair pasta really **hit the spot**. So, what **are** you **up to** tonight?

RENEE: **Same old, same old**! I'm really **in a rut**. I wish something new and exciting would happen in my life. I'm **fed up** with staying home every night and **vegging** in front of the tube.

MONA: What you need is a man.

RENEE: You're telling me! Actually, you know that one guy who works with Charlie? That real **hip** guy? I kind of **have a crush on** him.

MONA: You've got me **stumped**! A hip guy that works with Charlie? Hold on, I'm going to **go out on a limb** here; you don't mean Peter, do you?

RENEE: Yeah, that's the one! He's cute! Ask Charlie if he'll **fix** me **up with** him.

MONA: **Fat chance**!

RENEE: Why not? I'm not good enough? I'd do it for you **in a heartbeat**!

MONA: **Hello**! Peter is gay!

RENEE: Get out of here! I wouldn't have **pegged** him **for** gay, but now that you mention it, I guess it doesn't seem so **far-fetched**.

MONA: So, do you still want me to ask Charlie to fix you up with him?

RENEE: **Drop it**. He is a pretty cool guy though; maybe we could just be friends. He seems like the kind of person I'd **see eye-to-eye** with on most things. How about you, what are you up to tonight?

MONA: I've got that huge paper due next week. I'm going to have to **pull an all-nighter** to get it done. I've really been **slacking off** since I met Vic. I've got to get **on the ball** and seriously **hit the books** or I'll be **cramming for** my thesis like I was a freshman! I wish I could hang out and veg in front of the tube with you, but I'm off to the library. And don't worry, you **are bound to** meet someone. You know what they say; "**There are a lot of fish in the sea**!"

What do you mean, this new slang has you stumped! Well, don't just sit there and veg. Connect with a partner and see if you can see eye-to-eye on the meanings. There shouldn't be any need to pull an all-nighter on this. (answers on page 146)

1. **hit the spot** verb_____

2. **be up to** verb_____

3. **same old, same old** exp_____

4. **in a rut** adj_____

5. **fed up** adj_____

6. **veg** verb_____

7. **hip** adj_____

8. **have a crush on** verb_____

9. **stump** adj_____

10. **go out on a limb** verb_____

11. **fix up with** verb_____

12. **fat chance** exp_____

13. **in a heartbeat** adv_____

14. **hello!** exp_____

15. **peg for** verb_____

16. **far-fetched** adj_____

17. **drop it** exp_____

18. **see eye-to-eye** verb_____

19. **pull an all-nighter** verb_____

20. **slack off** verb_____

21. **on the ball** adj_____

22. **hit the books** verb_____

23. **cram for** verb_____

24. **be bound to** verb_____

25. **there are a lot of fish in the sea** exp_____

A. to baffle or confuse

B. to put someone in a category

C. to be efficient, to be alert

D. to agree, have similar views

E. to arrange a date

F. to study intensely shortly before an exam

G. "the same old thing"

H. "are you stupid?" or "don't be so foolish"

I. sick and tired, frustrated

J. doing, involved or occupied with

K. "there are many prospects to choose from"

L. improbable

M. in an instant

N. to be stuck in a boring routine

O. to stay up the entire night and study

P. to relax with an inert mental state, behave like a vegetable

Q. to decrease in intensity

R. cool, stylish

S. to be destined

T. to take a risk

U. to study intensely

V. "highly unlikely"

W. to be infatuated with someone

X. to be perfect

Y. "forget it"

TALK TURKEY!

If you're fed up with trying to figure out the new slang, then this should hit the spot. Hook up with a partner, go out on a limb and answer all the questions truthfully. Too far-fetched? Then make up a few white lies.

1. What was the last new English word you heard (not including this lesson, hello!) that had you **stumped**? Did you **go out on a limb** and guess the meaning of the word or did you look it up in a dictionary?

2. When was the last time you felt that you were **in a rut** and everything in your life was the **same old, same old**? How did you get yourself **out of the rut** or are you still **in a rut**?

3. Do you **see eye-to-eye** on your future with your parents? Name something that you'll never **see eye-to-eye** on with your parents. Is there someone in your life that you never **see eye-to-eye** with? Do you end up getting **fed up** when you talk to them?

4. What is something you would do **in a heartbeat**? If your best friend tried to **fix** you **up with** a person who's always **hitting the books**, would you go out with that person **in a heartbeat**, or say "**fat chance!**"

5. What are you **fed up** with at your house or school? Why? What are you **fed up** with about the US? Why? Find out if your teacher is **fed up** with anything in his/her life.

6. What have you **been up to** lately? Have you been **hitting the books** or **slacking off** and **vegging** in front the tube? What **are** you **up to** this coming weekend?

7. Who was the last person you **had a crush on**? Did you try to get someone to **fix you up** with the person you **had a crush on** or did you think that the two of you were **bound to** get together eventually?

8. Who's the **hippest** person you know in the US? Who's the **hippest** person you know in your native country? Who would you **peg for** as more **hip**, young people in your country, or young Americans? When Americans meet you, what nationality do they **peg** you **for**?

9. Do you procrastinate when it comes time to study and end up **cramming** and **pulling all-nighters**? Name a question from a recent exam that had you **stumped**. Who's the most **on the ball** person in your class? Before the last exam, do you think this person had to **pull an all-nighter** and **cram for** the exam?

10. What's the last meal you ate that really **hit the spot**? On a hot summer day, what would really **hit the spot** for you?

WRITE UP A STORM!

By yourself, come up with a story about fixing someone up. Make it as far-fetched as you can, and use as least fifteen new slang terms in your story. When you finish, don't just sit there and veg! Share the story with the person sitting next to you, or if you're really on the ball, read it out loud to your classmates.

"I'm Up To My Ears In Work."

1. When you had problems in a university class, who would you turn to for help? Do graduate students in your country work as teacher's assistants? Is it a desirable or difficult job to have? Does a TA's job involve teaching the class, grading papers, or just helping students? Have you or anyone you know ever worked as a TA during your university career? Has your teacher ever worked as a TA?

2. When someone at work, school, or home does something that bothers you, do you tell this person how you feel or do you tend to keep your feelings inside? If you do discuss your feelings, is your tone of voice quiet, at the top of your lungs, or somewhere in between?

Mona **lucked out** and is working as a TA for one of her professors. She and another TA, Lucy, help teach class, grade papers, and give the students a hand with their assignments. One student, Colin, is **in a bind** and heads over to the TA's office for help...

MONA: Hey, Colin, what's up?

COLIN: I was wondering if you could give me a hand. I still haven't **figured out** what to write my term paper on.

MONA: You still haven't selected a theme? You were supposed to have that done last week!

COLIN: I've narrowed it down to a few topics. Uh... here's the list.

MONA: Colin, you must have thirty items on this list! I don't have time to look over that many! I'm **up to my ears** in work as it is; and to **top things off**, this list is so messy, I can't even **make out** what you've written!

COLIN: Can't I just **run** these **by** you?

MONA: No, you can't run them by me. When you've pulled your weight on this assignment, I'll give you a hand; but don't come back here until you've done your part!

Colin leaves the office...

LUCY: Wow, you really **bit his head off**, but you sure **set him straight**! Must be **that time of the month**, huh?

MONA: You **hit the nail on the head**; but it really **gets on my nerves** when these **peabrains** come in here and try to con us into doing their **measly** assignments for them. Do **I look like I was born yesterday**? I mean, **get with the program**! We're so **bogged down with** work right now, and for the **peanuts** they pay us, it's just not worth the hassle! This is too much for me to take today.

LUCY: **Chill out**, Mona! We all did the same thing when we were undergrads!

MONA: **Not by a long shot**! Guys like that can't **cut** it and get **weeded out** before the graduate program.

LUCY: You're getting yourself all **worked up over** nothing. The assignment **went over his head** and he was stumped. He was just looking for the easy way out. Why don't we **call it a day** and go chow down.

MONA: Yeah, I guess you're right. Just give me a sec to **wrap up** what I'm doing. Is it cool if I ask Vic to come along?

LUCY: Sure, just don't blow your top with him like you did with poor Colin!

Did that conversation go over your head? Can't quite make it out on your own? Well, get with the program; grab yourself a partner and figure out the meanings together! (answers on page 146)

1. **luck out** verb_____   A. to scold and speak very angrily at someone

2. **in a bind** adj_____   B. a stupid or foolish person

3. **figure out** verb_____   C. to be slowed because of too much work

4. **up to one's ears** adj_____ D. small or insignificant

5. **to top things off** exp_____ E. "relax" or "calm down"

6. **make out** verb_____   F. to be precisely correct

7. **run by** verb_____   G. to be able to read or recognize

8. **bite someone's head off** verb_____ H. to get rid of less desirable persons

9. **set someone straight** verb_____   I. to correct someone

10. **that time of the month** noun_____   J. "wake up and realize what's going on"

11. **hit the nail on the head** verb_____ K. a small amount of money

12. **get on one's nerves** verb_____   L. the time for a woman's monthly period

13. **peabrain** noun_____   M. to become agitated or upset

14. **measly** adj_____   N. to annoy or bother someone

15. **look like one was born yesterday** exp_____ O. to stop working for the day

16. **get with the program** exp_____   P. to have a problem

17. **bog down with** verb_____   Q. to not understand

18. **peanuts** noun_____   R. "very unlikely" or "not remotely"

19. **chill out** exp_____   S. to solve a problem, to understand

20. **not by a long shot** exp_____ T. to ask for one's advice or opinion

21. **cut** verb_____   U. "and even worse..."

22. **weed out** verb_____   V. to have good fortune

23. **work up over** verb_____   W. deeply involved, overwhelmed

24. **go over one's head** verb_____ X. "do I look stupid?"

25. **call it a day** verb_____   Y. to make the grade

26. **wrap up** verb_____   Z. to conclude, to finish

TALK SHOP!

If you think it's "talking time" you hit the nail on the head. Now don't get yourself all worked up over something that goes over your head, just sit down with your partner and figure it out!

1. When you're **in a bind** in the US, who do you turn to for a hand? How about when you were home in your native country? When was the last time you found yourself **in a bind**? When you find yourself **in a bind** do let yourself get all **worked up over** it or do you just **chill** and let the problem take care of itself?

2. Does your teacher **bog** you **down with** assignments to the point where you're **up to your ears** in homework? When you were in high school, did your teachers **bog** you **down with** homework? If you were a head honcho would you **bog** your employees **down with** work?

3. When something tells you something that **goes over your head**, do you pretend that you understood, or do you tell them you couldn't quite **make out** everything and ask them to **run** it **by** you one more time? When was the last time you found yourself **in a bind** like this? How often does American slang **go over your head**?

4. Suppose the person you live with does a couple of things that really **get on your nerves**! What's the worse thing they do? Use "**and to top things off...**" in your answer. Come up with some advice on how to **set** your roommate **straight**!

5. Are you good at **figuring out** math problems? Are you good at **figuring out** the new slang meanings? Are you good at **figuring out** what to do when you're **in a bind**?

6. Imagine that you are the director of the first mission to Mars. You have narrowed down the potential candidates to twenty but you can only send ten. How will you **weed out** those that will have to stay behind? How will you decide who will **cut** it? Have you ever been in a situation where you just couldn't **cut** it? What was it?

7. Suppose your significant other is a **peabrain** and let himself get **up to his ears** in bills! Do you **bite his head off** when you find out, or would you just **chill out** and **figure out** how to get **out of the bind**? Would try to **figure out** what to do on your own, or would you **run** it **by** an accountant? What's the last thing you found yourself **up to your ears in**?

8. When is the last time you **lucked out** because your teacher let you **call it a day** early?

LET'S WRITE!

OK guys, just chill out and don't let yourselves get bogged down with this. Find a new partner and come up with a humorous dialogue between two roommates who get on each other's nerves. Use tons of slang in your story. When you wrap it up, run it by your teacher, and then share it with your classmates!

CROSSWORD REVIEW

Good job! You've almost completed <u>Unit Six</u>, but there's one more piece of business to take care of. Try to complete the crossword from the clues on the next page without looking back at the slang lists for this unit. If that's too tough, don't throw in the towel, just sneak a peek back at the lessons. Good luck, and remember to pay attention to verb tense and form. (solution on page 146)

Across

1 That friend of yours, Pamela, is really hot! Do you think you could ___ me __ ____ her?

3 Here's your chance to ___ Nathan _____ . You need to tell him that he's mistaken.

6 My life has become a boring routine. I'm really __ _ ___ right now.

9 Melissa was promised a fifteen percent increase in her salary. Instead, she got a _____ three percent raise!

10 Your excuse that your dog ate your homework sounds pretty ___ _____ to me.

13 Rebecca is sick of her diet. She told me that she's ___ __ with starving herself all the time.

15 I've been working twelve hours a day for the last six months. I'm really ____ ___ !

16 I don't have any plans for the weekend. What ___ you __ __ ?

18 _____ ___ would you? You need to calm down.

20 After ten straight hours of cramming, my _____ __ _____. I can't think anymore!

21 I've haven't cracked a book all semester. I need to ____ ___ the midterm next week or I'll fail.

22 If the boss finds out you lied on your job application, your promotion will go right ____ __ ____ .

23 Stop criticizing her. You're always __ ___ ____ about her friends.

24 Carissa is really angry. I asked her a question and she just about ___ __ ____ ___ !

25 I couldn't understand what the professor was talking about. It ____ ____ __ ____ .

27 That dweeb Ricardo asked me if I'd go out with him sometime. I told him "___ _____ !"

29 Jack has really been _____ __ for the last few weeks. If he doesn't start hitting the books soon, he's going to fail the course.

33 I don't want you sponging off of us any longer. If you don't start _____ ____ _____ , you're going to have to find another place to live.

35 Beth exaggerates everthing she ways. She's always talking _____ ___ ____ .

38 What an annoying person! Her constant whining really ____ __ __ ____ .

39 The writing on this prescription is so messy I can't ____ ___ what it says.

40 With my job, nightschool and house chores, I'm really _____ ____ ____ work this weekend.

41 ____ __ would you? You've been going on about the same thing for over an hour!

Down

2 Why do you get so _____ __ ____ over his comments? I'm sure he didn't mean to upset you.

4 I've never agreed with him on politics. We just don't ___ __ __ __ .

5 Stop by my office on your way out. I'd like to have a ____ with you.

7 This is a tough class. You have to be __ ____ ____ if your going to pass.

8 Man, you _____ ___ ! The teacher won't collect our papers until next week, so now you have time to get yours finished.

11 Those kids are driving me crazy! They've been __ __ ____ all morning!

12 I'm in love with that new girl. I ____ _ _____ __ her.

14 There are hundreds of jobs listed in the paper. You ___ _____ __ find one if you keep looking.

17 You ___ ___ ____ __ ___ ____ when you identified that problem.

19 You're my friend, so if you need help, you just say the word and I'll be there __ _ _____ .

26 I've had a rough day. I'm going to go home and ___ in front of the tube tonight.

28 A tall, cold glass of lemonade really ____ ___ ____ on a hot day.

30 Stop evading my questions. I want you to ____ _____ and tell me the truth.

31 Lisa didn't come to school yesterday. She ___ class and went shopping instead.

32 Could you help me out here? I'm really __ _ ____ . My regular babysitter just called to say she's sick, and I'm already late for my job interview.

34 He buys a new car every year. He must be _____ !

36 The boss will want to see this contract. Why don't you ___ it __ him before you sign it.

37 I had no idea what the correct answer was. I was completely _____ .

Blowing It

1. What would you do if you were supposed to meet your boyfriend or girlfriend but forgot? Have you ever been in this situation? Tell your partner about it.

2. What's the typical age for marriage in your native country? Have any of your friends gotten married? How did you feel when they told you they were getting married? Why?

Vic and Charlie are out **shooting the breeze**, when Vic realizes that he has screwed up...

VIC: What's the time dude?

CHARLIE: It's nearly 10:00.

VIC: You're **full of it**! That can't be!

CHARLIE: I'm dead serious. Why, what gives?

VIC: Oh man, I **blew** it! I was supposed to hook up with Mona and a friend of hers at 9:00! I'd better call her.

CHARLIE: **Screw it,*** man; just chill. She can **chew** you **out** tomorrow.

VIC: Let me borrow your cell phone, I'll get this over with **in a flash**.

Vic calls Mona to offer an excuse. After they talk briefly, Vic hangs up...

CHARLIE: I wouldn't have done that if I were you.

VIC: You think I shouldn't have called her to tell her I spaced on our date?

CHARLIE: I would've come up with a white lie.

VIC: You know Mona; she's no **dummy**! She would've **seen straight through me**!

CHARLIE: Yeah, you're probably right. She'll **play it cool** with you on the phone but you're **in for** a big surprise when you **show up** at her place! All **hell is going to break loose**! You'll be **in the doghouse** for sure!

VIC: Nah, I think she'll **let me off the hook**. Besides, if I lied to her and she found out about it, I could have been **out of the picture** completely. This way she'll be **pissed*** for a couple of days but I **saved my skin**. You know, this is more than just a **fling**. I'm falling pretty hard for Mona.

CHARLIE: Aww man, don't tell me you're **wimping out on** me! You're serious about Mona? You're not thinking of **popping the question** are you? If you join the ranks of **henpecked husbands**, I'll be all alone to take on all of the hot, young babes! Dude, you're too young to die!

VIC: Buddy, this didn't just **creep up on** me. I **knew right off the bat** there was something special about Mona. She's the one for me.

           * see dictionary for caution note regarding use of this term

You guys are no dummies, so you can get this done in a flash! Sit down with a partner and hook up the new slang with their meanings. Check out the conversation if you need a hand. (answers on page 147)

1. **shoot the breeze** verb_____

2. **full of it** exp_____

3. **blow** verb_____

4. **screw it** exp_____

5. **chew out** verb_____

6. **in a flash** adv_____

7. **dummy** noun_____

8. **see straight through** verb_____

9. **play it cool** verb_____

10. **be in for** verb_____

11. **show up** verb_____

12. **hell breaks loose** verb_____

13. **in the doghouse** adj_____

14. **let someone off the hook** verb_____

15. **out of the picture** adj_____

16. **piss off** verb_____

17. **save one's skin** verb_____

18. **fling** noun_____

19. **wimp out on** verb_____

20. **pop the question** verb_____

21. **henpecked husband** noun_____

22. **creep up on** verb_____

23. **know something right off the bat** verb_____

A. to be in serious trouble

B. to make angry

C. a foolish or stupid person

D. to back out, lose one's nerve

E. to relax, talk or converse idly

F. to develop a state of chaos or rage

G. to remain calm and collected

H. to release someone from blame or responsibility

I. to know someone is lying

J. to be uninvolved

K. a casual love affair

L. in trouble, in disfavor

M. to advance slowly or stealthily

N. to make a mistake

O. "I don't believe you"

P. to arrive

Q. to save one's reputation

R. fast, quickly

S. "forget it"

T. a weak husband who is dominated by his wife

U. angrily criticize someone

V. to propose marriage

W. to realize something immediately

TALKING TIME!

It's time to blab your secrets left and right, but if you'd rather try to pull a fast one on your partner, go for it! Will they fall for it, or see straight through you?

1. Have you ever seriously **blown** it with a good friend? What did you do? How did you get yourself **out of the doghouse**? How about with a boyfriend or girlfriend? Give your partner the scoop. When was the last time you were **in the doghouse**? Did you get **chewed out** big-time? How did you **get yourself off the hook**?

2. When you were a child, could your mom **see straight through you**? As a teenager, was it easier or more difficult for her to **see straight through** you? Can your teacher **see straight through** you, or can you basically get away with murder in class?

3. Who was the last person you were **pissed** at? Why were you **pissed** at them? How long did it take you to **let them off the hook**? Who was the last person who was **pissed** at you? Why were they **pissed** at you? How did you **get yourself off the hook**?

4. This question is for you guys. Suppose your best buddy gives you a call and is all like "Guess what dude, I **popped the question**!" Do you reply with A; "**You're full of it**!" B; "Congratulations, who's the lucky girl?" or C; both. Have you ever thought of **popping the question**? Girls, when your best friend calls to tell you her new boyfriend of only one week **popped the question** and she wants to say "yes", are you all like "Don't be such a **dummy**, it's just a week-long **fling**!" or "Congratulations!" Have you ever been close to having **the question popped** but the guy **wimped out of** it? Was that grounds for telling them "You are **out of the picture**?"

5. When you are out in public with someone special who does something out of line, do you show your emotions and let all **hell break loose**, or do you **play it cool** until you get home and then let all **hell break loose**? Do they realize what they **are in for**, or is it all a big surprise? Give your partner the dirt!

6. If it's an hour before English class and you haven't done your homework yet, do you say "**screw it**" and blow off doing your homework, or get it done **in a flash**?

7. Is your dad a **henpecked husband**? What makes you think he is or isn't? Girls, would you like to have a **henpecked husband** or would you find this situation difficult to put up with? Guys, do you think you'll turn into **henpecked husbands**? Why or why not?

8. Suppose the time **creeps up on you** and you **show up** late for a dinner date at a friend's house. Would you try to **save your skin** with a white lie, or would your friend **know right off the bat** that you weren't telling the truth?

WRITING TIME!

With a new partner, write a dialogue between a young couple that is having a fight. The disagreement can be about anything; another person, money, housework, etc. Use at least fifteen examples of slang from this lesson in your conversation.

"You Need To Blow Off Some Steam!"

1. If you are hanging out with a friend who gets angry with someone, how do you usually handle the situation?

2. If you are hanging out with a friend and you get angry with someone, how would you like your friend to handle the situation?

Mona and Lucy are hanging out waiting for Vic to show up. He's already an hour late when Mona's cell phone suddenly rings…

MONA: Hello? Vic, where are you? You **spaced out** on the time? Oh, I see. OK, I'll see you in about an hour at your place.

Mona hangs up the phone…

LUCY: Vic spaced out on the time? Wow, is he in for a big surprise! No way you'll **let that slide**!

MONA: **Damn straight**! He's not going to **weasel out of** this. I wonder what kind of **lame** excuse he'll come up with this time.

LUCY: What do you mean, "this time?" You mean this has happened before?

MONA: It's not like I've **kept track of** every time he's late, but he picked the wrong day to **mess with** me. I've had such a **crappy*** day! Tons of work at the office, that **flaky** student trying to worm out of doing his homework and now, to top things off, a **flake** for a boyfriend who thinks he's **got me wrapped around his finger** and can blow me off whenever it suits him.

LUCY: Whoa, Mona! Chill out! I think you're **reading** way too much **into** this! He just made an honest mistake. It could happen to anyone!

MONA: Why are you **sticking up for** that bonehead? His excuses won't **fly** with me! He must think I'm some airhead that'll just **fall for** his excuses and giggle after he's stood me up.

LUCY: **What's eating you**? You're really going off the deep end! Snap out of it!

MONA: What do you mean, "what's eating me?" Blowing me off in front of a friend **takes the cake**! He's going to have to do something really good to **make up for** this! I'm **seeing red**! How could he have just "spaced" on the time!

LUCY: I still don't see why you're **getting** so **riled up**!

MONA: How do I know he's really with Charlie and not out making **goo-goo eyes** at some airhead?

LUCY: It sounds like you've been keeping this **bottled up** for a long time! You really need to vent! Maybe you should **call off** tonight and **blow off some steam** before you see him.

MONA: Yeah, right, like that's going to happen! I can't wait to see him and **give him the third degree** to see if his excuses will **hold water**!

* See dictionary for caution note about use of this term

Grab a partner or two, or three; no one's keeping track! Just don't try to worm you way out of figuring out the meaning of the new slang. (answers on page 147)

1. let something slide verb_____

2. damn straight exp_____

3. weasel out of verb_____

4. lame adj_____

5. keep track of verb_____

6. mess with verb_____

7. crappy adj_____

8. flaky adj_____

9. flake noun_____

10. have someone wrapped around one's finger verb_____

11. read into verb_____

12. stick up for verb_____

13. fly verb_____

14. fall for verb_____

15. what's eating someone? exp_____

16. take the cake verb_____

17. make up for verb_____

18. see red verb_____

19. get riled up verb_____

20. goo-goo eyes noun_____

21. bottle up verb_____

22. call off verb_____

23. blow off some steam verb_____

24. give someone the third degree verb_____

25. hold water verb_____

A. an unreliable person

B. to work properly or successfully

C. weak, inadequate

D. to avoid an obligation in a devious manner

E. to be outstanding in some respect, good or bad

F. "absolutely right"

G. to be believable, to be valid

H. to become agitated or upset

I. flirtatious eye movements

J. to keep a record of something

K. to cancel

L. "what's bothering someone?"

M. to be furious or indignant

N. to have complete control over another person

O. to ignore or be flexible about a problem

P. to bother or annoy

Q. bad, worthless

R. unreliable, undependable

S. to get rid of anger, release one's frustrations

T. to be deceived, to be tricked

U. to question or interrogate someone

V. to speak or act in defense of

W. to find an unintended meaning in something one has done or said

X. to keep one's feelings inside

Y. to compensate for

TALK IT OUT!

Time to make up for all the silence! Sit down with your partner and answer all the questions. If your partner doesn't use the new slang in their answers, don't let it slide. Let them know you're not someone to mess with!

1. What's the last thing you were supposed to do, but **weaseled out of**? How did you manage to **weasel** your way **out of** it? Is there somthing coming up that you would like to **weasel** your way **out of**?

2. If somebody is **messing with** your best friend, do you **stick up for** your friend? Who **stuck up for** you when you were a kid? Who did you **stick up for**? What's your most memorable story about **sticking up for** someone?

3. Fill in the blank. "If someone **messed with** my _____ it would make me **see red**!" Why?

4. Do you try to **keep track of** how much money you spend? Are you good at **keeping track of** your expenses? Why or why not? Does your teacher usually **keep track of** the time in class or do you end up having to stay longer than you should?

5. What's the **lamest** excuse you've ever come up with for not completing a school assignment on time? Did your teacher **fall for** it? What's the **lamest** excuse you can come up with for cutting class? Ask your teacher if this excuse would **fly** with her! Check out all of your classmates' **lame** excuses. Which one **takes the cake**? Do any of them seem like they would **hold water**?

6. Who's the **flakiest** person you know in your native country? Why makes you think they are such a **flake**? Do you know any **flakes** in this country? What's the last thing they **flaked out** on?

7. You're studying for a big exam when your best friend calls and spends an hour telling you about his **crappy** day. Yikes! How do you **make up for** lost time when you finally get off the phone?

8. Have you made **goo-goo eyes** at anyone since coming to the US? Has anyone made **goo-goo eyes** at you? Demonstrate your best **goo-goo eyes** for your partner, but don't let them **read** too much **into** it!

10. Do you tend to keep your feelings **bottled up**? When you need to vent, who do you talk to?

11. What's the last thing that got you all **riled up**? Do you think you were **reading** too much **into** it or was your anger justifiable? How did you **blow off steam**? What do you usually do when you need to **blow off some steam**?

12. What's the last thing you **called off**? Why did you **call** it **off**? Have you ever known anyone who **called off** a wedding?

13. When you were a kid did you have your parents **wrapped around your finger**? Is it a piece of cake for you to **wrap someone around your finger**? How do you do it? Have you ever made **goo-goo eyes** at your boyfriend or girlfriend to get them **wrapped around your finger**?

14. If your boyfriend or girlfriend is an hour late for an important date do you **let it slide** or **give them the third degree**? Why?

WRITE IT UP!

Grab a partner; one of you is Vic, the other is Mona. Vic is late, and Mona is reading so much into it, she's seeing red! Write down the conversation that goes down between them when they meet at her place. Keep track and make sure that you use at least fifteen slang terms.

"What's Got You Looking So Down In The Dumps?"

1. Have you ever gotten so angry that you did something you later regretted? What was it? What did you do to make the situation better?

2. Have you ever told a boyfriend or girlfriend that you never wanted to see them again, but later changed your mind? Were you able to make the situation better? How?

Renee comes home from work and finds Mona looking pretty bummed. Mona gives Renee the lowdown on what happened with Vic the previous night…

RENEE: Hey? What's up? What's got you looking so down **in the dumps**?

MONA: It's Vic and me.

RENEE: Trouble in paradise, huh? A **lovers' spat**?

MONA: Nope, it's bigger than that. I think we **broke up**.

RENEE: Come on! You're **playing with** me, right?

MONA: No, I'm **dead serious**.

RENEE: Get out of here! Who **dumped** who? You guys were like two peas in a pod!

MONA: I dumped him.

RENEE: Have you **lost your marbles**? You must be out of your mind! He was **the best thing since sliced bread** to come along in your life!

MONA: **You're telling me**? I don't know **what got into** me. We were supposed to **hook up** the other night and he never showed. He totally **blew** me **off**!

RENEE: It's really not like him to be such a flake. Did he at least **come up with** a half decent excuse?

MONA: He was all like "I was out with a friend and it just **slipped my mind**."

RENEE: I can see **getting bent out of shape** over being blown off, but to **call it quits**? Isn't that going a little too far? Hold it, I bet I know what's going on!

MONA: Yeah, yeah, I was **PMSing**.* I completely **blew things out of proportion** and **hit the ceiling**. I drove over to his apartment, told him I never wanted to see him again, and **stormed out of** the place before he could even say anything.

RENEE: You said and did that? Are you nuts?

MONA: Well not exactly those words. I think I was more like "It'll be a cold day in hell before I see you again **Honey**!"

RENEE: You're **screwed**!* You really **botched** this **up**! You'd better come up with something good to get yourself out of this mess and back into his arms again, fast!

* see dictionary for caution note about use of this term

94

You'll need to be on your toes to match up the expressions and their meanings. Find a partner and give it your best shot. (answers on page 147)

1. in the dumps adj____

2. lover's spat noun____

3. break up verb____

4. play with verb____

5. dead serious adj____

6. dump verb____

7. lose one's marbles verb____

8. best thing since sliced bread adj____

9. you're telling me exp____

10. what has gotten into someone? exp____

11. hook up with verb____

12. blow off verb____

13. come up with verb____

14. slip one's mind verb____

15. get bent out of shape verb____

16. call it quits verb____

17. PMS noun____

18. blow things out of proportion verb ____

19. hit the ceiling verb____

20. storm out of verb____

21. honey exp____

22. screwed adj____

23. botch up verb____

A. completely honest

B. "why are you behaving strangely?"

C. to become annoyed or upset

D. sad, depressed

E. "I am well aware of that"

F. to forget, to overlook

G. to become crazy or insane

H. a small argument between a girlfriend and boyfriend.

I. to stop an activity

J. to explode in anger

K. very good, the best and latest development

L. to ignore a commitment or responsibility

M. to leave a place forcefully because of anger

N. to leave a boyfriend or girlfriend

O. to make a situation seem more serious than it really is

P. to end an intimate relationship

Q. to meet someone

R. joke or kid with someone

S. a term of endearment, sometimes used sarcastically when angry

T. a bad mood that may proceed a woman's monthly cycle

U. to ruin or destroy

V. in serious trouble or difficulty

W. to make up, produce, or invent

TALK IT UP!

Time to exercise those red things on your mugs; that's right, your lips! Find a partner and get those lips flapping. Use the new slang in your answers!

1. Imagine that you're **in the dumps** because your **honey** just **dumped** you, **broke up** with you, and **called it quits**! How do you get yourself **out of the dumps**?

2. Who was the last person you **dumped**? Why did you **dump** them? Have you ever been **dumped**? What excuse did your ex **come up with** for **dumping** you? How did it make you feel?

3. Lately, people have been **coming up with** a lot of new inventions and technological advances. What do you think is **the best thing since sliced bread**? Say in your own words: "I think _____ is **the best thing since sliced bread**!" Why do you think this way?

4. Who was the last person you **hooked up with**? Where did you **hook up**? Why did you **hook up**?

5. When you were in high school and you totally blew a test, did your parents **hit the ceiling**, or did they **blow** it **off** and say "no biggy, who needs calculus anyway"? Did your parents often **hit the ceiling** over your grades? Go ahead, spill your guts and tell your partner about it!

6. If you and a friend planned to **hook up** at 2:00 but she hasn't arrived by 2:30, do you **get all bent out of shape** and **blow** her **off** or do you hang out a little longer, hoping she hasn't **blown** you **off**?

7. Hey girls, when your best friend suffers from **PMS** do they tend to **lose their marbles** and **blow things out of proportion**? How about you guys, have you ever experienced this with your girlfriends? Do you have more **lover's spats** at a certain time of the month? Go ahead, let it all out! Give your partner the dirt!

8. Who was the last person you felt like asking "**what's gotten into you**?" How were they acting at the time? What was strange about their behavior?

9. Can you remember a situation in which someone thought you were **playing with** him or her but you were **dead serious**? What was it that you were **dead serious** about? Did this person end up believing you?

10. What's the last thing you **botched up**? Were you **screwed** after you **botched** it **up**? Why or why not? Give you partner the scoop about the last time you were really **screwed**.

WRITE IT OUT!

No playing around – we're dead serious here. Grab a sheet of paper and jot down the conversation that takes place when Mona tries to make up with Vic. Use as much new and old slang as possible.

CROSSWORD REVIEW

Have you been keeping the new slang bottled up? Here's your chance to give it a go. Don't flake out now! See how much you can remember by doing the crossword review. If you space on a word and need to save your skin, take a peek back at the lessons. Remember to use the correct form of the word. (solution on page 147)

Across

1 I'm going to _____ __ _____ and act like nothing happened. But, when we get back to my place, I'm really going to let him have it.

2 Cindy has to go back in for surgery again because the doctor _____ __ her boob job.

5 I know you're upset, so why don't we go for a run so you can _____ ___ ___ _____?

8 I'm __ ___ _____ with my girlfriend. First, I forgot her birthday, and then I missed our aniversary.

9 Any time I get pissed at my girlfriend, she gives me these ___ ___ _____ and I forget why I was mad.

10 Scott ___ ___ _____ when his apartment was burglarized. I've never seen him so mad!

12 I had a brief romance when I was on vacation. Nothing serious - just a little _____.

17 Brian didn't mean to miss your appointment. I'm sure it just _____ ___ _____.

18 Candice has been really depressed lately. She's been __ ___ _____ for the last several weeks.

23 If this rain doesn't let up, we're going to have to ___ ___ our picnic.

24 I tend to _____ __ my feelings instead of letting them out. This has caused a lot of problems in my relationships.

26 Let's _____ ____ our homework tonight and go out to a club instead.

27 You can't rely on Lucy. She's really a _____.

29 Carlos and Maria patched up the little argument they had the other night. It was just a _____ _____.

30 You'd better lie low. The boss is looking to _____ you ___ for being late again this morning.

31 Jessie's old man is really pissed off. He's all _____ ___ __ _____ because she totalled his new car.

32 Richard _____ his old girlfriend when she refused to shack up with him.

Down

1 Chris is going to ask his girlfriend to marry him. He's thinking about _____ ___ _____ on New Year's Eve.

2 John _____ __ with Erica after he walked in on her with another guy.

3 The company will reimburse you for all business expenses on this sales trip, so make sure to _____ _____ __ every cent you spend.

4 I hope you're not going to _____ ___ __ skydiving this weekend. Your excuse that you might be coming down with a bug sounds pretty lame.

6 I don't believe your lame story for a second. You're _____ __ __!

7 Anne is really angry this morning. Her boss rated her job performance as 'poor' and she's _____ ___!

11 That _____ excuse will never fly with our teacher. You'd better come up with a more convincing one than that!

13 This was the first time I'd been late with an assignment, so the teacher ___ __ _____, but she won't let me get away with it next time.

14 Sandra has such a suspicious nature. She's always _____ _____ everything that she's told.

15 I'm not kidding around with you. I'm _____ _____.

16 I expect you to honor your promise to clean out the garage this weekend, and don't try to _____ ___ __ it just because you'd rather hang with your friends.

19 What a colossal blunder! You've made some big mistakes in the past, but this one _____ ___ _____!

20 We've wasted a lot of time in this slow freeway traffic, but if I exit and take surface streets, I can _____ __ ___ lost time and we'll make it to the show.

21 The way Linda _____ ___ ___ the room means she's didn't get the raise she was expecting.

22 My older brother never let the bigger kids take advantage of me. He always _____ __ ___ me when I was a kid.

25 I used my dad's car without his permission and got into a wreck. I'm totally _____!

28 Janet's no _____. She'll see through your lame excuse in no time flat.

"This Blows Away Your Problem"

1.   Being a single mother in modern-day America is becoming increasingly common. This may occur as a result of divorce or unplanned pregnancy. Are single mothers commonplace in your native country? Why do you think they are or are not? Why do you think it is so prevalent in the US?

2.   Does the government help single mothers in your country? Do you have any friends who are single mothers? What is their life like?

Mona and Renee are **working out** at the gym. Mona wants to bitch about her problem with Vic, but Renee has bigger things to talk about…

MONA: These machines are a **drag** and it takes forever and a day to see any results! I want to get rid of this **potbelly** and these **flabby** arms fast!

RENEE: OK, let's **hit the weights** instead.

MONA: You know, Vic still hasn't called me. Do you think I should give him a call?

RENEE: I have a story that will take your mind off of Vic for a minute! It's **all the buzz** at the restaurant. Remember Melanie, the girl who's been in that **off again, on again relationship** for the past year?

MONA: Which I hope isn't what my relationship with Vic turns into!

RENEE: Well, for the last month it's really been **on the rocks**. **Here's the deal**; she just found out she's **got a bun in the oven**! And to top it off, her boyfriend's been **messing around on** her! She **burst into** tears when she told me that he said "Are you sure it was me who **knocked** you **up**?"

MONA: What a jerk! She needs to hear that like **she needs a hole in the head**! Then what happened?

RENEE: He freaked over the responsibility and **split**. She thinks he'll come back, but she was all "At least he offered to **put** me **up** at his mom's house until I find a place to stay."

MONA: Find a place to stay?!

RENEE: That was my **gut reaction** too, but I played dumb and pretended that it **flew over my head**. Then she goes "Renee, you seem to have your head on straight, maybe you could help me out." I was all like "Sure, what do you need?" but I wondered what she was **driving at**.

MONA: What was she driving at?

RENEE: It seems that she was shacking up with this guy, 'cause she got **kicked out of** her apartment for some reason. Now, she needs a new place to stay.

MONA: She didn't ask you to put her up, did she?

RENEE: That's where I thought it was going too! But she just **hit** me **up for** a couple hundred bucks.

MONA: Did you give it to her?

RENEE: If I had the money, I probably would have, but right now I'm just about broke. I'm trying to **get back on my feet** and I don't have any dough to spare.

MONA: I wonder how she makes it through the day at work! If I were in her shoes, I'd be **falling to pieces**!

RENEE: I heard this morning that her job might be **on the line** too. Poor Melanie, lately she's been **getting the short end of the stick**.

MONA: Well, she won't have to make any excuses for having a potbelly! Come on Renee, time for another set of killer sit-ups! Are you up for it?

Time to give your minds a workout. It's a drag, you say? That's just your gut reaction. Sit down with your partner and match the new slang terms with their meanings. (answers on page 148)

1. **work out** verb_____

2. **drag** noun_____

3. **potbelly** noun_____

4. **flabby** adj_____

5. **hit the weights** verb_____

6. **all the buzz** adj_____

7. **off again, on again relationship** noun_____

8. **on the rocks** adj_____

9. **here's the deal** exp_____

10. **have a bun in the oven** adj_____

11. **mess around on** verb_____

12. **burst into** verb_____

13. **knock up** verb_____

14. **need something like one needs a hole in the head** verb_____

15. **split** verb_____

16. **put up** verb_____

17. **gut reaction** noun_____

18. **fly over one's head** verb_____

19. **drive at** verb_____

20. **kick out of** verb_____

21. **hit up for** verb_____

22. **get back on one's feet** verb_____

23. **fall to pieces** verb_____

24. **on the line** adj_____

25. **get stuck with the short end of the stick** verb_____

A. to lift weights with intensity

B. to be pregnant

C. to have neither a need nor a desire for something

D. the main topic of conversation

E. to exercise

F. loose, lacking firmness

G. to regain one's financial solvency

H. a fat stomach

I. first reaction or emotional response

J. an activity that is boring or tedious

K. "here are the details"

L. spoiled or ruined

M. to leave

N. to suddenly begin an activity

O. to accommodate visitors at one's house

P. to receive the less desirable part of the deal

Q. to get a woman pregnant

R. at risk

S. to be unfaithful to one's significant other

T. to be beyond one's understanding

U. to mean to say or do

V. to force to leave

W. a romantic relationship in which the couple repeatedly breaks up and gets back together

X. to lose control of one's emotions

Y. to impose on someone, usually for money

TALK IT OVER!

That wasn't such a drag, now was it? Go ahead and talk up a storm! Hook up with a partner and make your partner burst into laughter with the answers you come up with! Remember that white lies are always cool as long as you use the slang!

1. What's **all the buzz** in your class right now? What's **all the buzz** in the tabloids? Whose relationship is **on the rocks** this week? Any stars with **a bun in the oven**? Who's **messing around on** whom?

2. Imagine what would happen if you were a seventeen-year-old girl who told her parents that she **had a bun in the oven**. Would your mom **burst into** tears? Would your dad's **gut reaction** be to **kick** you **out of** the house? What would be your **gut reaction** to the situation? Were there any girls in your high school who got **knocked up**? Was it **all the buzz** when people found out about it? What was your **gut reaction** when you found out?

3. What's something you **need like a hole in the head**? Answer with: "I need _____ like I need a hole in the head!" Why do you **need this like you need a hole in the head**? Have you ever bought anything that you **needed like a hole in the head**?

4. Who was the last person you **put up** at your place? Why did you **put** them **up**? Have they ever **put** you **up**? If you had to travel on business to a distant city, would you want your company to **put** you **up**? Why?

5. Have you or anyone you know ever been **kicked out of** a bar, school, a movie, a class, or anywhere else? Why did you end up getting **kicked out of** this place? Did you find yourself **bursting into** tears or **bursting into** laughter after you were **kicked out**? Why? Was the place a real **drag** anyway?

6. If you needed some dough quickly, who is the first person you would **hit up for** some cash? Why? When was the last time you **hit** your parents **up for** cash?

7. How often do you **work out**? What's the **flabbiest** area of your body? If you go to the gym, what's the first thing you **hit** to help get rid of this **flabby** area?

8. Do jokes tend to **fly over your head**? What was the last thing that **flew over your head**? Do the slang dialogues tend to **fly over your head** until you have figured out the meanings of the terms?

9. Have you ever helped a friend **get back on his feet**?

10. If you felt your job was **on the line**, would you A; **fall to pieces**, B; **split** before you were canned, or C; **hit** your friends **up for** loans before they find out that you're joining the ranks of the unemployed?

11. If your eight-month-long relationship with your significant is **on the rocks** because you caught them **messing around on** you, would you **split** or stick it out and try to work things out?

WRITE IT DOWN!

With your partner, sit down and make up a funny, trashy tabloid story about a star who is all the buzz right now. Read the completed story to your classmates so that they can burst into laughter.

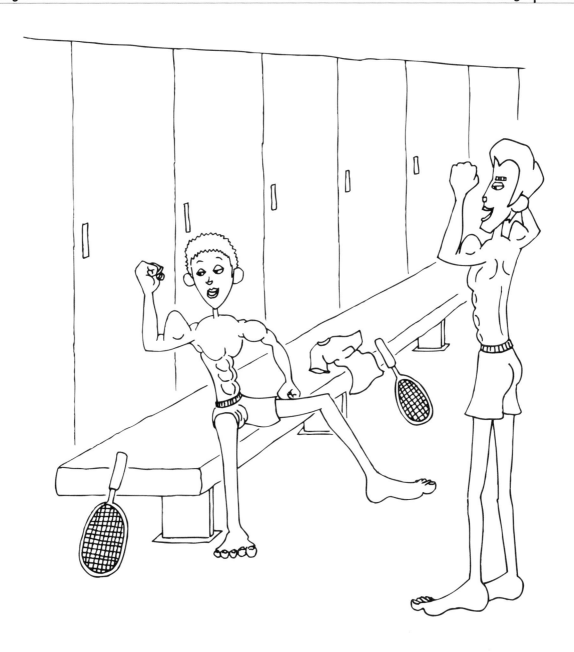

"I'm Going To Whip Your Butt!"

1. Are you good at sports? What are the most popular sports in your native country? When you were in high school, did you use to look forward to, or dread physical education class? Why? Has the situation changed since, or are you still the same as you were in high school?

2. Is exercising popular in your native country? How often do you exercise? What kind of exercise do you like to do? Do you consider yourself to be physically fit or are you in bad shape?

Charlie and Vic are in the locker room at the gym. They are about to play some racquetball...

CHARLIE: Buddy, are you ready to have **your butt whipped**?

VIC: What *do* you mean have my butt whipped? If anyone's butt is going to get kicked it'll be yours!

CHARLIE: You kick my butt? Don't make me **crack up**! I think you've finally **gone off the deep end**! For as long as I've known you you've never even come close to beating me! But if you're so sure, why don't you **put your money where your mouth is**?

VIC: OK, you're on. Loser **springs for** beers. I'm going to make you eat your words.

Vic **strips down to** his trunks...

CHARLIE: Whoa! Get a load of your **abs** dude, where did you get that **six-pack**? And those **guns**! Where did they come from? They look almost as good as mine! What happened to the **beer-belly** and those **scrawny** little arms?

VIC: I got myself a personal trainer. I buckled down and got serious about **working out**.

CHARLIE: I've heard those guys can cost **an arm and a leg**! It must have **run** you about fifty bucks an hour!

VIC: You're **in the ballpark**, but it'll be worth every penny. I'm really going to **get a kick out of** finally whipping your butt!

CHARLIE: Don't go **counting your chickens before they hatch**! Being **cut** doesn't make up for being a **klutz**! Reflex and coordination are what this game **comes down to**!

VIC: **Cut the crap!*** I'm all **fired up** and **raring to go**! Now, are you still up for this or am I hearing a little chicken in your voice?

CHARLIE: I'm as ready as I'll ever be. Let's hit the courts!

Charlie and Vic have been working up a sweat on the courts. Vic has been winning left and right...

CHARLIE: Man I'm beat, what do you say we call it a day and go have a couple of brewskies?

VIC: Dude! Don't break my concentration here! I'm **on a roll**, baby! One more win and the beers are on you if my memory serves me right!

CHARLIE: Yeah, yeah. I hear you. Hey, what's up with you and Mona?

VIC: You were dead on about her, man! I've been trying to get in touch with her and patch things up, but every time I call her she just slams down the receiver!

* see dictionary for caution regarding use of this expression

Time to give your minds a work out. Connect with a partner, and get yourself fired up to match up the new slang with their meanings. (answers on page 148)

1. whip someone's butt verb_____

2. crack up verb_____

3. go off the deep end verb_____

4. put your money where your mouth is exp_____

5. spring for verb_____

6. strip down to verb_____

7. abs noun_____

8. six-pack noun_____

9. guns noun_____

10. beer-belly noun_____

11. scrawny adj_____

12. work out verb_____

13. an arm and a leg noun_____

14. run verb_____

15. in the ballpark adj_____

16. get a kick out of verb_____

17. count one's chickens before they hatch verb_____

18. cut adj_____

19. klutz noun_____

20. come down to verb_____

21. cut the crap exp_____

22. fired up adj_____

23. raring to go adj_____

24. on a roll adj_____

A. upper arm and chest muscles

B. to cost

C. to partially remove one's clothing

D. having a well defined and muscular body

E. to laugh loudly

F. an uncoordinated person

G. continually successful

H. to go crazy, lose one's mind

I. very small and thin

J. to defeat badly

K. a lot of money

L. a feeling of excitement or a thrill

M. eager to begin

N. "stop talking nonsense"

O. a large, flabby stomach

P. abdominal muscles

Q. to engage in a physical exercise program

R. to pay for something

S. a well-defined muscular stomach

T. "back up your position by risking your money"

U. excited, enthusiastic

V. in a general range

W. to make plans based on events that may not occur

X. to simplify to

TALK TURKEY!

Time to cut the crap. Are you fired up and raring to flex your mug muscles? Go ahead, hook up with a partner or two. Are your answers on the up-and-up or do they leave your partner cracking up?

1. Do your **abs** fall into the **six-pack** category, the **beer-belly** category, or somewhere in between? Would you like to sport a **six-pack**? Do you think it's sexy for girls to have a **six-pack**?

2. Do you know anyone who is really **cut**? Is anyone in your class really **cut**? Is it all the rage for guys in your native country to be **cut**? Girls, do you like to go out with guys who are **cut**?

3. What do you **get a kick out of** doing? Do you **get a kick out of working out**? Why or why not? How often do you **work out**? What do you do?

4. What's the last thing that made you **crack up**? When you're in an aerobics class and you catch a glimpse of yourself in the mirror, are you such a **klutz** that it makes you **crack up**? Who is the biggest **klutz** you know? Do their body movements **crack** you **up**?

5. When you're in Las Vegas playing blackjack and you're really **on a roll**, do you **count your chickens before they hatch** and tell your buddies to go and upgrade your little hotel room to a master suite? Why or why not? Have you ever **counted your chickens before they hatched** about a job, good grades, or money you expected? Did everything end up OK? Why or why not?

6. When you were in high school did you have to **strip down** in front of your classmates before PE class? Did you **get a kick out of** trashing the **scrawny** kids, or were you one of the **scrawny** kids? Ask your teacher about her high school.

7. How much does your place **run** you? Does it cost **an arm and a leg** or is it reasonable? How much would a similar place **run** you in your native country? Is housing affordably priced there, or does it cost **an arm and a leg**?

8. When you are playing tennis with your best friend, do you **whip your opponents butt** or do they **whip your butt**? What sport do you think could **whip everyone's butt** at? Would you want to **put your money where you mouth is**? How much are you willing to risk?

9. Has any of your friends or acquaintances ever **gone off the deep end**? Do you know why? The last time you went to make a big purchase, was it **in the ballpark** of what you had planned to spend, or would everyone think you had **gone off the deep end** if you spent that much money?

10. What was the last thing you **sprang for**? Why did you **spring for** it? Who was the last person that **sprung for** something for you? What did they **spring for**? Why did they **spring for** it?

WRITE UP A STORM!

So, you think you're on a roll? Now that you're all fired up and raring to go, grab a new partner and try this one on for size: It's your first day at a new gym that you and your partner have joined. Write down the conversation that the two of you have at the gym. Use a lot of slang, and when you're done, act it out for you classmates so that they can get a kick out of it too!

"Something's Screwy Here"

1. Are gyms popular in your native country? Are they expensive? Did you belong to one? What did you use to do at the gym? Find out about gyms in the US from your teacher.

2. Have you ever gotten really angry at someone while talking to them on the phone? How did you act? Was your behavior acceptable in your native country? If not, then what is normal behavior? Ask your teacher what people in the US do in this situation.

Vic has been trying to call Mona to talk about what happened last week. While working out at the gym, he **spots** someone he thinks is Mona's roommate Renee. Renee has her back to Vic when he walks up to her…

VIC: Excuse me, haven't we met before?

RENEE: Oh, come on! Couldn't you be a little bit more original with your **pick up line**? That must be the oldest one in the book!

Renee turns around and sees Vic…

RENEE: Oops! I guess I put my foot in my mouth. Hey, Vic. **Where have you been hiding yourself?**

VIC: Hi Renee, I thought it was you. I don't blame you for giving me a hard time; a lot of **lowlifes** come here with one thing on their minds and it sure isn't exercising! So, what's up with your roommate? I wish she would **cut me some slack**! She **hangs up on** me every time I try to talk to her. It's not like she **busted** me with another chick or something; I just screwed up on the time.

RENEE: The last thing she would do is hang up on you! She's been **kicking herself** ever since she blew up at you. She thought you were still pissed at her! Something's **screwy** here. What number have you been dialing?

VIC: 555-2323.

RENEE: Oh that explains it. You've been dialing the wrong number. Our new number is 555-7756.

VIC: And I was thinking she just **had it in for me**. But now that I've got you here I might as well **pump you for** some **information**. Tell me, how do I **stack up to** her old **flames**?

RENEE: Now you sound like the **bonehead** I thought you were before! You're not supposed to ask questions like that! But if you must know, what it **boils down to** is that she's **head over heels** for you, although I can't figure out for the life of me why. You should give her a ring later tonight and see if you can **patch** things **up**.

VIC: Well, if she thinks I've been **giving her the cold shoulder**, I guess I'd better do a little **kissing up**. Do you think I should go the **whole nine yards** and send a dozen roses before calling?

RENEE: That might help you out of the doghouse. Sorry about thinking you were some **weirdo**! Have a good work out!

Find yourself a partner and see if you can suss out the meanings of the new slang. Don't let the teacher bust you looking up the meanings in the dictionary, use your heads!
(answers on page 148)

1. **spot** verb_____
2. **pick up line** noun_____
3. **where have you been hiding yourself?** exp_____
4. **lowlife** noun_____
5. **cut someone slack** verb_____
6. **hang up on** verb_____
7. **bust** verb_____
8. **kick one's self** verb_____
9. **screwy** adj_____
10. **have it in for someone** verb_____
11. **pump someone for information** verb_____
12. **stack up to** verb_____
13. **flame** noun_____
14. **bonehead** noun_____
15. **boil down to** verb_____
16. **head over heels** adj_____
17. **patch up** verb_____
18. **give someone the cold shoulder** verb_____
19. **kiss up to** verb_____
20. **whole nine yards** noun_____
21. **weirdo** noun_____

A. to catch someone doing something wrong
B. to persistently question someone for news or facts
C. to compare
D. to repair, set right
E. a lover
F. degenerate, unsophisticated person
G. to be flexible or lenient with someone
H. a stupid or foolish person
I. the entire thing, everything that is relevant
J. to ignore someone
K. to regret something that one has said or done
L. "it's been a long time since we last met"
M. strange or unusual
N. to intend to harm
O. persuasive words used to attract a potential lover
P. to simplify or summarize
Q. to seek favor by flattery
R. to end a telephone conversation abruptly
S. to locate, identify, or see
T. a strange or odd person
U. crazy about, infatuated with

TALK SHOP!

What it boils down to is that it's time to get your lips in motion! Don't forget to use the new slang in your answers!

1. Hey gals, have you heard any **pick up lines** since you came to the US? Dudes, have you used any **pick up lines** since you came to the US? If you're not sure about American **pick up lines**, ask your teacher to give you the inside scoop on the most common ones. What are some common **lines** in your native country?

2. What's the last thing that you could **kick yourself** for doing? Why did you do such a **boneheaded** thing? How does your partner's **boneheaded** mistake **stack up to** yours?

3. Have you ever gotten **busted** for cheating on a test? Hey **bonehead**, how did the teacher **bust** you? Did you ask the teacher to **cut you some slack** and let you off the hook?

4. Do you have a lot of old **flames**? How do they **stack up to** your latest or last **flame**? Have you ever **busted** a significant other cheating on you? Did you end up **patching** things **up** or did you dump him or her?

5. Have you ever **kissed up to** a boss, a teacher, or your parents? Why did you **kiss up to** them? Did you end up getting what you wanted or did they just **give you the cold shoulder**?

6. Just about everyone has **hung up on** someone at some point in his or her life. Have you ever **hung up on** someone? Why did you **hang up on** them? Did you **patch** things **up** or have you thought of them as a **lowlife** ever since they made you so angry that you **hung up on** them? Have any of your old **flames** ever **hung up on** you?

7. If you were **head over heels** about your best friend's brother or sister, would you **pump** your best friend **for information** or just keep your trap shut?

8. Say you've just **spotted** a friend that you haven't seen in forever and a day! What new slang phrase do you say to them?

9. What is your main reason for studying English? Answer using: "What it **boils down to** is that I'm studying English because..."

10. Have you ever had a teacher that you thought **had it in for your**? What made you think they **had it in for you**?

LET'S WRITE!

Grab your hats and your pencils. Write a "I can't put it down" story about a teacher that had it in for you. Go the whole nine yards and put everything it. If no teacher ever had it in for you, go ahead and make up a story. When you're finished, see how your story stacks up to those written by your classmates.

CROSSWORD REVIEW

Way to go! You've got one more unit under your belt. You guys are really on a roll. Make sure none of the new slang has flown over your head by doing the crossword review. Remember to use the correct form of the word. (solution on page 148)

Across

6   Everyone at the office is worried about the rumored layoffs. It's ___ ___ _____.

7   My ex is in town and wants me to ___ him __ over the weekend, but I don't want him staying at my place.

8   Eric and Steven finally _____ __ their differences and reached an agreement on sharing royalties for the song they co-wrote.

15 Julie ____ __ ___ me again! She must really be pissed to slam the phone down like that!

17 If you want a six-pack you really have to start working your ___.

21 I'm not surprised that Carlo and Maria finally broke up. Their relationship had been __ ___ _____ for some time.

22 I'll loan some money until you can land a job, but once you ___ ____ __ ____ ____, I'll expect prompt repayment.

24 Your instructions ____ ____ Arnie's head. You'll have to simplify your explanation and go over it again more carefully.

25 That new guy, Walt, is always talking to himself. He's a real _____ don't you think?

27 Colleen is pregnant again, but not by her husband. She got _____ __ by her personal trainer.

29 This party is a ____. Twenty guys, one six-pack, and no chicks. Let's bail and find some real action.

30 I can hardly get my jeans on anymore. I need to start eating right and exercising if I want to get rid of this _____.

31 Great sound, huh? So, how do you think my new stereo _____ __ __ the old one?

33 This doesn't make sense! I set my watch this morning, but now it's one half hour ahead of the correct time. Something's _____ here.

Down

1   I'm going to head over to the gym and ____ ___.

2   Tom's job is __ ___ ____ because he's been goofing off and coming in late. If he doesn't shape up soon, he's going to get canned.

3   Miranda is bound to break a piece of your best china if you let her handle it. She's a real _____.

4   I thought I could defeat Ted at tennis, but he beat me in straight sets. He really _____ __ ____!

5   My boss is on my case about everything I do. He really __ __ __ for me.

9   Jim's teacher has agreed to ___ ___ ____ _____ and accept his assignment late, but she won't give him a break like that again.

10 That's an expensive watch you're sporting. It must have cost you __ ____ __ __ ___.

11 Sheila had the nerve to ___ __ __ ___ another loan when she still hasn't paid me back for the C note I loaned her last month.

12 I knew Scott would _____ __ when he heard that joke. He laughed so hard there were tears in his eyes.

13 I really ___ _ ____ ___ __ downhill skiing! It's such a blast!

14 Donna and Gary are crazy in love. They're ____ ____ ____ for each other.

16 Munir has won every hand of Black Jack he's played for the last half hour. He's really __ _ ____!

18 I'll pay for the movie tickets if you'll _____ ___ the munchies.

19 If you go camping with Joe, he brings every piece of equipment known to man. Tent, lantern, stove, fridge, generator, the _____ ____ _____.

20 You'll have to ____ __ _ the boss if you want a raise. He expects everyone to suck up to him.

23 Those friends of yours have no jobs, ambition, or prospects for the future. They're just a bunch of _____.

26 Elmer was last in line when brains were being passed out. He's a real _____.

28 Claire dumped Josh when she _____ him with another chick.

32 I can't believe I did such a stupid thing. I could ____ myself!

Hanging At The Mall

1. What's your favorite thing to shop for? Do you prefer to shop for it in the US or in your native country? Why? Do you prefer shopping for clothes in the US or in your country? Why? Describe your favorite area to shop for clothes in your country. How does it compare to malls in the US? Does your teacher enjoy shopping? Find out some good places to shop in your city from your teacher.

2. Would you rather shop alone or with friends? Why?

Mona and Renee are hanging at the mall. Renee has a blind date and is window-shopping in the hopes of finding something to wear on her date tonight...

MONA: So, what's the scoop on this guy that your friend fixed you up with?

RENEE: Well, his name is Mark, but I don't know much else except that he's from up north, and he's been here for only a few months.

MONA: What do you guys have **in store** for tonight?

RENEE: Beats me. Our plans are still **up in the air**, but since he's new in town, I thought I'd show him around. That new restaurant downtown is all the buzz. Everyone says it's **the bomb**, but I don't think I can get a reservation so late.

MONA: You must be talking about Daddy O's.

RENEE: Yeah, that's the one, they've always got a killer swing band playing there.

MONA: I think you're in luck. One of my students is a waiter there. Let me see if I can **pull a few strings** and get you guys a table. He **can't not** do this for me! **It's a long story**, but he owes me big-time.

Mona **whips out** her cell phone and gives her student a ring...

MONA: "Hi, Gary? Mona here. Sorry to bother you at home but do you think you could get my roommate and her date a table at Daddy O's tonight? You can? Thanks Gary, you're a sweetheart! She's going to **flip** when I tell her. See ya next Monday."

             Well Renee, I **scored**! You're in! The **word is** that everyone gets pretty **decked out** for Daddy O's, so what are you going to wear?

RENEE: How about this lovely red velvet shirt with red fur trim? You know, fur trim **is all the rage** this year!

MONA: Have you lost it? Do you want to look like a **cheesy** version of Mrs. Claus two months before Christmas?

RENEE: Oh come on, **get real**, would you! I **wouldn't be caught dead** wearing that. Seriously though, how about the same one in black?

MONA: Yeah, I can **picture** you in that, and check it out; it's a **steal**! Only a hundred bucks!

RENEE: Are you **tripping**? **In my book** that's pretty **steep**! I can't see **shelling out** a hundred bucks for a **teensy** shirt like that!

MONA: Well, let's head over to that other shop, Street Scene. They've got the same stuff at **rock bottom** prices. Hmm, doing all this shopping for dates is making me miss Vic even more. I wish he would call me. I guess I really blew it with him.

RENEE: Oops, Mona, don't kill me but uh... I have something kind of important to tell you. Last night when I was at the gym I **ran into** Vic, and to make a long story short, he's been trying to call you but he had our old number. Sorry, it just **slipped my mind**.

MONA: It slipped your mind? Damn, Renee, sometimes you really are an **airhead**!

You can't not know what's in store for you now! Whip out a pencil and collar a new partner. The word is that you guys are not a bunch of airheads, so you'll be able to get this done in no time flat. (answers on page 149)

1. **in store** adj_____	A. "the rumor is..."
2. **up in the air** adj_____	B. to imagine, to form a mental image
3. **the bomb** adj_____	C. to be obligated or required
4. **pull a few strings** verb_____	D. small in size or amount
5. **can't not** verb_____	E. to use one's influence
6. **it's a long story** exp_____	F. "the details are complicated and lengthy"
7. **whip out** verb_____	G. to become very enthusiastic
8. **flip** verb_____	H. not have anything to do with
9. **score** verb_____	I. dressed up, wearing nice clothes
10. **word is** exp_____	J. in bad taste, tacky
11. **decked out** adj_____	K. to pull out something rapidly
12. **be all the rage** verb_____	L. to accomplish a goal
13. **cheesy** adj_____	M. the best
14. **get real** exp_____	N. undecided
15. **not be caught dead** exp_____	O. "in my opinion"
16. **picture** verb_____	P. overpriced
17. **steal** noun_____	Q. to act crazily or foolishly
18. **trip** verb_____	R. the very lowest
19. **in my book** exp_____	S. to be very popular
20. **steep** adj _____	T. to forget, to overlook
21. **shell out** verb_____	U. "be serious"
22. **teensy** adj_____	V. planned, in readiness
23. **rock bottom** adj_____	W. stupid or forgetful person
24. **run into** verb_____	X. to pay, use money
25. **slip one's mind** verb_____	Y. a bargain
26. **airhead** noun_____	Z. to meet by chance

TALKING TIME!

Are you ready for what's in store for you? You can't not be! Word is that you've done this quite a few times before! Hook yourself up with a partner or two and get those lips flapping! Don't let it slip your mind to use the new slang in your answers!

1. Name something that you would **not be caught dead** wearing. **In your book**, what's the **cheesiest** clothing item you could wear? If your blind date showed up all **decked out** in this **cheesy** thing thinking he or she was all **the bomb**, would you insist on going to a place where you're not likely to **run into** any of your friends?

2. What is something you **can't not** do for your best friend?

3. Name a shop in your native country that had pretty **steep** prices. How about **rock bottom** prices? How much are you willing to **shell out** to buy a sweater? **In your book**, do you find prices in the US to be pretty **steep**? Which local stores sell clothing at **rock bottom** prices? Get the lowdown from your teacher.

4. When was the last time you got all **decked out**? Have you gotten all **decked out** since you came to the US?

5. Can you **picture** what the future has **in store for** you? Tell your partner about it. When Friday night arrives, are your plans for the weekend still **up in the air** or do you know what the weekend has **in store for** you?

6. When it's time to pay for something do you usually **whip out** some plastic or **shell out** cold, hard cash? Which type of payment is more common in your native country? Why?

7. What's the last thing that **slipped your mind**? Did you feel like a total **airhead** when you realized it had **slipped your mind**?

8. What's the last thing you bought that you felt was a **steal**? How much did you have to **shell out**?

9. What flick **is all the rage** right now? **In your book** what band **is all the rage**? Do you and your partner see eye-to-eye on this or is one of you all like "**get real**, they suck!" Is it difficult to **score** tickets to one of their concerts?

10. When was the last time you felt like asking someone "Are you **tripping**?" What were they doing or talking about at the time?

WRITING TIME!

Picture this: you and your partner are hanging at the mall and shopping together. You can't not know the lingo before you hit the shops, so whip out your pencils, and write down the conversation that goes on between the two of you while you shop. Use at least fifteen example of the new slang.

Vic's New Set Of Wheels

1. If money was no object and you could buy any brand of car, what would you purchase? Why? If you could buy anything you wanted, what would you buy? Why?

2. Do your friends consider you a careful and safe driver or are they scared stiff when you get behind the wheel?

3. Have the police in the US ever stopped you? Why? How did you deal with the situation? How about in your native country?

4. Have you bought anything expensive recently? What was it? Why did you buy it?

Vic has just bought his dream car and he's dropped by Charlie's place to show off his new **set of wheels...**

CHARLIE:	Whoa, you **lucky dog**! You got the **Vette**! I wish I were **in your shoes**.
VIC:	**Hop in**! I'll take you out for a **spin**.
CHARLIE:	Why don't you **ride shotgun** and let me get behind the **wheel**?
VIC:	Are you **out of your mind**? **What do you take me for**? Nobody gets behind this wheel of this baby but me, and besides you're too much of a **leadfoot**!
CHARLIE:	OK, you drive. Man, what a beauty! She must've cost you a **pretty penny**!
VIC:	**You can say that again**! But I've **had my heart set on** it for a long time and now that business has picked up, it seemed like the perfect time to buy.
CHARLIE:	So, how much did she **set** you **back**? Thirty **grand**?
VIC:	Yeah, right! **In your dreams**! Try doubling that. I had to **pay through the nose** for this baby!
CHARLIE:	Man, I am definitely in the wrong line of work. It'll be a cold day in hell before I can lay my hands on a set of wheels like this! My car is such an old **lemon**!
VIC:	Check it out! Listen to that engine! Here we go!
CHARLIE:	Let's see how fast she can go! **Floor** it!
VIC:	Zero to sixty in under five seconds! Pretty impressive, huh?
CHARLIE:	Yeah, looks like the cop behind us must be pretty impressed, too! He's having a hard time **catching up to** us! You'd better **pull over**.
OFFICER:	Nice car. License and registration please.
VIC:	Here you go, sir. So, what's the problem officer?
OFFICER:	I clocked you at 98, but I'm going to give you a break and say an even 95 here on the ticket. Just a piece of friendly advice, sir. The next time you have a leadfoot, **keep your eyes peeled** for cops!

Hook up with a partner and match the new slang with the meanings. If you need a hand, use the conversation to figure out their definitions. (answers on page 149)

1. **set of wheels** noun_____

2. **lucky dog** noun_____

3. **Vette** noun_____

4. **in someone's shoes** adj_____

5. **hop in** exp_____

6. **spin** noun_____

7. **ride shotgun** verb_____

8. **wheel** noun_____

9. **out of one's mind** adj_____

10. **what do you take me for?** exp_____

11. **leadfoot** noun_____

12. **pretty penny** noun_____

13. **you can say that again** exp_____

14. **have one's heart set on** verb_____

15. **set back** verb_____

16. **grand** noun_____

17. **in one's dreams** exp_____

18. **pay through one's nose** verb_____

19. **lemon** noun_____

20. **floor** verb_____

21. **catch up to** verb_____

22. **pull over** verb_____

23. **keep one's eyes peeled** verb_____

A. a lot of money

B. to ride in the front passenger seat of a vehicle

C. "do you think I'm a fool?"

D. to establish a goal

E. to cost

F. something that is unsatisfactory or defective, particularly when unreliable

G. crazy or foolish

H. "get in the car"

I. to watch carefully for

J. a lucky person

K. a steering wheel

L. "I strongly agree with you"

M. a short drive

N. one thousand US dollars

O. to drive one's car to the side of the road and stop

P. to pay an excessive amount of money

Q. a Corvette

R. in the same situation as another

S. a person who drives fast and aggressively

T. to press the gas pedal of a car to the floor

U. to come up from behind and overtake

V. "never" or "no way"

W. an automobile

1. Who was the last person you thought was a **lucky dog**? Why did you think they were a **lucky dog**? Did you wish you were **in their shoes**? Why or why not? Do you think your buddies back in your native country want to be **in your shoes** now? Why or why not?

2. Who was the last person you felt like asking "**are you out of your mind**?" What were they doing, saying, or thinking about doing at that time? Did they go through with it, or did they chicken out?

3. What do you **have your heart set on** doing or buying? Are you going to buy it or do it in the near future? Why or why not?

4. If you could buy something in the US that would **set** you **back** at least a **grand**, what would you buy? How much would it end up **setting** you **back**? Would you feel you had **paid through the nose** for it or that it was a steal?

5. On a beautiful Sunday afternoon, would you rather go out for a **spin**, veg on the couch in front of the tube, or hit the beach? Would you react to your partner's answer by replying "**you can say that again**!" or by saying "**are you out of your mind**?"

6. When you get behind **the wheel** do you have a **leadfoot** and **floor it,** or stay within the speed limit? Do you always **keep your eyes peeled** for cops? Have the cops ever had a tough time **catching up to** you?

7. What is the last thing you owned that was a **lemon**?

8. Suppose a stranger pulled up to you in a **Vette** and said "**hop in**!" Would you get in, or say "**in your dreams! What do you take me for**?"

"Don't Look Now, But You're In For A Surprise"

1. Do your acquaintances consider you the kind of person who gets angry easily? Do you agree with their opinion of you? Why or why not? Who was the last person you got angry at? Why did you end up getting angry with them? Did you end up forgiving them or is forgiveness difficult for you?

2. Who was the last person you ran into? Were you happy to see them? Have you ever been walking down the street and hidden from someone you didn't want to see? Why didn't you want to see them? Did you get away with hiding?

Vic and Charlie **pull up to** the mall and spot Mona and Renee heading out…

CHARLIE: Don't look now, but there's Mona and Renee. Maybe we'd better **keep a low profile**.

VIC: Too late, they're looking in our direction. I think they spotted us.

At that same moment, Renee and Mona are walking out of the mall and heading toward the parking lot…

RENEE: Mona, correct me if I'm wrong but isn't that Vic over there in that hot new Vette?

MONA: I think you're right, but don't say…

RENEE: (yells) Hey, Vic, Charlie, over here!

MONA: Renee, you're such a **big mouth**! Why did you do that?

RENEE: Oh, come off it Mona! You and I both know you're dying to see him! What's wrong, do you **have butterflies in your stomach**?

Vic pulls up to Renee and Mona…

VIC: Hi, Mona. What's up? Long time, no see. Looking good as always! How's life been treating you?

MONA: Pretty good. I see you got yourself those snazzy new wheels you were going on about.

VIC: Hop in and I'll take you for a spin. Uh… Charlie, time to hit the road pal!

MONA: What do you say you let me get behind the wheel?

VIC: Uh, sure, no problem. She's all yours, have a **ball**! But don't **get carried away**, I'm still breaking her in.

RENEE: Watch out, keep an eye on the speedometer. She's known for her leadfoot!

Mona **tears out of** the parking lot…

VIC: Maybe you should ease up, I already got a speeding ticket. Listen Mona, about the other night, I'm really sorry. I've been trying to call you but I was dialing the wrong number.

MONA: I know, Renee just told me. I'm the one who should apologize. I don't know **what came over me**. I just lost it. So where do we go from here?

VIC: It's your **call**. You can head back to the mall if you want.

MONA: Vic, I was talking about our relationship, not the car!

VIC: Sorry, it's just that your leadfoot is making me a little nervous.

MONA: I **get the picture**. Is 25 OK for you? So where do we go from here?

VIC: We need to **have a heart-to-heart**, but this isn't the time or the place for it. What do you say we head back to the mall and I'll spring for some **grub** for the bunch of us?

MONA: Are you sure? Renee can really **put** it **away**. This could **wind up** costing you an arm and a leg!

VIC: That's OK, I've **got it covered**. I'll call you later tonight and we can make a date for our heart-to-heart.

MONA: OK, but let me **jot down** my new number so you don't **screw up on** it again.

Renee and Charlie see Vic and Mona driving towards them…

RENEE: Check it out, **ear-to-ear grins**! I guess they must've **made up with** each other! That was pretty **cut-and-dried**! They were gone, what, all of three minutes?

CHARLIE: I knew she had him **hooked** when he let her behind the wheel of his new Vette!

You get the picture don't you? It's pretty cut-and-dried. Sit down with your partner, put your heads together and match up the slang terms with their meanings. (answers on page 149)

1. **pull up to** verb____

2. **keep a low profile** verb____

3. **big mouth** noun____

4. **have butterflies in one's stomach** verb____

5. **ball** noun____

6. **get carried away** verb____

7. **tear out of** verb____

8. **what came over someone?** exp____

9. **call** noun____

10. **get the picture** verb____

11. **have a heart-to-heart** verb____

12. **grub** noun____

13. **put away** verb____

14. **wind up** verb____

15. **have something covered** verb____

16. **jot down** verb____

17. **screw up on** verb____

18. **ear-to-ear grin** noun____

19. **make up with** verb____

20. **cut-and-dried** adj____

21. **hooked** adj____

A. to leave somewhere very quickly

B. to have a feeling of nervous anticipation

C. to make a mistake

D. to understand

E. to eat a lot

F. to have a sincere or candid conversation

G. to hide

H. to settle differences

I. food

J. "why is one behaving strangely?"

K. to write something quickly

L. simple

M. fun, a great time

N. a very big smile

O. to drive one's car to a certain point and stop

P. to lose one's self control

Q. decision, choice

R. to result in

S. fascinated or devoted to something

T. a person who can't keep a secret

U. to assume a responsibility

TALK IT UP!

Let yourself get carried away and put your big mouth into action! Get rid of those butterflies in your stomach and make your partner sport an ear-to-ear grin. Make up a story or two if you have to, but be sure to use the new slang in your answers!

1. Would you have **butterflies in your stomach** if you had to give a speech in front of the class? If you have to tell your parents you failed an important exam, would you have **butterflies**? Do you have **butterflies in your stomach** if you're about to ask somebody out on a date? When was the last time you had **butterflies in your stomach**? Why?

2. Which one of your friends is considered such a **big mouth** that they couldn't keep a secret to save their own life? What was the last secret they blabbed all over the place? Do you have a **big mouth**? Did you ever get **carried away** and **wind up** blabbing a secret all over the place? Tell your partner what is was.

3. What is the last thing that put an **ear-to-ear grin** on your face? How often do you find yourself sporting an **ear-to-ear grin**?

4. Who's the last person you **had a heart-to-heart** with? What was it about? How often do you **have a heart-to-heart** with your parents, friends, boyfriend or girlfriend?

5. How much **grub** can you **put away** when it dinnertime and you are starving? How much **grub** did you **put away** last night?

6. Do the instructions to a VCR or DVD player seem pretty **cut-and-dried**? Can you explain something very complicated in such a manner that it sounds **cut-and-dried**? Think of an example. Explain it and see if your partner agrees that it's **cut-and-dried**!

7. What's something you've gotten **hooked** on since coming to the US? When you get back to your native country will you still be able to have it? Why or why not?

8. What are you supposed to do tonight? Do you think you'll do it or will you **wind up** doing something else? When was the last time you got lost? Where did you **wind up**?

9. Are you good at **jotting down** directions given over the phone in English? How about in your native language?

10. If you are hanging at the mall when you see an ex heading in your direction, do you **keep a low profile** and **tear out of** there when you get the chance, or do you get **carried away** and start waving?

11. Who's the last person you blew up at? Did you **make up with** them? Why or why not?

WRITE IT OUT!

Everyone knows someone who is a big mouth. On your own, whip up a story involving a big mouth. The story can be funny, sad, embarrassing, crazy, etc. as long as you wind up using at least fifteen examples of the new slang. When you are finished with your story, share it with the person next to you.

CROSSWORD REVIEW

Dudes, you've wrapped up <u>Unit Nine</u>? Not so fast! Don't let yourself get carried away and think it's a done deal. Has something slipped your mind? Wipe that ear-to-ear grin off your face and jot down the answers to the crossword review. Remember to use the correct form of the word. (solution on page 149)

Across

4 Close your eyes and _____ yourself lying in the warm sun on a white sand beach, sounds of gentle surf, an ice-cold beer at your side... Now will you go to Fiji with me?

7 Frankie and Johnny had a big fight last weekend, but they ____ __ ____ each other. I saw them walking hand-in-hand this morning.

9 Don't tell him any secrets unless you want the whole world to know. He's a real ___ _____.

12 The procedure for replacing the toner cartridge in your printer is very ___ ___ _____. It's simple and routine.

13 She has terrible taste in clothing. Her closet is full of _____ outfits.

14 Karen is all _____ ____ tonight - fancy dress, heels, makeup, new do - I wonder what's up?

17 They really hold you up in that new restaurant. Their prices are pretty _____.

18 That cake is really scrumptious. Maybe I'll have just a _____ weensy bit more.

19 You have a choice of going to a play or seeing a movie. It's your ____.

21 This truck set me back about twenty-five thousand, but Jeff paid over sixty _____ for his new car.

22 Mandy is as thin as a rail, but she has quite an appetite. She can really ___ __ _____ when she sits down to eat.

24 I'm so tired of driving this _____. It's always breaking down, and as soon as I have one thing fixed, something else goes wrong.

25 Candice ___ ___ _____ __ _ a sports car, but with her limited budget she's going to have to settle for an economy model.

28 Look at what I was able to get! I _____ two tickets to that sold-out concert you want to go to!

30 Chet is such a _____ ___! He doesn't have to take the final because he got 'A's in all the regular exams. I wish I were in his shoes.

31 You're still living with your roommate after she stole money from you? Are you _____?

32 Can I borrow a piece of paper and a pen so I can ___ ____ your address and phone number?

Down

1 Yoko and Yoshihiro wanted to catch that new romantic comedy, but tickets were all sold out. They _____ __ renting a video instead.

2 That handbag normally sells for over a hundred bucks and you paid only thirty? What a _____!

3 You'd better ____ ____. There's a cop car behind you with its red lights flashing.

5 Mindy would forget her head if it weren't attached to her body. She is such an _____.

6 There's no need to explain it to me again, I ___ ___ _____.

8 I can't believe I botched up the easiest question on the test. I totally _____ __ __ it.

10 Ata and Najdah haven't decided what to do for summer break. Their plans are still __ __ ___ ___.

11 Don't worry about being short of cash, I've ___ ___ _____. You can treat me next time.

15 Go topless? Have you lost it? I wouldn't __ _____ ___ without my top at the beach.

16 I've got connections in the TV industry, so I'll ____ _ ___ _____ and set up an audition for you.

20 All of us had great time at the party. We had a ____.

23 Have you heard that great new Beck CD? It's ___ ____!

26 I'm so _____ on that late night TV soap opera that I can't stop watching it!

27 Wow, did you see those cops burning rubber? The way they ____ ___ __ here, they must be after someone.

29 I'd like to go for a _____ in your new car. How about taking me for a short ride?

"Are You Getting Cold Feet?"

1. How long on average do people in your native country know each other before marriage? Ask your teacher about the US. How long *do* you think you would have to know someone before marrying him or her? Why?

2. What's the custom for proposing in your native country? Do guys ask the girl first or do they have to ask the girl's parents for her hand? Are there any traditional gifts that are given at this time? If yes, who gives these gifts and what are they?

3. In the US, parties are thrown for the bride and groom separately before the actual wedding ceremony. Are there any traditional parties before the wedding ceremony in your native country? If yes, tell your partner about them. Ask your teacher about bachelor parties, bachelorette parties, and bridal showers in the US.

Vic, Charlie, Mona, and Renee have just polished off their lunch at the mall. Mona and Renee are about to hit the road, while Vic and Charlie have some shopping to do…

MONA: Well, it was great running into you guys, but we've got to **get going**. Renee's got a hot date **lined up for** tonight.

CHARLIE: I don't mean to be **nosy**, but is it anyone I know?

RENEE: I doubt it. Somebody at work hooked me up with this guy.

VIC: A blind date? Good luck.

RENEE: I think I'll be OK. I only have to put up with him for a couple of hours. Besides, blind dates aren't always bad. You and Mona were pretty **gone** the first night you met, and now the two of you are head over heels for each other!

VIC: I'll give you that. Especially the last part!

MONA: Enough **dillydallying**! Come on Renee. We'll catch you guys later.

While Vic and Charlie are **window shopping**, Vic hesitates in front of a jewelry store window…

VIC: Check out the size of that **rock**! Pretty cheesy, huh? It looks like something a chick would get from her **sugar daddy**!

CHARLIE: Wow, twenty-five grand! Of course, with the way you've been **blowing** money, it wouldn't surprise me if you **forked out** the dough for a ring like that. Wait a minute, there's something **fishy** here! Why are you **eyeing** those rocks? You've got marriage on your mind again. I thought you **nixed** that idea!

VIC: Yeah, I was **getting cold feet** about asking Mona to **tie the knot**. But after seeing her again, I realize she's the one. I just don't want to **jump the gun**, because I don't know if either one of us is ready to get hitched. I think I want to pop the question, but maybe now is not right time.

CHARLIE: Hey, we're talking marriage here! Either you do or you don't–you can't be **wishy-washy** about it. But, if you decide to take that trip down the aisle buddy, I'll be there to back you up one hundred percent!

VIC: I don't want to rush into this. I know we **smoothed** things **over** between us just now, but there are still a few **bugs to work out** in the relationship. Besides, I thought you were **dead against** my getting married! What makes you so **gung ho** about it now?

CHARLIE: **Use your head**, man! I'm thinking of the bachelor party! I would **go all out** for a bash like that. Mona would be pissed if she heard me now, but you'd be kissing up to her for the rest of your life for that one evening! A wild bachelor party, the **cornerstone** of any good marriage!

VIC: Maybe in your book, but I think it'd be a cold day in hell before you could find a woman who would see eye-to-eye with you on that!

This is no time for dillydallying! Grab a partner and match up the new slang terms with their meanings. (answers on page 150)

1. **get going** verb_____

2. **line up for** verb_____

3. **nosy** adj_____

4. **gone** adj_____

5. **dillydally** verb_____

6. **window shop** verb_____

7. **rock** noun_____

8. **sugar daddy** noun_____

9. **blow** verb_____

10. **fork** verb_____

11. **fishy** adj_____

12. **eye** verb_____

13. **nix** verb_____

14. **get cold feet** verb_____

15. **tie the knot** verb_____

16. **jump the gun** verb_____

17. **wishy-washy** adj_____

18. **smooth over** verb_____

19. **bugs to work out** noun_____

20. **dead set against** adj_____

21. **gung ho** adj_____

22. **use one's head** verb_____

23. **go all out** verb_____

24. **cornerstone** noun_____

A. foundation

B. minor problems to fix

C. to correct problems

D. to delay or procrastinate

E. to use one's intellect to solve a problem

F. to act or begin before the proper time

G. indecisive

H. to observe carefully

I. strange, unusual

J. to prepare to leave

K. adamantly opposed

L. to reject

M. a rich older man who takes care of a young girl financially in exchange for companionship

N. involved or infatuated

O. to get married

P. to spare no expense or effort

Q. to pay or contribute

R. to plan an series of activities or events

S. a gemstone, usually a diamond

T. to view goods for sale without any intention of purchasing

U. to lose one's courage

V. annoyingly inquisitive

W. to spend money extravagantly

X. enthusiastic

TALK IT OVER!

Time to talk your heads off! Grab a partner and hop to it! Give him or her the scoop on the questions lined up for you and don't dillydally!

1. Do you have anything special **lined up for** this weekend?

2. How often do you go **window shopping** in the US? How often did you go **window shopping** in your native country? With who did you usually go **window shopping**? How about here in the US?

3. Are you **dead set against** smoking in public places? Why or why not? In your native country are most people **dead against** smoking in public places? Ask your teacher about American attitudes toward smoking.

4. Do **sugar daddies** exist in your native country? If so, are they a common sight? Why or why not?

5. Before **tying the knot** in your native country is it common for the girl to receive a **rock** from her husband-to-be? If not, is there another customary gift? What is it? Which custom do you prefer? Why? Guys, do you think you would **go all out** if you had to purchase a **rock** for your wife-to-be? Do people **go all out** in your native country when giving the traditional gift?

6. Who was the last person you caught **eyeing** you? If you walking down the street and you catch some wacko **eyeing** you, what would you do?

7. After having a disagreement with your boyfriend/ girlfriend, do you prefer to **smooth** things **over** with words, gestures, or gifts? How about with a friend, colleague, or boss? Who was the last person you had to **smooth** things **over** with? Did you get **cold feet** before doing it? Why or why not?

8. When two people **tie the knot** in your country, do they usually **go all out** on the wedding? Give your partner the scoop when it comes to weddings in your country! When you **tie the knot** do you want to **go all out** on your wedding ceremony? Why or why not?

9. Time to **use your head**! In your opinion, what is the **cornerstone** of a good marriage? Why?

10. Who's the **wishy-washiest** person you know? What was the last thing they couldn't make up their mind on?

WRITE IT DOWN!

Sit down with a partner. One of you is wishy-washy about getting hitched and the other must help him or her to make a decision. Find out as much as you can about the imaginary potential mate, then use your head and write a dialog in which one talks the other into, or out of, tying the knot. Remember to use the new slang in your conversation.

"He Just Rubbed Me The Wrong Way"

1.   Are blind dates popular in your native country? Have you ever been on one? Who fixed you up? How did it turn out?

2.   If you were on a date, where would you take someone you wanted to impress? Why? What kind of place would give a bad impression on a first date? Why? Have you ever experienced going to a place like that on a first date?

Mona is at home watching the tube when Renee comes home early looking totally **frazzled**!

MONA: Geez, is that you Renee? You **scared the living daylights out of me**! What are you doing back so early?

RENEE: That is the first and last time I go on a blind date!

MONA: What happened?

RENEE: What happened is I told that jerk to **take a hike**!

MONA: This I've got to hear! Give me the dirt!

RENEE: Well, from the minute he picked me up, I was getting **bad vibes**. There was something about him I couldn't quite **put my finger on**.

MONA: You're telling me! I didn't want to **put my nose where it doesn't belong**; you know the old saying, "**different strokes for different folks**!" But now I can **spill the beans** and tell you he really **rubbed me the wrong way**. We're talking **creepy**!

RENEE: I thought the same thing, but there was no polite way for me to back out of the date with him standing at the door!

MONA: I hope you at least had a good time at that new restaurant!

RENEE: We didn't even go there! When we drove up to the place, he was all like "This place is **too rich for my blood**!" We ended up at some horrible burger joint, where all the waitresses wear teensy skirts and even teensier shirts!

MONA: I know the place you mean! You should've **ditched** him then!

RENEE: Well, **it goes without saying** that he was eyeing the waitresses and they were making goo-goo eyes back at him. Of course, they were just **sucking up to** him in hopes of a bigger tip. I wish I'd **had the nerve** to walk out. But get this! While we were waiting for our food, he tells me that he can help me **get my foot in the door** for a position as a waitress there! He was all like "that would be a step up for you in your career!"

MONA: You've got to be kidding! Is this guy for real?

RENEE: I know! I was getting more pissed with each word he said, and believe me, this jerk was **talking my ear off**! Then, he started getting on me, telling me he had been trying to **break the ice** all evening, that I was too uptight, and needed to **let my hair down**. Then, just when I thought things were as bad as they could get, the evening took another nosedive! He tried to kiss me! I told him to **back off**, but it went right over his head! At that point I **let him have it** and told him exactly what I thought of him.

MONA: You didn't throw a **fit** in the restaurant, did you?

RENEE: Well, I wasn't planning to, but then he told me he didn't have any money with him and I ended up having to **foot the bill**! What a **nightmare**!

With the help of a partner, see if you can put your finger on the meaning of the slang. If you get stuck, put your nose where is doesn't belong, and ask the guy or gal next to you for help. (answers on page 150)

1. frazzled adj_____

2. scare the living daylights out of someone verb_____

3. take a hike exp_____

4. bad vibes noun_____

5. put one's finger on something verb_____

6. put one's nose where it doesn't belong verb_____

7. different stroke for different folks exp_____

8. spill the beans verb_____

9. rub someone the wrong way verb_____

10. creepy adj_____

11. too rich for one's blood adj_____

12. ditch verb_____

13. it goes without saying exp_____

14. suck up to verb_____

15. have the nerve verb_____

16. get one's foot in the door verb_____

17. talk someone's ear off verb_____

18. break the ice verb_____

19. let one's hair down verb_____

20. back off exp_____

21. let someone have it verb_____

22. fit noun_____

23. foot the bill verb_____

24. nightmare noun_____

A. weird, scary

B. bad feelings from someone

C. "it is obvious"

D. "get lost!"

E. too expensive

F. to reveal a secret

G. to relieve a tense and uncomfortable situation

H. frayed, upset

I. to offer unsolicited advice, to interfere in another's affairs

J. to abandon or discard

K. a tantrum, an emotional reaction

L. to seek favor by attention or flattery

M. "every person has different tastes and preferences"

N. to identify the cause or source of a problem

O. to pay expenses

P. to talk incessantly

Q. an unpleasant or terrifying experience or situation

R. to lose one's inhibitions

S. to have the audacity or courage to act

T. to unintentionally irritate or annoy someone

U. "retreat" or "stop bothering me"

V. to take the first step towards a goal

W. to frighten severely

X. to angrily and loudly criticize

TALK TURKEY!

Time to talk each other's ears off. Put your nose where it doesn't belong and get all kinds of dirt on your classmates. Do you have the nerve to let your hair down and answer the questions truthfully? If not, make up a few white lies. Be sure to use the new slang in your answers.

1. Has anything happened to you in the US that **scared the living daylights out of you**? What **scared the living daylights out of you**? Have you met or seen any **creepy** persons here in the US? What made you think they were **creepy**? Would they **scare the living daylights out of you** if you were surprised by them in a dark alley, or was this person just a tad **creepy**?

2. Come on, **spill the beans**! Have you ever **ditched** someone? Where and why did you **ditch** them?

3. What would be your dream job? How would you **get your foot in the door**?

4. Who's your favorite movie star? If you saw him or her walking down the street would you **have the nerve** to say something? What would you say?

5. What really **rubs you the wrong way** when you are out in public? People smoking next to you? People making goo-goo-eyes at you? People who **talk your ear off** on public transportation? Is there anything else? When someone is doing something that **rubs you the wrong way** do you **have the nerve** to tell him or her to stop?

6. Who was the last person you **sucked up to**? Why did you **suck up to** them? Did you end up getting what you wanted?

7. What do you do when you are in a situation that gives you **bad vibes**? When was the last time this happened?

8. When you meet someone for the first time what sort of questions do you ask to **break the ice**? How long do you have to know someone before you **let your hair down** with him or her?

9. If you were at a party and someone walks by you, trips, and spills coffee all over your expensive new clothes, would you throw a **fit**? When was the last time you had a **fit**? When was the last time you **let somebody have it**? Why?

10. In your country who usually **foots the bill** for a university student's education? Who's **footing the bill** for your education?

11. Are you good at **putting your finger on** what's wrong with something that's on the blink? When you try to start your car, but it won't cooperate, are you able to **put your finger on** the problem?

12. Which one of your friends usually **puts their nose where it doesn't belong**? What's the last thing they were too nosy about? Does **it go without saying** that this friend usually **talks your ear off** too?

WRITE UP A STORM!

Select a partner. Imagine that the two of you are on a date, and one of you finds the other a tad creepy. Bad vibes are filling the air! Write down the conversation that you have. Let the other person have it, or even throw a fit if they rub you the wrong way. Just be sure to use fifteen example of new slang in your conversation.

"I've Got A Few Skeletons In My Closet"

1. What's the last thing in your life that you were very nervous about doing? Why did it make you nervous? How did the situation turn out?

2. Describe your favorite secret spot in your native country? Have you found a new favorite place in your new city? Where is it?

3. Has there ever been anything about you that you would rather keep a secret from most of the world?

Mona and Renee are hanging at their place waiting for Vic to show up…

RENEE: So where are you and Vic heading?

MONA: Vic suggested a walk on the beach because it's such a beautiful day. Then, we'll probably end up having some breakfast; that is, if I can manage to **keep** anything **down**. I'm so **antsy** right now, I feel like I'd **lose my lunch** if I ate anything.

RENEE: If I were in your shoes I'd be feeling the same way! Today's your big heart-to-heart. Maybe you won't see eye-to-eye on anything and break up! You know, he could even be thinking of popping the question!

MONA: Gee Renee, when you **put it that way** I feel so much better. I know who not to turn to for advice when I'm feeling **on edge**. I'd probably **pass out** if he popped the question.

The doorbell rings…

MONA: Renee, could you get the door? My **legs** are **like Jell-O**.

RENEE: Sure. (Renee opens the door) Oh, hi Vic. Mona will be right down.

VIC: Hey Mona, you look great as usual! Ready to go?

MONA: Sure. See you Renee.

RENEE: (Whispers in Mona's ear) Don't **sweat** it Mona. I'll **keep my fingers crossed for you** for you.

Mona and Vic arrive at a beautiful secluded beach…

MONA: This place is beautiful! How did you ever find it?

VIC: I grew up along the coastline here so I **know it like the back of my hand**. But I didn't bring you here for **small talk**. I'm not good at making speeches so I'm just going to **wing** it and I hope it comes out OK. Mona, I know this may sound **corny**, but I'm not **goofing around** here. The first time I saw you, I knew you were made for me. When we had that **falling-out**, I was so lonely and lost without you… What I'm trying to say is I don't ever want to be without you. I want us to spend our lives together, grow old together. Mona, will you marry me?

MONA: Oh, Vic. But there's more to me than meets the eye. I want to be **up-front** with you. I **have a few skeletons in my closet**.

VIC: If you're talking about your high school days, I knew about that from day one. That's ancient history. Besides everyone has a secret or two!

MONA: Charlie **let you in on** my big secret? What a **lousy** thing to do! He's such a **blabbermouth**! But what skeleton could you have in your closet?

VIC: I never told this to anyone but, I've **got two left feet**!

MONA: Not being able to dance doesn't really qualify as a skeleton!

VIC: Well, I just thought I should let you know so I wouldn't **let** you **down** when we have our first dance at our wedding reception. (Vic takes the ring out his pocket and begins to place it on Mona's finger.) So, what do you say, will you make me the happiest man in the world and be my wife?

MONA: Oh Vic, yes! We're going to be so happy together.

*(Mona checks out the size of the rock and thinks to herself: "All of my friends are going to **eat their hearts out** when they see this!")*

Quit goofing around and grab a partner. Don't sweat this matching exercise because it should be a piece of cake. (answers on page 150)

1. **keep down** verb_____

2. **antsy** adj_____

3. **lose one's lunch** verb_____

4. **put it that way** verb_____

5. **on edge** adj_____

6. **pass out** verb_____

7. **legs like Jell-O** adj_____

8. **sweat** verb_____

9. **keep ones' fingers crossed** verb_____

10. **know something like the back of one's hand** verb_____

11. **small talk** noun_____

12. **wing** verb_____

13. **corny** adj_____

14. **goof around** verb_____

15. **falling-out** noun_____

16. **up-front** adv_____

17. **have a skeleton in one's closet** verb_____

18. **let someone in on something** verb_____

19. **lousy** adj_____

20. **blabbermouth** noun_____

21. **have two left feet** verb_____

22. **let down** verb_____

23. **eat one's heart out** verb_____

A. to faint

B. to improvise

C. candid, frank

D. to be thoroughly familiar with something

E. to worry about

F. fidgety, nervous

G. to joke or play around

H. to have a shameful secret

I. unpleasant, bad

J. to express one's opinion in an irritating or annoying fashion

K. to disappoint

L. to be jealous or envious of someone

M. silly, cliche, or childishly sentimental

N. to inform someone

O. unimportant or idle conversation

P. to vomit

Q. anxious, irritable

R. said of one whose legs are unsteady because of nervousness

S. to be able to keep food or drink in one's stomach

T. to wish for good luck

U. a person who can't keep a secret

V. to be poor dancer

W. an argument or disagreement

TALK UP A STORM!

Goof around and be corny because there's no reason why you have to be up-front about everything. Got some skeletons in your closet? Keep 'em there! You don't have to let everyone in on your secrets!

1. When you are really hungry, or when you must be polite, will you eat foods that you really don't like? Have you ever had to eat something you didn't like? Were you able to **keep it down** or did you wind up **losing your lunch**?

2. When you think about the city you lived in your native country, did you **know it like the back of your hand**? How about the city you live in now–do you **know it like the back of your hand**?

3. Suppose you are at a party and there are tons of new people there speaking English. Are you good at making **small talk** in English or do your **legs turn into Jell-O** at the thought of having to approach strangers and speak to them in English? Are you good at making **small talk** in your native tongue? Dancing is the same in any language! Are you good at it or do you **have two left feet**?

4. You've about to take your driving test! Are you **sweating** it? Do you tell all of your friends to **keep their fingers crossed**?

5. When's the last time someone **let** you **down**? Did you feel **lousy** afterwards? How do you make yourself feel better when you are in a **lousy** mood?

6. What do you own that makes all of your friends **eat their hearts out**? If they were touching or using it would you be **antsy**?

7. Do you have any **skeletons in your closet**? If you were about to get married would you **let** your future spouse **in on** any secrets you have? Why or why not?

8. When a tough situation presents itself, are you good at **winging** things and finding a way out? If your teacher called on you to give a speech in English about your native country, could you **wing** it or would you be **sweating** the entire way through it?

9. Are you one of those persons who always **goofs around** in English class? If not, name one of the persons who always **goofs around** in class.

10. Who is someone in your life right now that you wish would be **up-front** with you? Would you say that if they aren't **up-front**, a **falling-out** is inevitable?

LET'S WRITE!

You have to write this on your own, so you may have to wing it. Write a story about someone who winds up eating his or her heart out. If you're sweating it, it could be about you and all the new slang you've learned! Be sure to use at least fifteen new slang terms and as many old ones as you like.

CROSSWORD REVIEW

Now that you know slang like the back of your hand, this crossword puzzle should be a breeze! Don't sweat it, just quit goofing around and give it your best shot! Remember to use the correct form of the word. (solution on page 150)

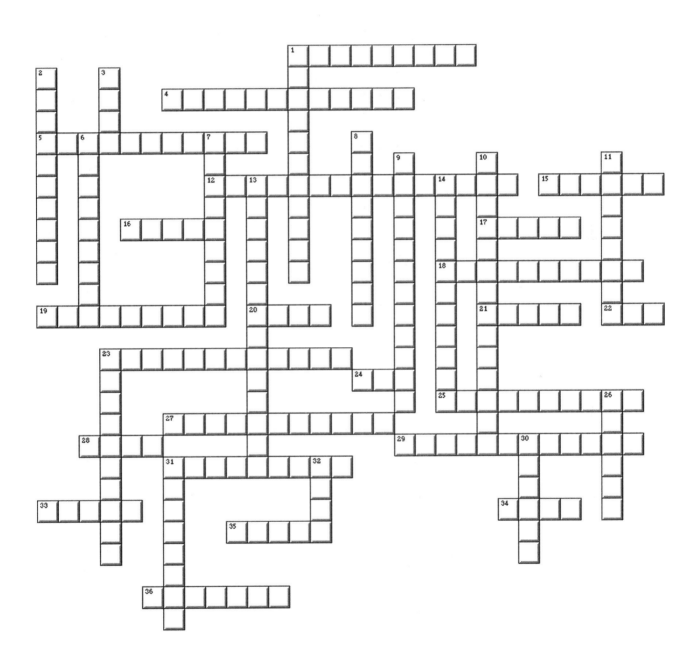

Across

1 I was stunned. I nearly _____ ___ when he told me the bad news.

4 You really _____ ___ ___ when you told my mom that Bill and I are getting married. He hasn't even proposed yet!

5 This is making me sick. I'm going to ____ __ _____ if he doesn't stop talking about his job in the emergency room.

12 This is not the time to be _____ ____ ____ . You can't back out now.

15 This hotel is _____ . It's dark and dank; it reminds me of a funeral parlor.

16 Don't _____ it. We've got everything under control so there's no reason to worry.

17 The crook wanted to abandon his getaway car, so he tried to _____ it at a wrecking yard.

18 So, you're going to ___ ___ ____ ! It's hard to believe that you are getting married.

19 I told that jerk to ____ _ _____ when he tried to pick me up at the dance.

20 Look at the size of that _____ on her finger!

21 I'm really _____ today. I just can't seem to sit still.

22 I just heard we're not going to attend the conference this year. The boss told me to ___ our plans to go.

23 Your mom is really going to ___ ___ ____ __ when she sees what you spilled on the carpet!

24 She was furious and had a ___ when her friends ditched her at the restaurant and stuck her with the bill.

25 I'm in great shape. I've got a job _____ __ ____ me as soon as I graduate.

27 You have a brain. I expect you to ___ _____ ____ and think for yourself.

28 I'm going to have to _____ over a lot of dough to get my car fixed.

29 We settled our differences and got everything _____ ____ .

31 Please __ __ _____ with me about my illness. I'd appreciate your honesty.

33 His brand of humor isn't very sophisticated. I hope you don't mind his _____ jokes.

34 I lost my notes for my speech, so I had to ____ it.

35 The room is too small, the air conditioning doesn't work, and the food is terrible. These accommodations are _____ .

36 David ___ _____ his friend when he failed to keep his end of the bargain.

Down

1 This problem has me puzzled. I just can't ___ __ _____ on what is wrong.

2 Don't _____ or we'll miss our flight.

3 He had a few drinks and he was ____ . You'd better take him home and put him to bed.

6 I hate these social functions where everyone engages in idle conversation. I'm just not good at _____ ____ .

7 Everything that could have gone wrong, did go wrong. Our vacation was a _____ !

8 That brownnoser always _____ __ __ the boss when our annual evaluations are held.

9 What a _____ ! That guy cannot keep a secret!

10 My parents are very opposed to this. They're ____ ___ _____ us getting married so young.

11 I'm pretty queasy this morning. I don't know if I can ____ ____ any food.

13 Let's not sit with Tim because he'll ____ ___ ____ __ . He's a real motormouth.

14 My boyfriend wrecked my car, but he won't pay for repairs. He expects me to ____ ___ ____ !

23 I shouldn't be telling you this, but I'm going to ___ ___ __ __ this secret.

26 I'm sorry I've been so irritable lately, but trying to make this deadline really has me __ ___ .

30 That weird guy has been _____ you for quite a while. He's been staring over at your side of the table all night.

31 I'm getting ___ _____ from that guy. He gives me the creeps.

32 That woman is always poking around and asking questions. She's so ____ !

Unit One Matching Exercises

Lesson One		Lesson Two		Lesson Three	
1. E	13. X	1. F	12. Q	1. N	13. P
2. V	14. U	2. S	13. A	2. O	14. W
3. O	15. K	3. O	14. B	3. A	15. C
4. F	16. J	4. U	15. J	4. F	16. L
5. M	17. P	5. K	16. V	5. S	17. D
6. D	18. G	6. D	17. H	6. E	18. H
7. W	19. B	7. P	18. N	7. U	19. G
8. I	20. A	8. I	19. M	8. R	20. V
9. T	21. H	9. C	20. L	9. Q	21. T
10. Q	22. C	10. T	21. R	10. K	22. M
11. L	23. R	11. E	22. G	11. I	23. J
12. S	24. N			12. B	

Unit One Crossword Solution

Unit Two Matching Exercises

Lesson One		Lesson Two		Lesson Three	
1. O	14. D	1. O	13. B	1. W	14. N
2. R	15. J	2. H	14. U	2. H	15. K
3. N	16. B	3. F	15. W	3. P	16. T
4. E	17. H	4. P	16. D	4. Y	17. C
5. W	18. Y	5. M	17. K	5. D	18. G
6. C	19. I	6. I	18. C	6. R	19. Q
7. G	20. P	7. Q	19. L	7. A	20. O
8. Q	21. T	8. E	20. S	8. J	21. X
9. M	22. X	9. A	21. J	9. M	22. V
10. U	23. K	10. V	22. G	10. B	23. U
11. A	24. L	11. T	23. N	11. I	24. L
12. V	25. F	12. R		12. S	25. F
13. S				13. E	

Unit Two Crossword Solution

Unit Three Matching Exercises

	Lesson One		
1.	L	13.	J
2.	K	14.	P
3.	T	15.	A
4.	U	16.	H
5.	M	17.	Q
6.	F	18.	O
7.	B	19.	S
8.	G	20.	I
9.	R	21.	V
10.	C	22.	N
11.	D	23.	E
12.	W		

	Lesson Two		
1.	C	14.	J
2.	V	15.	S
3.	G	16.	P
4.	M	17.	H
5.	Q	18.	Y
6.	X	19.	B
7.	U	20.	K
8.	R	21.	T
9.	I	22.	W
10.	O	23.	N
11.	F	24.	D
12.	A	25.	L
13.	E		

	Lesson Three		
1.	O	13.	W
2.	I	14.	Q
3.	E	15.	U
4.	G	16.	C
5.	P	17.	T
6.	R	18.	J
7.	K	19.	N
8.	V	20.	F
9.	D	21.	A
10.	S	22.	M
11.	L	23.	B
12.	H		

Unit Three Crossword Solution

143

Unit Four Matching Exercises

Lesson One		Lesson Two		Lesson Three	
1. K	14. M	1. B	13. S	1. N	13. D
2. V	15. Y	2. O	14. L	2. S	14. H
3. T	16. G	3. D	15. M	3. E	15. C
4. B	17. L	4. F	16. R	4. Q	16. W
5. O	18. J	5. H	17. P	5. M	17. O
6. W	19. N	6. A	18. T	6. V	18. P
7. E	20. X	7. C	19. J	7. A	19. T
8. F	21. P	8. G	20. N	8. U	20. G
9. H	22. R	9. U	21. K	9. I	21. L
10. D	23. Q	10. E	22. V	10. X	22. K
11. S	24. I	11. I	23. Q	11. J	23. F
12. C	25. U	12. W		12. B	24. R
13. A					

Unit Four Crossword Solution

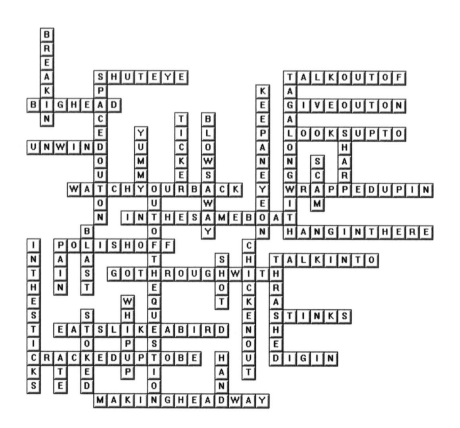

Unit Five Matching Exercises

Lesson One		Lesson Two		Lesson Three	
1. S	12. J	1. I	13. H	1. I	12. K
2. Q	13. G	2. W	14. V	2. R	13. F
3. N	14. C	3. L	15. O	3. P	14. J
4. O	15. V	4. K	16. J	4. L	15. S
5. F	16. L	5. F	17. R	5. E	16. D
6. B	17. U	6. X	18. Q	6. N	17. H
7. A	18. M	7. A	19. C	7. Q	18. C
8. T	19. K	8. S	20. U	8. B	19. T
9. H	20. R	9. D	21. B	9. A	20. O
10. D	21. I	10. E	22. N	10. G	21. U
11. E	22. P	11. M	23. P	11. M	
		12. G	24. T		

Unit Five Crossword Solution

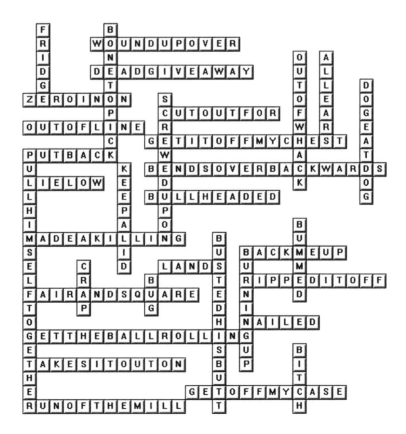

Unit Six Matching Exercises

Lesson One		Lesson Two		Lesson Three	
1. S	13. O	1. X	14. H	1. V	14. D
2. C	14. F	2. J	15. B	2. P	15. X
3. R	15. M	3. G	16. L	3. S	16. J
4. L	16. H	4. N	17. Y	4. W	17. C
5. V	17. Q	5. I	18. D	5. U	18. K
6. T	18. I	6. P	19. O	6. G	19. E
7. G	19. D	7. R	20. Q	7. T	20. R
8. A	20. P	8. W	21. C	8. A	21. Y
9. W	21. U	9. A	22. U	9. I	22. H
10. E	22. K	10. T	23. F	10. L	23. M
11. N	23. X	11. E	24. S	11. F	24. Q
12. B	24. J	12. V	25. K	12. N	25. O
		13. M		13. B	26. Z

Unit Six Crossword Solution

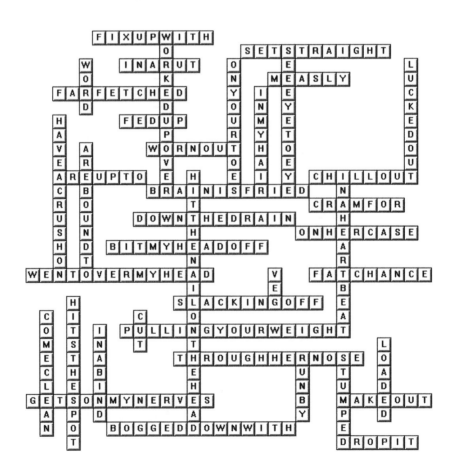

146

Unit Seven Matching Exercises

Lesson One		Lesson Two		Lesson Three	
1. E	13. L	1. O	14. T	1. D	13. W
2. O	14. H	2. F	15. L	2. H	14. F
3. N	15. J	3. D	16. E	3. P	15. C
4. S	16. B	4. C	17. Y	4. R	16. I
5. U	17. Q	5. J	18. M	5. A	17. T
6. R	18. K	6. P	19. H	6. N	18. O
7. C	19. D	7. Q	20. I	7. G	19. J
8. I	20. V	8. R	21. X	8. K	20. M
9. G	21. T	9. A	22. K	9. E	21. S
10. A	22. M	10. N	23. S	10. B	22. V
11. P	23. W	11. W	24. U	11. Q	23. U
12. F		12. V	25. G	12. L	
		13. B			

Unit Seven Crossword Solution

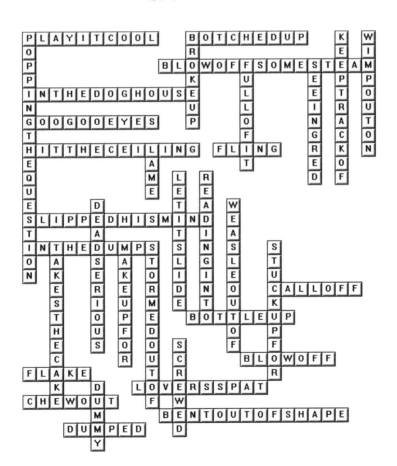

Unit Eight Matching Exercises

Lesson One		Lesson Two		Lesson Three	
1. E	14. C	1. J	13. K	1. S	12. C
2. J	15. M	2. E	14. B	2. O	13. E
3. H	16. O	3. H	15. V	3. L	14. H
4. F	17. I	4. T	16. L	4. F	15. P
5. A	18. T	5. R	17. W	5. G	16. U
6. D	19. U	6. C	18. D	6. R	17. D
7. W	20. V	7. P	19. F	7. A	18. J
8. L	21. Y	8. S	20. X	8. K	19. Q
9. K	22. G	9. A	21. N	9. M	20. I
10. B	23. X	10. O	22. U	10. N	21. T
11. S	24. R	11. I	23. M	11. B	
12. N	25. P	12. Q	24. G		
13. Q					

Unit Eight Crossword Solution

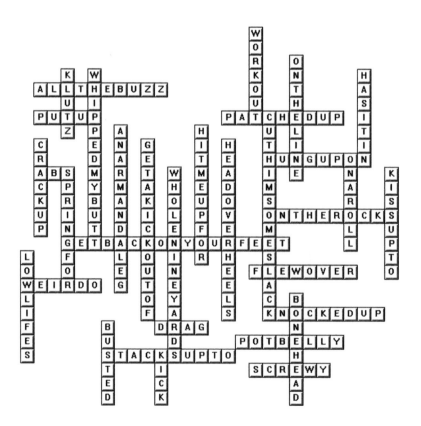

Unit Nine Matching Exercises

Lesson One

1. V	14. U
2. N	15. H
3. M	16. B
4. E	17. Y
5. C	18. Q
6. F	19. O
7. K	20. P
8. G	21. X
9. L	22. D
10. A	23. R
11. I	24. Z
12. S	25. T
13. J	26. W

Lesson Two

1. W	13. L
2. J	14. D
3. Q	15. E
4. R	16. N
5. H	17. V
6. M	18. P
7. B	19. F
8. K	20. T
9. G	21. U
10. C	22. O
11. S	23. I
12. A	

Lesson Three

1. O	12. I
2. G	13. E
3. T	14. R
4. B	15. U
5. M	16. K
6. P	17. C
7. A	18. N
8. J	19. H
9. Q	20. L
10. D	21. S
11. F	

Unit Nine Crossword Solution

Unit Ten Matching Exercises

Lesson One		Lesson Two		Lesson Three	
1. J	13. L	1. H	13. C	1. S	13. M
2. R	14. U	2. W	14. L	2. F	14. G
3. V	15. O	3. D	15. S	3. P	15. W
4. N	16. F	4. B	16. V	4. J	16. C
5. D	17. G	5. N	17. P	5. Q	17. H
6. T	18. C	6. I	18. G	6. A	18. N
7. S	19. B	7. M	19. R	7. R	19. I
8. M	20. K	8. F	20. U	8. E	20. U
9. W	21. X	9. T	21. X	9. T	21. V
10. Q	22. E	10. A	22. K	10. D	22. K
11. I	23. P	11. E	23. O	11. O	23. L
12. H	24. A	12. J	24. Q	12. B	

Unit Ten Crossword Solution

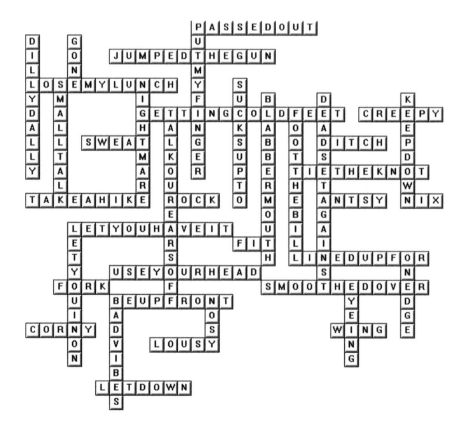

Relaxed Speech

When speaking casually or rapidly, consonant and vowel sounds are often shortened or even dropped. In some cases, the resulting words are known as contractions (e.g. **won't**, **can't**, **they're**, etc.) and will be seen in both print as well as heard in conversation. Other combinations are nonstandard and will rarely be seen in print or found in dictionaries. Some common examples of nonstandard forms are listed below to help non-native speakers of English improve their listening skills. The use of such speech forms is to be avoided in formal settings as it suggests that the speaker is poorly educated or lacks sophistication.

The bold-faced term indicates how the expression might be represented in print. It is followed by a pronunciation key (see page 160) and derivation. Finally, a sample sentence illustrates the term in spoken use. Underlined terms will be found elsewhere in the list. (A quick review of this list will demonstrate the importance of good diction in spoken communication.)

'a [ə] altered form of **of**

"Gimme a bite **'a** yer cake."

an or **'n** [æn/ən] altered form of **and** or **than**

"I'm tired **an/'n** I don't feel like goin' out tonight."
"My car is way faster **'n** yers."

arncha [ɑːrntʃə] shortened form of **aren't you**

"**Arncha** gonna do yer homework?"

bedder or **bedda** [bedɚ/bedə] altered form of **better**

"She'd **bedder/bedda** not tell 'em what happened."

'cause [kʌz] altered form of **because**

"I can't go **'cause** I'm broke."

coulda [kʊdə] shortened form of **could have**

"Ya **coulda** done a better job."

couldna [kʊdnə] shortened form of **couldn't have**

"I can't believe I ran into ya here. I **couldna** been luckier."

da [də] shortened form of **would have**

"Why dincha tell me you were gonna go? I **da** gone with ya."

dincha [dɪntʃə] shortened form of **didn't you**

"**Dincha** hear that the party was called off?"

doncha [doʊntʃə] shortened form of **don't you**

"**Doncha** know that chick over there?"

dunno or **donno** [dʌnoʊ/doʊnoʊ] shortened form of **don't know**

"I **dunno** what time it is."

'e [iː] altered form of **he**

"Where'd **'e** go?"

'em or **'im** [əm/ɪm] altered form of **him** or **them**

"Lookit **'em/'im**. He's on cloud nine 'cause he jus' popped the question."
"Ask **'im/'em** if ya kun borrow that new flick they rented."

'er [ɜːr/ɑːr] altered form of **or**, **are**, **her**, or **our**

"Ya wanna eat fish **'er** steak fer dinner?"
"These machines **'er** a drag."
"She's in a bad mood so stop buggin' **'er**."
"Izat **'er** new teacher?"

fer [fɜːr] altered form of **for**

"We'll be away **fer** three weeks."

gedda [gedə] *shortened form of* **get a**

"I heard <u>yer</u> <u>gonna</u> **gedda** a new laptop."

gimme [gɪmiː] *shortened form of* **give me**

"**Gimme** the dirt! What happened last night?"

godda [gɑːdə] *shortened form of* **got a**, **got to**, **have got a**, *or* **have got to**

"She's **godda** new set <u>'a</u> wheels."
"He's **godda** <u>gedda</u> new job."
"I **godda** new English teacher this term."
"<u>Ya</u> **godda** <u>gimme</u> the scoop."

gonna [gʌnə] *shortened form of* **going to**

"Are <u>ya</u> **gonna** give me a hand moving this weekend?"

hafta [hæftə] *shortened form of* **have to**

"<u>Ya</u> don't **hafta** help me if <u>ya</u> don't <u>wanna</u>."

hasta [hæstə] *shortened form of* **has to**

"The iron **hasta** warm up before <u>ya</u> <u>kun</u> use it."

howyabin [haʊjəbɪn] *shortened form of* **how have you been**

"Long time, no see. **Howyabin?**"

'im (*see* **'em**)

-in' [ɪn] *altered* **-ing** *endings*

"I'm **goin'** home 'cause I'm **havin'** trouble."

'is [ɪz] *altered form of* **his**

"Let's go hang out in **'is** Jacuzzi."

izat *or* **zat** [ɪzæt/zæt] *shorted form of* **is that**

"**Izat/zat** <u>'er</u> new teacher?"

ja [dʒə] *shortened form of* **did you**

"**Ja** go to that huge bash last night?"

jer [dʒɜːr] *shortened form of* **did your**

"**Jer** pictures turn out OK?"

jus' [dʒʌs] *altered form of* **just**

"**Jus'** <u>gimme</u> a sec. I'll be right down."

kun *or* **kin** [kʌn/kɪn] *altered form of* **can**

"I **kun/kin** give <u>ya</u> a lift if <u>ya</u> need one."

lemme [lemiː] *shortened form of* **let me**

"**Lemme** deal with the situation."

lookit [lʊkɪt] *shortened form of* **look at**

"**Lookit** that dude sporting a psychedelic tie! What year does <u>'e</u> think it is?"

maya [meɪjə] *shortened form of* **may have**

"They **maya** already left."

maynada [meɪnɑːdə] *shortened form of* **may not have**

"He **maynada** heard what <u>ya</u> said."

'member [membɚ] *altered form of* **remember**

"**Member** when we took that great trip to Spain?"

mighda [maɪdə] *shortened form of* **might have**

"She **mighda** gone shopping."

mighnada [maɪnɑːdə] *shortened form of* **might not have**

"He **mighnada** been able to find a parking place."

musta [mʌstə] *shortened form of* **must have**

"It's not like Cecelia to be so late. She **musta** forgotten about <u>'er</u> meeting."

musnada [mʌsnɑːdə] *shortened form of* **must not have**

"Eddie's wearing jeans? He **musnada** known this was a formal party."

prob'ly [prɑːbliː] *altered form of* **probably**

"We'll **prob'ly** spend the weekend at the cabin."

shoulda [tʃʊdə] *shortened form of* **should have**

"<u>Ya</u> **shoulda** helped that old lady with <u>'er</u> bags."

shouldna [tʃʊdnə] *shortened form of* **should not have**

"We **shouldna** brought so much luggage!"

sumthin' [sʌmθɪn] *altered form of* **something**

'We <u>shoulda</u> gotten **sumthin'** <u>fer</u> <u>yer</u> mom."

ta *or* **da** [tə/də] *altered form of* **to**

"Tell <u>'em</u> **ta** take <u>ya</u> out **da** dinner."

thad [ðæd] *shortened form of* **that would**

"**Thad** be great if we could take a vacation together."

wal [wɔːl] *altered form of* **while**

"He <u>musta</u> come over **wal** she was at the store."

wanna [wɑːnə] *shortened form of* **want to**

"<u>Ya</u> **wanna** hang out at the pool this weekend?"

whacha *or* **whadaya** [wʌtʃə/wʌtʌjʌ] *shortened form of* **what you**, **what are you** *or* **what do you**

"<u>Ya</u> <u>hafta</u> tell me **whacha** <u>wanna</u> do."
"**Whacha/whadaya** <u>doin'</u> tonight?"
"**Whatcha/whadaya** <u>wanna</u> do <u>fer</u> <u>yer</u> birthday?"

whad [wʌd] *shortened form of* **what did**

"**Whad** <u>'e</u> <u>wanna</u> talk <u>ta</u> <u>ya</u> about?"

whas [wʌs] *shortened form of* **what is**

"**Whas** <u>'e</u> <u>doin'</u>?"

whassup [wʌsʌp] *shortened form of* **what is up**

"Hey guys, **whassup?**"

where'd [werd] *shortened form of* **where did**

"Hey! **Where'd** everyone go?"

who'da [huːdə] *shortened form of* **who would have**

Who'da thought they'd get back together again after she busted <u>'im</u> with anther chick!

whydja *or* **whydya** [waɪdʒə/waɪdjə] *shortened form of* **why did you**

"**Whydja/whydya** come home so late last night?"

woncha [woʊntʃə] *shortened form of* **won't you**

"Why **woncha** change <u>yer</u> mind and come along with us?"

woulda [wʊdə] *shortened form of* **would have**

'If you had told <u>'er</u>, she **woulda** helped <u>ya</u>."

wouldna [wʊdnə] *shortened form of* **wouldn't have**

"If I were you, I **wouldna** done that."

ya [jʌ] *altered form of* **you**; *shortened form of* **do you**

"What are **ya** <u>doin'</u>?"
"**Ya** know what time it is?"

yer [jɜːr] *altered form of* **your**; *shortened form of* **you are**

"Izat **yer** mother? She looks like **yer** sister!"
"**Yer** <u>gonna</u> have a great time in Hawaii."

yers [jɜːrz] *altered form of* **yours**

"This one is **yers**. Mine is over there."

Verb Tenses

Using this chart and the diagrams beginning on page 157, you can form all tenses for any of the verbs used in the dialogues.

BASE VERB	SIMPLE PAST	PRESENT PARTICIPLE	PAST PARTICIPLE	BASE VERB	SIMPLE PAST	PRESENT PARTICIPLE	PAST PARTICIPLE
babble	babbled	babbling	babbled	charge	charged	charging	charged
back	backed	backing	backed	check	checked	checking	checked
bag	bagged	bagging	bagged	chew	chewed	chewing	chewed
bail	bailed	bailing	bailed	chicken	chickened	chickening	chickened
barf	barfed	barfing	barfed	chill	chilled	chilling	chilled
barge	barged	barging	barged	chip	chipped	chipping	chipped
bark	barked	barking	barked	chow	chowed	chowing	chowed
be	was/were	being	been	chug	chugged	chugging	chugged
beat	beat	beating	beat	clam	clammed	clamming	clammed
end	bent	bending	bent	come	came	coming	come
bitch	bitched	bitching	bitched	count	counted	counting	counted
bite	bit	biting	bitten	crack	cracked	cracking	cracked
blow	blew	blowing	blown	cram	crammed	cramming	crammed
blurt	blurted	blurting	blurted	crash	crashed	crashing	crashed
boil	boiled	boiling	boiled	creep	crept	creeping	crept
bomb	bombed	bombing	bombed	cut	cut	cutting	cut
book	booked	booking	booked	die	died	dying	died
booze	boozed	boozing	boozed	dig	dug	digging	dug
bottle	bottled	bottling	bottled	do	did	doing	done
break	broke	breaking	broken	down	downed	downing	downed
breeze	breezed	breezing	breezed	drag	dragged	dragging	dragged
buckle	buckled	buckling	buckled	drive	drove	driving	driven
bug	bugged	bugging	bugged	drop	dropped	dropping	dropped
bum	bummed	bumming	bummed	dump	dumped	dumping	dumped
bump	bumped	bumping	bumped	eat	ate	eating	eaten
burst	burst	bursting	burst	end	ended	ending	ended
bust	busted	busting	busted	eye	eyed	eyeing	eyed
butt	butt	butting	butt	fall	fell	falling	fallen
buy	bought	buying	bought	figure	figured	figuring	figured
call	called	calling	called	fix	fixed	fixing	fixed
can	canned	canning	canned	flake	flaked	flaking	flaked
catch	caught	catching	caught	flip	flipped	flipping	flipped

BASE VERB	SIMPLE PAST	PRESENT PARTICIPLE	PAST PARTICIPLE	BASE VERB	SIMPLE PAST	PRESENT PARTICIPLE	PAST PARTICIPLE
floor	floored	flooring	floored	lose	lost	losing	lost
flop	flopped	flopping	flopped	luck	lucked	lucking	lucked
fool	fooled	fooling	fooled	make	made	making	made
foot	foot	footing	foot	mess	messed	messing	messed
freak	freaked	freaking	freaked	mooch	mooched	mooching	mooched
get	got	getting	gotten	motor	motored	motoring	motored
give	gave	giving	given	nix	nixed	nixing	nixed
go	went	going	gone	nurse	nursed	nursing	nursed
goof	goofed	goofing	goofed	pass	passed	passing	passed
grill	grilled	grilling	grilled	patch	patched	patching	patched
gulp	gulped	gulping	gulped	peg	pegged	pegging	pegged
guzzle	guzzled	guzzling	guzzled	pick	picked	picking	picked
hand	handed	handing	handed	picture	pictured	picturing	pictured
hang	hung	hanging	hung	pig	pigged	pigging	pigged
haul	hauled	hauling	hauled	pipe	piped	piping	piped
have	had	having	had	piss	pissed	pissing	pissed
head	headed	heading	headed	play	played	playing	played
hear	heard	hearing	heard	polish	polished	polishing	polished
hit	hit	hitting	hit	pop	popped	popping	popped
hog	hogged	hogging	hogged	pour	poured	pouring	poured
hold	held	holding	held	psyche	psyched	psyching	psyched
hook	hooked	hooking	hooked	puke	puked	puking	puked
hop	hopped	hopping	hopped	pull	pulled	pulling	pulled
iron	ironed	ironing	ironed	pump	pumped	pumping	pumped
jerk	jerked	jerking	jerked	punch	punched	punching	punched
jet	jet	jetting	jet	put	put	putting	put
jot	jotted	jotting	jotted	rack	racked	racking	racked
jump	jumped	jumping	jumped	rake	raked	raking	raked
keep	kept	keeping	kept	read	read	reading	read
kick	kicked	kicking	kicked	ring	rang	ringing	rung
kill	killed	killing	killed	rip	ripped	ripping	ripped
kiss	kissed	kissing	kissed	rock	rocked	rocking	rocked
knock	knocked	knocking	knocked	rub	rubbed	rubbing	rubbed
know	knew	knowing	known	run	ran	running	run
land	landed	landing	landed	sack	sacked	sacking	sacked
let	let	letting	let	save	saved	saving	saved
look	looked	looking	looked	scam	scammed	scamming	scammed

BASE VERB	SIMPLE PAST	PRESENT PARTICIPLE	PAST PARTICIPLE	BASE VERB	SIMPLE PAST	PRESENT PARTICIPLE	PAST PARTICIPLE
score	scored	scoring	scored	swallow	swallowed	swallowing	swallowed
scare	scared	scaring	scared	sweat	sweated	sweating	sweated
scram	scrammed	scramming	scrammed	swing	swung	swinging	swung
scratch	scratched	scratching	scratched	swipe	swiped	swiping	swiped
screw	screwed	screwing	screwed	sugarcoat	sugarcoated	sugarcoating	sugarcoated
see	saw	seeing	seen	tag	tagged	tagging	tagged
set	set	setting	set	take	took	taking	taken
shack	shacked	shacking	shacked	talk	talked	talking	talked
shake	shook	shaking	shaken	tear	tore	tearing	torn
shell	shelled	shelling	shelled	tell	told	telling	told
shoot	shot	shooting	shot	throw	threw	throwing	thrown
show	showed	showing	showed	tie	tied	tying	tied
sink	sank	sinking	sunk	toss	tossed	tossing	tossed
slack	slacked	slacking	slacked	toy	toyed	toying	toyed
sleep	slept	sleeping	slept	trash	trashed	trashing	trashed
slip	slipped	slipping	slipped	trip	tripped	tripping	tripped
smooth	smoothed	smoothing	smoothed	turn	turned	turning	turned
snap	snapped	snapping	snapped	twist	twisted	twisting	twisted
sneak	sneaked	sneaking	sneaked	unwind	unwound	unwinding	unwound
space	spaced	spacing	spaced	use	used	using	used
spill	spilled	spilling	spilled	vedge	vedged	vedging	vedged
split	split	splitting	split	vent	vented	venting	vented
sponge	sponged	sponging	sponged	wake	woke	waking	woken
sport	sported	sporting	sported	walk	walked	walking	walked
spot	spotted	spotting	spotted	watch	watched	watching	watched
spring	sprang	springing	sprung	weasel	weaseled	weaseling	weaseled
stack	stacked	stacking	stacked	weed	weeded	weeding	weeded
stall	stalled	stalling	stalled	whip	whipped	whipping	whipped
stand	stood	standing	stood	wimp	wimped	wimping	wimped
stick	stuck	sticking	stuck	wind	wound	winding	wound
stiff	stiffed	stiffing	stiffed	wing	winged	winging	winged
stink	stank	stinking	stunk	wipe	wiped	wiping	wiped
storm	stormed	storming	stormed	work	worked	working	worked
strip	stripped	stripping	stripped	worm	wormed	worming	wormed
stuff	stuffed	stuffing	stuffed	wrap	wrapped	wrapping	wrapped
suck	sucked	sucking	sucked	zero	zeroed	zeroing	zeroed

Past Tenses (using the verb **go** as an example)

SIMPLE

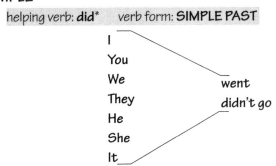

helping verb: **did***   verb form: **SIMPLE PAST**

I
You
We
They
He
She
It

went
didn't go

CONTINUOUS

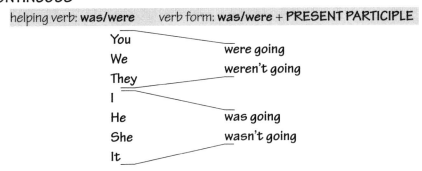

helping verb: **was/were**   verb form: **was/were** + **PRESENT PARTICIPLE**

You
We
They
I
He
She
It

were going
weren't going

was going
wasn't going

PERFECT

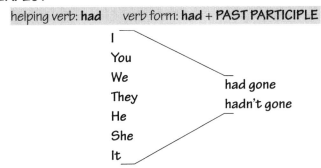

helping verb: **had**   verb form: **had** + **PAST PARTICIPLE**

I
You
We
They
He
She
It

had gone
hadn't gone

PERFECT CONTINUOUS

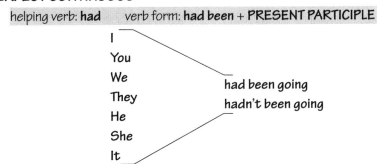

helping verb: **had**   verb form: **had been** + **PRESENT PARTICIPLE**

I
You
We
They
He
She
It

had been going
hadn't been going

* the verb **be** in simple past form is **were** or **was**. A helping verb is not needed. For example: **He was/wasn't here**.

Present Tenses (using the verb **go** as an example)

SIMPLE

helping verb: **do/does***   verb form: **BASE VERB/BASE VERB +s/es**

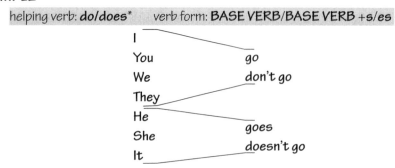

CONTINUOUS

helping verb: **am/are/is**   verb form: **am/are/is + PRESENT PARTICIPLE**

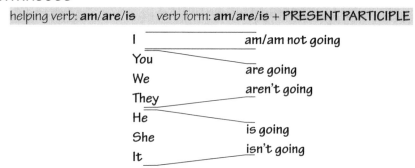

PERFECT

helping verb: **have/has**   verb form: **have/has + PAST PARTICIPLE**

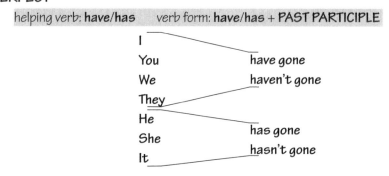

PERFECT CONTINUOUS

helping verb: **have/has**   verb form: **have/has been + PRESENT PARTICIPLE**

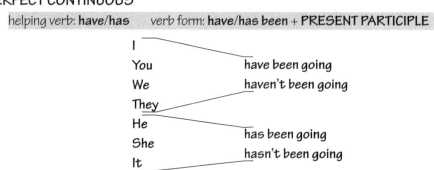

* the verb **be** in the simple present is **am**, **are** or **is**. A helping verb is not needed. For example: **He is/isn't here.**

Future Tenses *(using the verb **go** as an example)*

SIMPLE

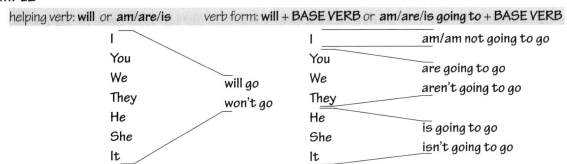

helping verb: **will** or **am/are/is**   verb form: **will + BASE VERB** or **am/are/is going to + BASE VERB**

I
You
We
They
He
She
It

will go
won't go

I   am/am not going to go
You
We   are going to go
They   aren't going to go
He
She   is going to go
It   isn't going to go

CONTINUOUS

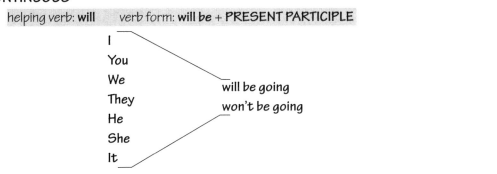

helping verb: **will**   verb form: **will be + PRESENT PARTICIPLE**

I
You
We
They
He
She
It

will be going
won't be going

PERFECT

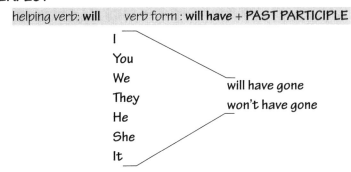

helping verb: **will**   verb form : **will have + PAST PARTICIPLE**

I
You
We
They
He
She
It

will have gone
won't have gone

PERFECT CONTINUOUS

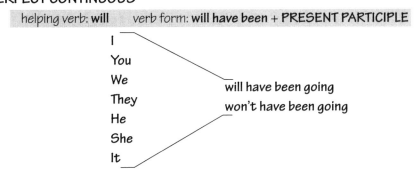

helping verb: **will**   verb form: **will have been + PRESENT PARTICIPLE**

I
You
We
They
He
She
It

will have been going
won't have been going

Glossary of Grammar Terms and Dictionary Notes

All vocabulary terms in the dictionary are arranged in character-by-character alphabetical order. Each bold-faced term is followed by an IPA pronunciation and a functional label (*e.g.* **adj**, **verb phrase**, etc.) A frequency-of-use estimate is provided in the form of asterisks (from one to five). The term is defined in Standard English, and a sample sentence illustrates typical use and context. If appropriate, a **grammar point** and/or **usage warning** will be included.

IPA Pronunciation Key

Vowels

ɪ as in 'p<u>i</u>t'

e as in 'p<u>e</u>t'

æ as in 'c<u>a</u>t'

ʌ as in 'c<u>u</u>t'

ʊ as in 'b<u>oo</u>k'

uː as in 'cl<u>ue</u>'

ə as in 'Americ<u>a</u>'

iː as in 'k<u>e</u>y'

ɑː as in 'f<u>a</u>ther'

ɔː as in 'c<u>au</u>ght'

ɜːr as in 'b<u>ir</u>d'

eɪ as in 'b<u>ai</u>t'

oʊ as in 'b<u>oa</u>t'

aʊ as in 'h<u>ou</u>se'

aɪ as in 'h<u>igh</u>'

ɔɪ as in 'b<u>oy</u>'

ɚ as in 'moth<u>er</u>'

Consonants

b as in '<u>b</u>ee'

d as in '<u>d</u>og'

g as in '<u>g</u>un'

v as in '<u>v</u>at'

ð as in '<u>th</u>at'

z as in '<u>z</u>ip'

ʒ as in 'mea<u>s</u>ure'

l as in '<u>l</u>ip'

r as in '<u>r</u>ed'

j as in '<u>y</u>ellow'

w as in '<u>w</u>et'

dʒ as in '<u>j</u>ump'

p as in '<u>p</u>ea'

t as in '<u>t</u>ea'

k as in '<u>k</u>ey'

f as in '<u>f</u>at'

θ as in '<u>th</u>in'

s as in '<u>s</u>ip'

ʃ as in '<u>sh</u>ip'

h as in '<u>h</u>at'

m as in '<u>m</u>ap'

n as in '<u>n</u>ap'

ŋ as in 'ha<u>ng</u>'

tʃ as in '<u>ch</u>in'

Functional Labels

Adjective (adj)
Adjectives are words that modify nouns and specify color, size, number, etc.

Adverb (adv)
Adverbs are words that modify verbs, adjectives, or other adverbs. They specify where, when, in what manner, and how much.

Expression (exp)
For the purposes of this book, an expression is defined as a single word or phrase that is almost exclusively used in spoken form, e.g., "**Bingo**!" or "**As if**!"

Noun (noun)

A noun is the name of a person, place, thing, or idea. They are classified in the following two catagories.

Count Noun (count noun)

A count noun is a noun that forms a plural and can be used with the indefinite article **a** or **an**, with words such as **few** or **many**, or with a numeral. A singular count noun (for example, **brewskie**) can be preceded by one of the following; an article (**a**, **an**, or **the**), a demonstrative adjective (**this**, **that**, **another**, or **the other**), or an adjective pronoun (**my**, **your**, **his**, **her**, **our**, or **their**). A speaker may correctly state; "I want **a brewskie**", "I want **that brewskie**" or "I want **her brewskie**", but "I want **brewskie**" would be incorrect.

Non-Count Noun (non-count noun)

A non-count noun (also called a **mass noun**) has only a singular form and the letter **s** will never be added as an ending. A non-count noun can be used with **some**, while the articles **a** and **an** are usually not used. Using the non-count noun **dough** as an example; one can say "I need **some dough**", "I need **that dough**" or "I need **your dough**", but "I need **a dough**" is incorrect.

Particles

Particles are the same words as prepositions; **in**, **on**, **with**, **away**, etc, but with a different function. While a preposition shows the relationship between two nouns, e.g., "the book is **on** the table", a particle is used to change the meaning of a verb. Consider the verb **get**; on its own it has many different meanings. Adding the particle **away**, yields **get away**, and a new meaning. Add another particle **with**, to produce **get away with**, and the meaning changes again.

Phrases

A phrase is a closely related group of words that has no subject or predicate. Phrases may function as adjectives, adverbs, nouns, or verbs.

Adjective Phrase (adj phrase)

Adjective phrases, e.g., **bent out of shape**, limit or describe nouns and pronouns. They are often used with the verb **be** and its counterparts; **look**, **seem**, **feel**, **get**, and **become.**

Adverb Phrase (adv phrase)

Adverb phrases, e.g., **fair-and-square**, modify verbs, adjectives or other adverbs.

Noun Phrase (noun phrase)

Noun phrases, e.g., **little girls room**, function as nouns and have been classified in this book as count noun phrases or non-count noun phrases.

Prepositional Phrase (prep phrase)

The prepositional phrases used in this book, e.g., **on the blink**, function as adjectives or adverbs.

Verb Phrase (verb phrase)

Verb phrases contain a verb, e.g., **give someone the ax**. Because the verb phrase functions as a verb, proper use requires attention to correct tense and form.

Simple Verb (verb)

A verb indicates an action or state of being, or the time of action or being. Verbs may be transitive or intransitive.

Transitive (T)

A transitive verb needs a direct object (a person, place, or thing immediately following the verb) that takes the action of the verb. A transitive verb may be used in either the active or passive voice. The active voice is used when the subject performs the action represented by the verb, e.g., "Jack **hit** the baseball." The passive voice is used when the subject is affected by the action represented by the verb ("Jack **was hit** by the baseball.") or when the person or thing performing the action is unimportant or unknown to the sense of the sentence ("Mary **was mugged**!") To form the passive voice, use the verb **be** in the desired tense (past; **was**, **were**; present perfect; **has been**, **have been**; present continuous; **am being**, **is being**, **are being**) and add the past participle of the verb. "Help, we **are being beaten**!" The verb **get** is commonly used instead of the verb **be**, e.g., "Mary **got knocked** off!" or "Mary **is getting killed**!"

Intransitive (I)

An intransitive verb takes no object so there is no noun directly after the verb. Therefore, a sentence with an intransitive verb can be used only in the active voice, e.g., "Shelly **ran** to the store."

Two Word Verb (2 word verb)

A two word verb is made up of a verb and a particle, e.g., **blow off** or **blow up**. Two word verbs fall into two categories, separable or inseparable and may be either intransitive or transitive with the majority of them falling into the latter category.

Separable (sep)

When a two word verb is separable, the object can go between the verb and its particle. When the object is a regular or a proper noun it may be positioned either between the verb and its particle, or after them. However, if the object is an object pronoun (**me, you, him, her, us, them**, or **it**) the object can only come between the verb and its particle. For example, one can say "Johnny **blew off** his homework", "Johnny **blew** his homework **off**", or "Johnny **blew** it **off**", but "Johnny **blew off** it" would be incorrect. Note that separable two word verbs are always transitive.

Inseparable (insep)

Inseparable two word verbs are used as one complete word because nothing can come between the verb and its particle. Using the inseparable two word verb **think about** as an example, one can say "You must **think about** your future!" or "You must **think about** it!" However, "You must **think** it **about**!" would be incorrect. In addition, inseparable two word verbs can be intransitive and take no object. For example, **blow up** can be used as follows; "He **blew up**!" If an object is needed, a preposition is added and the two word verb grows into a pseudo three word verb, e.g., "He **blew up at** her!"

Three Word Verb (3 word verb)

True three word verbs are made up of a verb and two particles. For example, the verb **put** and the particles **up** and **with** produces **put up with**. There are two important points to remember when it comes to three word verbs: 1. they are usually used in the active voice; 2. an object is necessary. "It's OK dude, I can **put up with** it!" is correct form. "It's OK dude, I can **put up with**" or "I can **put up**!" is incorrect.

Usage, Grammar, and Warnings

Sure you know the new slang, but you may find yourself wondering "How often is this stuff actually used?" or "Is this OK to use in all situations or could I find myself munching on a knuckle sandwich after saying some of these things?"

Frequency of Use
Look for the number of asterisks following the functional label for each dictionary entry. Refer to the chart below to get an idea of how often each term will be used.

*   Rarely used, perhaps once every few months.

**   Used occasionally, about once a month.

***   Used two to three times a month

****   Used weekly

*****   Used daily or more often

Grammar Point
Watch for the symbol ⓖ which identifies a Grammar Point. These notes will provide valuable information for proper grammatical use of each term.

Usage Warning
Keep your eyes peeled for the warning signs ⚠ and the notes following it to make sure you don't end up with your foot in your mouth, or worse!

Explanatory Chart

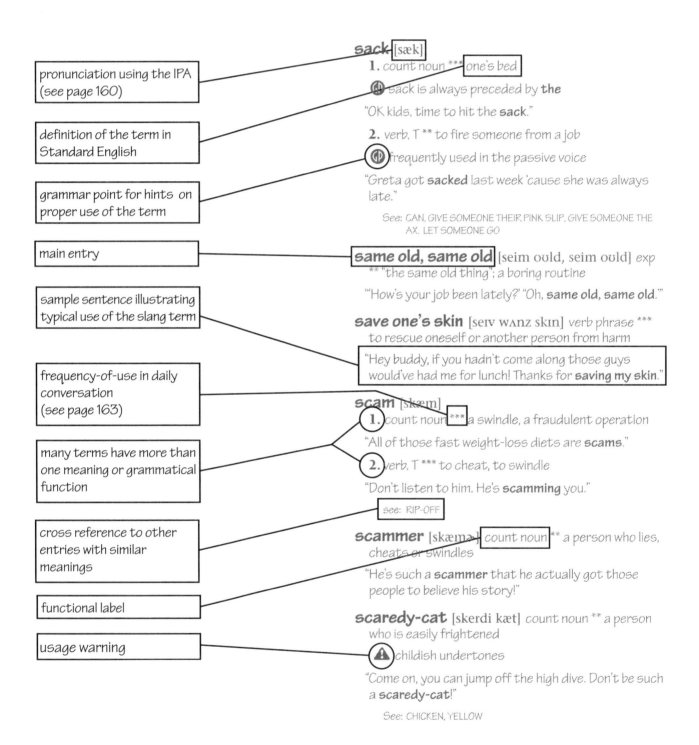

pronunciation using the IPA (see page 160)

definition of the term in Standard English

grammar point for hints on proper use of the term

main entry

sample sentence illustrating typical use of the slang term

frequency-of-use in daily conversation (see page 163)

many terms have more than one meaning or grammatical function

cross reference to other entries with similar meanings

functional label

usage warning

sack [sæk]
1. count noun *** one's bed
sack is always preceded by **the**
"OK kids, time to hit the **sack**."
2. verb, T ** to fire someone from a job
frequently used in the passive voice
"Greta got **sacked** last week 'cause she was always late."
See: CAN, GIVE SOMEONE THEIR PINK SLIP, GIVE SOMEONE THE AX, LET SOMEONE GO

same old, same old [seim ould, seim ould] exp ** "the same old thing"; a boring routine
"'How's your job been lately?' 'Oh, **same old, same old**.'"

save one's skin [seiv wʌnz skin] verb phrase ***
to rescue oneself or another person from harm
"Hey buddy, if you hadn't come along those guys would've had me for lunch! Thanks for **saving my skin**."

scam [skæm]
1. count noun *** a swindle, a fraudulent operation
"All of those fast weight-loss diets are **scams**."
2. verb, T *** to cheat, to swindle
"Don't listen to him. He's **scamming** you."
see: RIP-OFF

scammer [skæmə] count noun ** a person who lies, cheats or swindles
"He's such a **scammer** that he actually got those people to believe his story!"

scaredy-cat [skerdi kæt] count noun ** a person who is easily frightened
childish undertones
"Come on, you can jump off the high dive. Don't be such a **scaredy-cat**!"
See: CHICKEN, YELLOW

A

abs [æbz] *count noun* ** abdominal (stomach) muscles

⓪ always used in the plural form

"I hate working on my **abs** when I go to the gym!"

airhead [erhed] *count noun* ** a stupid or forgetful person, often used in regard to girls. Literally, one's head contains air instead of brains

⚠ mild insult; should not be said to a person's face unless in jest

"Mary is such an **airhead**. She would forget her head if it weren't attached to her body!"

See: BEANBRAIN, BIRDBRAIN, DINGBAT, DITZ, DUMMY, PEABRAIN, SPACE CADET

alcky [ælkiː] *count noun* *** a person who drinks too much alcohol, an alcoholic

⚠ derogatory; suggests that alcohol has begun to interfere with or destroy a person's daily life

"Her old man is an **alcky**."

See: BOOZER

all ears [ɔːl ɪrz] *adj phrase* *** listening attentively, eager to hear

"He was **all ears** when I mentioned how well the new job pays."

all-nighter

See: PULL AN ALL-NIGHTER

all the buzz [ɔːl ðe bʌz] *adj phrase* ** the main topic of conversation

"Have you seen that new horror movie? It's **all the buzz**."

an arm and a leg [æn ɑːrm ænd ə leg] *count noun phrase* **** a lot of money, an exorbitant price

⓪ always used in the singular form

"Susan had to pay **an arm and a leg** for her plane ticket home."

See: BUNDLE, PRETTY PENNY

antsy [æntsi] *adj* * fidgety, nervous

"Craig is always so **antsy** when I'm around him that I end up getting nervous too."

See: EDGY, ON EDGE

ASAP [eɪ es eɪ piː] *adv* ** quickly (abbreviation for **As Soon As Possible**)

"I don't think I can afford the rent much longer. I need to get a new roomie, **ASAP**."

as if [æz ɪf] *exp* **** "I can't believe it!" or "no way!"

"That gorgeous guy asked you out? **As if**!"

"'C'mon, tell me the secret!' '**As if** I'd tell you!'"

See: GET OUT OF HERE, GET OUT OF TOWN, NUH-UH, SHUT UP, YEAH RIGHT

at the crack of dawn [æt ðe kræk əv dɑːn] *prep phrase* *** very early in the morning

⓪ usually used with **be up** or **get up**

"Jommana went home early 'cause she has to be up **at the crack of dawn** tomorrow."

at the drop of a hat [ət ðe drɑːp əv ə hæt] *prep phrase* *** without delay, immediately

"If you need anything, call me. I'll be there **at the drop of a hat**."

See: IN A FLASH, IN A HEARTBEAT, IN A JIFFY, IN A NEW YORK SECOND, IN NO TIME FLAT, IN TWO SHAKES OF A LAMB'S TAIL

B

babble on [bæbl ɑːn] *2 word verb* *** to talk a lot about something that is unimportant

⓪ if the object is stated, it is preceded by **about**

"Miriam wanted to leave but Jose kept **babbling on** about his dog."

See: TALK SOMEONE'S EAR OFF

babe [beɪb]

1. *count noun* **** an attractive young person, usually female

⚠ generally used only by guys with this meaning

"Have you seen Marco's new girlfriend? She's a total **babe**!"

See: HONEY, HUNK

2. *exp* *** a term of endearment, used to address one's boyfriend, girlfriend, husband, wife, etc.

"**Babe**, you're the greatest. I love you."

See: HONEY

Note: other common terms of endearment are: **baby, candy, cookie, honey bun, lover, pumpkin, sugar, sugar pie, sweetie**

back off [bæk ɑːf] 2 word insep verb, I/exp *** to withdraw; "retreat!" or "stop bothering me!"

⚠ rude undertones

Ⓟ often used in the imperative form

"My boss was way out of line, so I told him to **back off**."

"You're really starting to get on my nerves! **Back off**, would you!"

back out [bæk aʊt] 2 word insep verb, I *** to withdraw from a situation or break an agreement

Ⓟ if the object is stated it is preceded by **of**

"You've got to be joking! Sharif **backed out** of that business deal? It was the chance of a lifetime!"

back up [bæk ʌp] 2 word sep verb ** to support or strengthen

Ⓟ typical usage: **back (someone) up on something** or **back something (a story) up**

"I know you'll find this hard to believe, but ask Joelle. She was there and she'll **back** me **up**/ she'll **back up** my story."

badass [bædæs] adj *** extremely good, stylish, or cool

⚠ crude, used mainly by younger males. May be shortened to **bad**, which is dated

"Dude, those are some **badass** wheels you've got."

See: HOT, KICK-ASS, RAD

bad vibes [bæd vaɪbz] count noun phrase **** bad feelings from a situation, someone, or something

"I don't think Joey and Rachel can pull this off. I've got **bad vibes** about this deal."

bag on [bæg ɑːn] 2 word insep verb, I ** to nag or criticize

⚠ slightly rude undertones

Ⓟ typical usage: **bag on someone for/about something** or **bag on someone to do something**

"When we were in high school, my dad constantly **bagged on** us about our homework/to do our homework."

bail [beɪl] verb, I ** to leave or give up on

⚠ usually used by the younger generations

Ⓟ if an object is used it is preceded by **on**

"This party sucks. Let's **bail**."

"The movie was a bore so we **bailed**."

See: BE OFF, BOOK, GET GOING, HIT THE ROAD, JET, SPLIT

bail out of [beɪl aʊt əv]

1. 3 word verb **** to rescue someone who is in a difficult situation

Ⓟ usage is typically **bail someone out of something**

"I don't know how I can ever repay you for this. You're always there to **bail** me **out of** my problems."

2. 3 word verb *** to withdraw from an unpleasant or trying situation

Ⓟ if the object is a person, **of** is replaced with **on**; **out** may also be dropped

"You said you would stay the entire week! I can't believe you're **bailing out** (**of** this/**on** me) after only two days!"

ball [bɔːl] count noun ** fun, a great time

Ⓟ always preceded by **a** and used in the singular form

"We had a **ball** at the party last night!"

See: BLAST, HOOT, RIOT, SCREAM

ballpark figure [bɔːlpɑːrk fɪgjɚ] count noun phrase *** an estimate, an approximation

"How many people are coming to the picnic? I just need a **ballpark figure**."

balls [bɔːlz] non-count noun **** courage

⚠ somewhat coarse. This word is usually heard only in male company as the term **balls** refers to a man's testicles

"He finally got the **balls** to walk out on her!"

See: GUTS

bananas [bənɑːnænəz] adj * crazy

⚠ slightly dated term

Ⓟ only used to describe people or people's feelings, never precedes a noun

"You want to ask the boss for a raise after she just told us how badly the company is doing? Are you **bananas**?"

See: BONKERS, CUCKOO, NUTS, NUTTY, OUT OF ONE'S MIND, OUT TO LUNCH, WACKO, WACKY

barf [bɑːrf] *verb, I/non-count noun* ** *to vomit, to throw up*

⚠ *somewhat crude*

"That food looks like **barf**! I think I'll **barf** if I have to eat it!"

See: LOSE ONE'S LUNCH, PUKE, TOSS ONE'S COOKIES

barge in [bɑːrdʒ ɪn] *2 word insep verb, T/I* *** *to enter suddenly or rudely*

🌀 *the object is often preceded by* **on**

"I wish John would stop **barging in** on our conversations!"

See: BUTT IN

bark up the wrong tree [bɑːrk ʌp ðe rɑːŋ triː] *verb phrase* ** *to waste one's effort by pursuing the wrong path, to misdirect effort*

"You're **barking up the wrong tree** if you think I'm going to bail you out of this mess."

bash [bæʃ] *count noun* ** *a party*

"Gail's having a big **bash** at her place this weekend. Are you going?"

be all like [biː ɔːl laɪk] *verb phrase* ***** *to say*

⚠ *among young persons, often heard more that the actual word* **say**

🌀 *can be used in either present or past tense regardless of the actual time, sometimes the word* **like** *or* **all** *is dropped*

"I saw Frank the other day and he **was all like** 'Where have you been hiding yourself?' and I **was like** 'I've been here, it's just that you haven't been calling!' and he **was all** 'What? I've called you, you just haven't been home!' and **I'm all** 'you're such a liar!'"

See: GO

be all over [biː ɔːl oʊvɚ]

1. *3 word verb* *** *to single out a person for angry criticism*

🌀 *the object is always a person*

"When Yutaro told his boss he couldn't finish the project, his boss **was all over** him! You could hear him going off all over the office!"

See: CHEW OUT, GO OFF ON, JUMP DOWN SOMEONE'S THROAT

2. *3 word verb* ** *to touch another person in a sexual way*

"Did you see Jill? She **was all over** that guy last night!"

be all the rage [biː ɔːl ðe reɪdʒ] *verb phrase* ** *to be very popular*

"Have you seen those new space-age watches? They **are all the rage** in Tokyo!"

See: HOT

beanbrain [biːn breɪn] *count noun* ** *a stupid or foolish person (literally, the brain is the size of a bean)*

"How could he have gone into business with such a **beanbrain**!"

See: BIRDBRAIN, BONEHEAD, DOOFUS, DOPE, DUMMY, NINCOMPOOP, PEABRAIN

beat [biːt] *adj* ***** *exhausted*

🌀 *when used in the first person present tense,* **I am beat**; *second person,* **you look/must be beat**; *third person,* **he looks/seems/must be beat**

"I can't believe we ran ten miles! I'm **beat**!"

See: DEAD, POOPED, WIPED OUT, WORN OUT

beat around the bush [biːt ə raʊnd ðe bʊʃ] *verb phrase* *** *to say something indirectly, to avoid the main issue*

🌀 *usually used in the negative imperative form*

"Don't **beat around the bush**!"

"Stop **beating around the bush**!"

"'John, why didn't you meet me last night?' 'Well, Sarah, uh, I went to work as usual, then after that I stopped at the store to pick up a few things, then I, um, got in my car and started to drive home. I was listening to the radio and…' 'John, stop **beating around the bush**! Why did you blow me off?'"

See: STALL

beat it [biːt ɪt] *verb phrase/exp* ** *a rude way of telling someone to leave; "get lost!"*

"You stupid dog! Look what you did to my garden! Get out of here! **Beat it**!"

See: SCRAM, TAKE A HIKE

beat(s) [biːts] *verb, T* **** *to surpass, to be better than*

🌀 *generally used when talking about activities, therefore* **it** *or gerunds are commonly used*

"'What do you say we go to a movie?' 'Good idea! It **beats** staying home and watching all of the crappy reruns on the tube.'"

beats me [biːts miː] *exp* **** "I don't know."

"'What's on the tube tonight?' '**Beats me**.'"

See: YOU'VE GOT ME

be better off [bi: betɚ ɑːf] *verb phrase* ***** a more favorable position

🅖 *object can be a gerund or a person*

"You **are better off** getting in the other lane now."

"Manny shouldn't be sad that Paula dumped him. He **is better off** without her!"

be bound to [bi: baʊnd tuː] *verb phrase* **** to be certain or destined

🅖 *always followed by the simple form of a verb*

"Just be patient. You **are bound to** find a job sooner or later."

be cool [bi: kuːl] *verb phrase* **** to act composed, nonchalant; to stay calm

🅖 *used mainly in the imperative form*

"There's Christopher. Just **be cool** and maybe he won't notice the dent on his car."

See: PLAY IT COOL

Beemer [biːmɚ] *count noun* *** term for any automobile manufactured by BMW (Bayerische Motoren Werke)

"I just saw Nathan in a new **Beemer**. He must be raking in the dough!"

beer belly [bɪr beli] *count noun phrase* * a large flabby stomach, often from drinking too much beer

⚠ *potentially insulting, even with friends*

"Christopher is really getting out of shape. He's even starting to get a **beer belly**!"

See: GUT, POTBELLY

beet red [biːt red] *adj phrase* * flushed and red from embarrassment

"Mikhail turned **beet red** when he realized he had been walking around with toilet paper hanging out of his pants."

be game [bi: geɪm] *verb phrase* *** to be ready, willing to proceed

🅖 *if the object is stated, it is preceded by* **for**

"'What do you say we go fishing this weekend?' 'I am **game** (for that).'"

See: BE UP FOR

be in for [bi: ɪn fɔːr]

1. 3 *word verb* * to be likely to experience or encounter

"From the looks of the weather, I'd say we **are in for** some rain today."

2. 3 *word verb* ** to be guaranteed punishment or trouble

"Your puppy dug up Mom's flowerbed? You **are in for** it now!"

be into [bi: ɪntuː] 2 *word verb* ***** to enjoy, to be interested

🅖 *sometimes the word* **get** *replaces* **be**. *The object can be anything from a band to a person or activity*

"'What/ Who **are** you **into**?' 'I **am into** the Red Hot Chile Peppers/ Christopher/ cooking.'"

be missing something upstairs [bi: mɪsɪŋ sʌmpθɪŋ ʌpsterz] *verb phrase* *** to be crazy or strange (literally, a person is missing part of their brain)

⚠ *used only to refer to people, can be used seriously or in jest*

"I think that guy **is missing something upstairs**. I asked him the same question three times and he gave me three different answers! What a weirdo!"

bend over backward [bend oʊvɚ bækwɚd] *verb phrase* ** to go to great lengths to accommodate someone

"I can't believe Sumiyo would try to hurt you. She's always **bending over backward** for you and everyone else around her."

bent out of shape [bent aʊt əv ʃeɪp] *adj phrase* ** annoyed or angry

🅖 *often preceded with* **all**

"Eric was all **bent out of shape** because I forgot to pick him up at the airport."

Benz [benz] *count noun* *** nickname for any model of automobile manufactured by Mercedes Benz

"Jack drives a **Benz** now. Business must be pretty good."

be off [bi: ɑːf]

1. 2 *word insep verb*, I ***** to leave, depart

🅖 *if the destination is stated, it is preceded by* **for**

"It's already eight? I'd better **be off** (for work). I'll call you later."

See: BOOK, GET GOING, HIT THE ROAD, JET, SPLIT

2. 2 word insep verb, T **** to stop using, or to no longer enjoy something that was enjoyed at one time

🔘 sometimes the object is preceded by **of**, and the object may be either people or things

"No coffee for me, please. I **am off** (of) coffee."

be on [bi: ɑ:n]

1. 2 word insep verb, I *** to be responsible for the bill

🔘 subject is always what is being paid for, object is always the person paying. The subject is often **it** (meaning the bill)

"Drinks **are on** me!"

"You got it last time, so this time **it's on** me."

2. 2 word sep verb, T *** to nag someone

"Sue **is** always **on** him about something!"

be out of [bi: aʊt əv] 3 word verb ***** to be lacking, to have nothing left

🔘 sometimes **all** is said between **be** and **out** for emphasis

"Honey, could you run to the store. We **are out of** OJ, eggs, and bread."

"'I'll have the fish' 'I'm sorry. We **are** all **out of** fish.'"

"I want to make another bet but I **am out of** money. Can I bum a few bucks?"

See: RUN OUT OF

best thing since sliced bread [best θɪŋ sɪnts slaɪst brɛd] adj phrase * very good, the best and latest development

⚠ slightly outdated, usually used by older generations

🔘 always preceded by **the**

"I couldn't live without my cell phone! It's the **best thing since sliced bread**!"

be there with bells on [bi: ðer wɪθ belz ɑ:n] verb phrase * eagerly looking forward to something, ready to celebrate

"You're going to deliver the commencement address? I'll **be there with bells on**!"

be up for [bi: ʌp fɔ:r] 3 word verb ***** to be interested or enthusiastic

🔘 the action can either be stated or implied

"'**Are** you **up for** seeing a movie tonight?' 'Sure, I **am up for** a movie. What do you want to see?'"

See: BE GAME

be up-front [bi: ʌp frʌnt] 3 word verb *** to be candid, frank

"OK doctor, I want you to **be up-front** with me; don't sugarcoat the truth."

be up to [bi: ʌp tu:] 3 word verb ***** involved or occupied with, doing

🔘 this 3-word verb always has a continuous meaning but is rarely used in the continuous form

"'What have you **been up to** the past month?' 'I haven't **been up to** much.'"

bighead [bɪghed] count noun *** an inflated ego, a conceited person

🔘 the subject is always the person referred to, usually used in the singular form preceded by **a**

"Maya has such a **bighead**! She always thinks she's the best at everything!"

bigheaded [bɪghedɪd] adj ** conceited, self-important

"Maya is so **bigheaded**!"

big house [bɪg haʊs] count noun phrase * a federal penitentiary, prison

⚠ often heard in movies

🔘 always used in the singular form, preceded by **the**

"If they nail you on a counterfeiting charge, you'll go to the **big house** for a long time."

See: CAN, JOINT, PEN, SLAMMER

big mouth [bɪg maʊθ] count noun *** a person who cannot keep a secret, one who gossips; a person who is loudmouthed

🔘 term can be used in two ways:

"You have a **big mouth**!" or "You are a **big mouth**!"

"Don't tell Ryo your secret, unless you want it to be all over town by tomorrow morning. She's such a **big mouth**!"

See: BLABBERMOUTH

big-time [bɪg taɪm] adv/adj ***** extensively, to an extreme degree

⚠ casual, used with the younger generations

"You ate it **big-time** on that last wave. I didn't know if you were going to come back up!"

bimbo [bɪmboʊ] count noun *** a sexually attractive woman who dresses suggestively, but is lacking in intelligence

⚠️ very derogatory! Should not be used directly to someone's face

"Pamela, the **bimbo**, got promoted? Not for her brains, that's for sure. She must have slept with the boss!"

bingo [bɪŋgoʊ] exp *** "that's right", "correct", or "exactly"

"'You look just like Yasmine; you must be her brother.' **'Bingo.'**"

> See: HIT THE NAIL ON THE HEAD

birdbrain [bɜːrdbreɪn] count noun ** a stupid or foolish person (literally one's brain is the size of a bird's)

⚠️ mild insult

"Don't be such a **birdbrain**! Of course those contests are a scam!"

> See: BEANBRAIN, BONEHEAD, DOOFUS, DOPE, DUMMY NINCOMPOOP, PEABRAIN

bitch [bɪtʃ] verb, I **** to complain, nag

⚠️ usually used with the above by the younger generation because the noun form is a vulgar term that refers to a mean-spirited woman

🅖 if an object is stated, it is usually preceded by **about**

"Pierre is never satisfied! He is always **bitching** about something."

bite [baɪt] count noun **** a small, quick meal

🅖 always used in the singular form with the word **a**

"What do you say we grab a **bite** before the movie?"

bite off more than one can chew [baɪt ɑːf mɔːr ðən wʌn kæn tʃuː] verb phrase ** to take on more responsibility than one can handle

"I know you offered to take care of the Miller account, but you're already in charge of three major accounts. Be careful not to **bite off more than you can chew**."

bite someone's head off [baɪt sʌmwʌnz hed ɑːf] verb phrase ** to scold and speak very angrily at someone

"The boss **bit my head off** when he saw me walking in late this morning."

> See: CHEW OUT, JUMP DOWN SOMEONE'S THROAT

blab [blæb] verb, T/I ** to chatter idly; to reveal a secret by indiscreet talk

"Julia **blabbed** my secret all over town."

blabbermouth [blæbɚmaʊθ] count noun *** a person who can't keep a secret

"If you want everyone to know about something, just tell Gunther. He's the biggest **blabbermouth** I know!"

> See: BIG MOUTH

blast [blæst] count noun *** a good time, fun

🅖 always preceded by **a** and used in the singular form

"We had a **blast** at the beach party."

> See: BALL, HOOT, RIOT, SCREAM

blow [bloʊ]

1. verb, T ***** to fail, make a mistake, do something wrong

🅖 usually used in the active voice; object is generally **it**

"I didn't study and I totally **blew** it (the exam)."

"I think I **blew** it (my chance) with her. I called her by my ex-girlfriend's name."

2. verb, T *** to spend money extravagantly

🅖 often followed by money

"Eric was **blowing** money right and left after he got his bonus."

"Scott **blew** a couple grand trying to get his old heap running."

blow a fuse [bloʊ ə fjuːz] verb phrase ** to lose one's temper, loudly express anger

"Ryan **blew a fuse** when he found out someone had taped over his favorite video."

> See: BLOW ONE'S TOP, FLY OFF THE HANDLE, HIT THE CEILING, LOSE IT

blow away [bloʊ əweɪ]

1. 2 word sep verb **** to surprise or shock

🅖 the object is always a person, used in both the active and passive voice

"The news of her death **blew** everybody **away**."

"Everybody was **blown away** by the news of her death."

> See: BLOW ONE'S MIND

2. 2 word sep verb *** to be much better, to be the best

"The movie Killer Attack 20 definitely **blew away** Killer Attack 19!"

3. 2 word sep verb *** to kill violently

⚠ when used with this meaning it will hopefully only be heard in the movies or on TV

"The cops **blew away** the terrorists!"

> See: BUMP OFF, KNOCK OFF, TAKE CARE OF

blow off [bloʊ ɑːf] 2 word sep verb ***** to ignore a commitment or responsibility

"'I wish I could go out with you tonight but I'm really bogged down with homework.' 'Oh, just **blow it off**. There's a great new flick playing downtown.'"

"I was supposed to meet Joe last night but he never showed up. He's such a flake. He's always **blowing people off**."

> See: CUT, DITCH, STAND UP

blow off some steam [bloʊ ɑːf sʌm stiːm] verb phrase *** to get rid of anger, release one's frustrations

"I'm so pissed off right now! I'm going out for a walk to **blow off some steam**."

> See: BITCH, VENT

blow one's mind [bloʊ wʌnz maɪnd] verb phrase *** to surprise or shock

🔊 commonly used in the adjective form **mind-blowing**

"The news was **mind-blowing**."

"I can't believe that happened to you! It just **blows my mind**!"

> See: BLOW AWAY

blow one's top [bloʊ wʌnz tɑːp] verb phrase *** lose one's temper, loudly express anger

"Dad is going to **blow his top** when he sees what you did to his golf clubs!"

> See: BLOW A FUSE, FLY OFF THE HANDLE, HIT THE CEILING, LOSE IT

blow the lid off [bloʊ ðə lɪd ɑːf] verb phrase *** to expose, call public attention to something

⚠ generally used in reference to a scandal or illegal activity

"His testimony at the trial **blew the lid off** the protection racket."

blow things out of proportion [bloʊ θɪŋz aʊt əv prəpɔːrʃən] verb phrase ** to exaggerate, to make a situation seem more serious than it really is

⚠ generally used in conversations where there is a problem

"Why are you so upset? I was only five minutes late. You're always **blowing things out of proportion**."

> See: MAKE A MOUNTAIN OUT OF A MOLEHILL

blurt out [blɜːrt aʊt] 2 word sep verb ** to say something suddenly without thinking

"'Why is Julie crying?' 'Alejandro **blurted out** that he saw her boyfriend with another girl.'"

bod [bɑːd] count noun ** a person's body

⚠ often used when admiring an attractive female figure

"Man, check out the **bod** on her! I'd love to jump her bones!"

bog down with [bɑːg daʊn wɪθ] 3 word verb ** to be slowed or stuck because of an excessive burden

"Shahala really wanted to come but she was **bogged down with** work from her class."

boil down to [bɔɪl daʊn tuː] 3 word verb *** to simplify or summarize

"There are a lot of reasons why Atsuro didn't get the promotion, but what it all **boils down to** is that he's not qualified for the position."

> See: COME DOWN TO

bomb [bɑːm]
　1. adj ** the best

🔊 always proceeded by **the**

"You've got to hear that new Janet Jones CD – it's **the bomb**!"

> See: BADASS, COOL, HOT, KILLER

　2. verb, T **** to perform poorly, fail

"George **bombed** the last test, so he's going to have to take the final."

> See: FLOP

bombed [bɑːmd] adj **** extremely intoxicated, drunk

"Lily got really **bombed** off of those tequila shots!"

> See: GONE, HAMMERED, LOADED, MESSED UP, RIPPED, SLOSHED, TOASTED, TRASHED, WASTED

bonehead [boʊnhed] count noun ** a stupid or foolish person

⚠ mainly used in jest with friends

"Don't be such a **bonehead** – I was only joking! You don't have to pay for the glass you broke."

> See: BEANBRAIN, BIRDBRAIN, DIMWIT, DOOFUS, DOPE, DUMMY, NINCOMPOOP, PEABRAIN

bone to pick [boʊn tuː pɪk] count noun phrase ** a complaint or grievance that needs discussion

🅖🅟 always preceded by **a**. If the name of the person being complained to is stated, the name is preceded by **with**

"I have a **bone to pick** with Eduardo. I'm really pissed off about his dog barking all night long."

bonkers [bɑːŋkəz] adj * crazy

🅖🅟 never used before a noun

"That guy over there is **bonkers**!"

> See: BANANAS, CRACKPOT, CUCKOO, LOONY, NUTS, NUTTY, OUT OF ONE'S MIND, OUT TO LUNCH, WACKO, WACKY

book [bʊk] verb, I **** to leave quickly

"This party is a drag! Let's **book**!"

> See: BAIL, BE OFF, GET GOING, HIT THE ROAD, JET, SPLIT

boom [buːm] adv/count noun ***** suddenly, abruptly, without warning; a loud noise

"I don't know what happened. We were sitting there having a nice conversation when **boom**! He snapped at me and walked off!"

> See: OUT OF THE BLUE

booze [buːz] non-count noun *** any kind of strong alcoholic drink, liquor

"There's always a ton of **booze** at frat parties."

boozer [buːzɚ] count noun ** a person who drinks a lot of alcohol or is constantly intoxicated

⚠ derogatory since it suggests that a person regularly drinks to excess

"How could she possibly think of marrying him? He's such a **boozer**!"

> See: ALCKY

booze up [buːz ʌp] 2 word sep verb ** to drink a lot of alcohol, to become intoxicated

"I don't want to go out with them because they're always **boozing** it **up**."

botch up [bɑːtʃ ʌp] 2 word sep verb *** make a mistake, ruin or destroy

"Conan was late, which totally **botched up** our surprise party."

> See: GOOF UP, MESS UP

bottle up [bɑːtl ʌp] 2 word sep verb ** to hold back or confine one's feelings

🅖🅟 generally used in the passive voice

"Yunsuke finally exploded. He'd been **bottling up** his anger for years."

"You have to talk about your feelings. It's not good for you to **bottle** things **up**."

bottomless pit [bɑːtəmləs pɪt] count noun *** a person who can consume large quantities of food or drink

"You'd better put a few more burgers on the grill. That friend of yours is a **bottomless pit**. He's been eating steadily for hours."

bottoms up [bɑːtəmz ʌp] exp ** a toast to encourage the drinker to finish (literally, the bottom of the glass is turned up to the ceiling.)

⚠ most commonly used when drinking alcohol, especially beer or hard liquor

"Hey everybody, bar's closing. **Bottoms up**!"

brain [breɪn] count noun *** a very intelligent person

"My high school history teacher was such a **brain**! She knew everything and anything about every subject."

brainy [breɪni] adj *** very intelligent

⚠ sometimes used with negative undertones

"'Why don't you want to go out with Chris?' 'He's too **brainy**.'"

bread [bred] *non-count noun* *** money

"I'm always broke. I really need to start making more **bread**!"

See: DOUGH

break in [breɪk ɪn] *2 word sep verb* **** to use something for the first time, to make something ready for everyday use

"Why don't we go back to my place? We could make some margaritas to **break in** my new blender."

break the ice [breɪk ðe aɪs] *verb phrase* ** to relieve a tense or uncomfortable situation

"I going to introduce the new office manager to the staff. That should help **break the ice**."

break up [breɪk ʌp] *2 word verb, I* **** to end an intimate relationship with a boyfriend/girlfriend, husband/wife

🔁 if the parting was mutual, **we broke up**; if the parting was one sided, **I broke up with her/him**

"Lisa and David aren't going out anymore. They **broke up** (with each other) two weeks ago."

"Mark **broke up** with Jenny."

See: CALL IT QUITS, SPLIT UP

breeze [briːz] *count noun* *** anything easily accomplished

🔁 always used with the word **a**

"'How was the exam?' 'It was a **breeze**!'"

See: PIECE OF CAKE, SNAP

breeze into [briːz ɪntuː] *2 word insep verb, T* ** to arrive in a casual way, often late

🔁 the word **into** changes to **in** when referring to time

"He **breezed in** at about eleven!"

"'So when did Judy finally show up?' 'She **breezed into** the office at about nine-thirty!'"

brewskie [bruːskiː] *count noun* * a beer, generic term for any brand

⚠️ beer is often ordered by brand name, but this term can be heard on TV or in the movies

"'What'll it be?' 'We'll have a couple of **brewskies**.'"

bring home the bacon [brɪŋ hoʊm ðe beɪkən] *verb phrase* *** make a living, earn a salary to support one's family

"It's good that Peggy got her MBA. Now that her husband has been laid off, she's the one who **brings home the bacon**."

broad [brɑːd] *count noun* * woman

⚠️ dated, disrespectful term used largely by men

"Did you see that **broad** Chuck brought to the party last night? She was old enough to be his mother!"

See: BABE, CHICK, DAME

broke [broʊk]

1. *adj* ***** to be temporarily out of money

"I'm **broke**! I've got to stop at the ATM and pick up some cash."

2. *adj* **** to be on a tight budget; for example a student or someone waiting for payday

"I can't go to the movies. I'm **broke**!"

3. *adj* *** to be penniless; for example a homeless person or a failed business

"I've been **broke** since the day I was born!"

See: BUSTED, HARD UP

brownnoser [braʊnnoʊzɚ] *count noun* ** a person who seeks to gain favor from a superior

⚠️ potential insult!

🔁 sometimes used as a verb: **to brownnose**

"Get a load of Mitch! He's complimenting the boss on that cheesy suit he's wearing! What a **brownnoser**!"

See: KISS-ASS

bubbly [bʌbli] *non-count noun* *** champagne

"You got promoted? Fantastic! Let's break out the **bubbly**!"

buck [bʌk] *count noun* ***** one US dollar

⚠️ only used to refer to whole dollar amounts

"My car was only a thousand **bucks**!"

See: CLAM, SMACKAROO

buckle down [bʌkl daʊn] *verb, I* *** to get serious and apply oneself

"If Yoshi wants to enter college he's going to have to **buckle down** and study for the TOEFL."

buddy [bʌdi]

1. count noun ***** friend, companion

"Najdah and I are **buddies**. We go way back!"

See: CHUM, PAL

2. exp a term of address for a stranger

⚠ used only in informal situations with one's peers

"Hey **buddy**, could you give me a hand loading this box in my car? It weighs a ton."

See: DUDE, PAL

buff [bʌf] adj *** very muscular, extremely toned muscles

"Check out Meg! She's gotten really **buff**! She must be going to the gym everyday."

See: CUT, FIT

bug [bʌg]

1. verb, T **** to bother, annoy, pester

"Will you stop **bugging** me about my grades? I'm doing the best that I can!"

"It really **bugs** me when someone leaves the cap off of the toothpaste!"

See: DRIVE SOMEONE UP A WALL, PICK ON

2. verb, T ** to install a hidden listening device

"When we go into the room, don't say anything incriminating. They've **bugged** the whole place."

3. count noun **** a virus, a non-specific illness; either a cold or the flu

"Kareem left school a little early because he felt like he was coming down with a **bug**."

Bug [bʌg] count noun *** nickname for the Volkswagen Beetle

"I needed a cheap car when I was in college, so I bought a used **Bug**."

bugs to work out [bʌgz tu: wɜːrk aʊt] count noun phrase *** minor problems to solve or fix

"Your computer is all set up. There are still a few **bugs to work out**, but basically it's ready to use."

bullheaded [bʊlheded] adj ** stubborn

"You'll never convince Shiro to change his mind. He's so **bullheaded**!"

See: HARDHEADED

bum [bʌm]

1. count noun **** a lazy person who has no ambition

"'Jim got laid off again?' 'Yeah, that **bum** just can't hold down a job.'"

2. adj ** injured, not working properly

"I can't play basketball 'cause I've got a **bum** knee."

bummed [bʊmd] adj ***** depressed or disappointed

"Everyone was **bummed** that Munir couldn't stay for the wedding."

See: DOWN, IN THE DUMPS

bummer [bʊmɚ] count noun **** a disappointment; "that's unfortunate" or "I'm disappointed"

⚠ used mainly by younger generations

ⓖ used in the singular form preceded by **a**, or on its own

"What a **bummer**!"

"You failed your test? **Bummer**, man!"

bum off of [bʌm ɑːf əv] 3 word verb **** to borrow, to sponge

ⓖ the use is always to **bum something off of someone**, sometimes **of** is dropped; can also be shortened to **bum something**

"Can I **bum a few bucks (off [of] you)** until payday?"

See: HIT UP FOR, SPONGE OFF OF

bum out [bʌm aʊt] 2 word sep verb **** to depress or disappoint; make someone sad

⚠ used mainly by the younger generation

"The bad news really **bummed** us **out**."

ⓖ commonly used in the adjective form; **out** is frequently dropped and **over** or **about** substituted

"Prim was **bummed (out)** about/over her test."

bump into [bʌmp ɪntuː] 2 word insep verb, T *** to meet someone by chance or accident

"Guadalupe **bumped into** Mike at the mall."

See: RUN INTO

bump off [bʌmp ɑːf] 2 word sep verb ** to kill, murder

⚠ usually heard only in movies

"They **bumped off** Manny and dumped his body in the river."

See: BLOW AWAY, KNOCK OFF, TAKE CARE OF

bum rap [bʌm ræp] *count noun phrase* ** a bad deal, a bad reputation that is undeserved

*"He didn't really do that crime. He got a **bum rap**."*

bunch [bʌntʃ] *count noun* ***** a lot, many

⚠ used only in casual situations

🅖🅟 always proceeded by **a**

*"Don't take my donut! There are a **bunch** of them over on the counter. Go get your own!"*

See: LOADS, MOUNDS, PLENTY, TON

bundle [bʌndl] *count noun* **** a lot, a sizeable sum of money

⚠ most commonly used when referring to money

🅖🅟 always proceeded by **a**

*"My teeth were in really bad shape. It cost me a **bundle** to have them fixed."*

See: AN ARM AND A LEG, PRETTY PENNY

burned out [bɜːrnd aʊt]

1. *adj* **** mentally or physically exhausted

*"Mayumi never goes out on week nights 'cause she's too **burned out** from school."*

See: BEAT, WIPED OUT, WORN OUT

2. *adj* **** sick of, bored with

🅖🅟 the object is preceded by **on**

*"Please, not burgers again! I'm so **burned out** on burgers! We've eaten them every night this week!"*

See: I'VE HAD IT UP TO HERE

burning up [bɜːrnɪŋ ʌp] *adj* **** extremely angry

*"Ralph was **burning up** when Kris showed up an hour late."*

burst into [bɜːrst ɪntuː]

1. *2 word insep verb, T* *** to suddenly begin an activity

🅖🅟 object is usually **tears**, **laughter**, **flames**, or **song**

*"The teacher kicked them out of the class because they **burst into** laughter while she was telling a very sad story."*

2. *2 word insep verb, T* *** to enter suddenly or rudely

*"Karen **burst into** my office without even knocking first."*

See: BARGE IN

burst someone's bubble [bɜːrst sʌmwʌnz bʌbl] *verb phrase* *** bring someone back to reality from a high emotional point

*"I hate to **burst your bubble**, but just because the professor said you could get an 'A' doesn't mean you will. You still need to work your butt off for the final."*

bust [bʌst]

1. *verb, T* **** to catch someone doing something wrong

🅖🅟 used in both the active and passive voice

*"The boss **busted** Tetsuya for sleeping at his desk."*

2. *verb, T* **** to arrest, place into police custody

🅖🅟 if an object is stated it is preceded by **for**

*"Did you hear? Jimmy was **busted** for shoplifting!"*

busted [bʌstd]

1. *adj* **** broken, inoperative

*"The coffee maker is **busted**. We'll have to go buy a new one this weekend."*

See: ON THE BLINK, SHOT

2. *adj* *** to be out of money

*"I'm **busted**. Could you loan me twenty bucks until payday?"*

See: BROKE, HARD UP

3. *adj* ** to be caught in the act, arrested

*"Oh man, the police can see us. We're **busted**!"*

bust one's balls/butt/hump [bʌst wʌnz bɑːlz/bʌt/hʌmp] *verb phrase* **** to work very hard

⚠ **balls** is generally used only by guys as it refers to a man's testicles and is considered vulgar; **butt** is crude

*"I **busted my balls/butt/hump** on that research paper but I only got a 'B'!"*

See: WORK ONE'S BUTT/BALLS OFF

butt in [bʌt ɪn] *2 word insep verb* **** to interrupt something, often a conversation, a queue, or a dance

*"Hey, you're not allowed to **butt in** line!"*

🅖🅟 sometimes the word **on** is added, especially when talking about conversations

*"He's always **butting in (on)** conversations!"*

See: BARGE IN, CUT IN

butterflies in one's stomach

See: HAVE BUTTERFLIES IN ONE'S STOMACH

buy [baɪ] verb, T ***** to believe, to accept

🌐 always used in the active voice; sometimes **for a minute** is added to the end of the statement for emphasis

"Jimmy was busted for shoplifting? I don't **buy** that (for a minute)!"

buzzed [bʌzd] adj *** slightly intoxicated; high on drugs or alcohol

⚠ a common variation is to **catch a buzz**

"I don't think I'll drink anymore tonight. I'm **buzzed (catching a buzz)** and I've got to drive home."

See: TIPSY

C

Caddy [kædi] count noun ** nickname for any automobile manufactured by the Cadillac Division of General Motors

"Look at all the **Caddies** parked outside the country club."

call [kɔːl] count noun **** a decision, choice

🌐 usually preceded by a possessive adjective

"'What do you feel like doing?' 'Anything is OK with me. It's your **call**.'"

call it a day [kɔːl ɪt ə deɪ] verb phrase ***** to stop working for the day

"I'm beat! What do you say we **call it a day** and start again tomorrow bright and early?"

call it quits [kɔːl ɪt kwɪts] verb phrase *** to stop an activity

🌐 always used in the active voice

"We've been working on this for twelve hours straight! Let's **call it quits** and get a bite to eat"

See: BREAK UP

call off [kɔːl ɑːf] 2 word sep verb **** to cancel

🌐 used in both the active and passive voice; sometimes **off** is dropped

"The game was **called (off)** because of the weather."

"I don't know what's gotten into Eriko! She **called off** the wedding!"

can [kæn]

1. count noun *** bathroom, toilet

⚠ somewhat coarse term, used mainly by guys

🌐 always preceded by **the**

"'Where's Jack?' 'He's in the **can**.'"

See: JOHN, LITTLE GIRLS ROOM

2. count noun ** prison, jail

🌐 always preceded by **the**

"You're on parole. If you're seen with a firearm, you'll go back in the **can**."

see: BIG HOUSE, JOINT, PEN, SLAMMER

3. verb, T ** to fire someone from a job

"I heard on the grapevine that the new boss is going to **can** the entire sales staff!"

🌐 often used with **get** in the passive voice

"I'm so bummed. I got **canned** yesterday."

See: GIVE SOMEONE THE AX, GIVE SOMEONE THEIR PINK SLIP, LET SOMEONE GO, SACK

can't not [kænt nɑːt] verb phrase **** to be obligated or required, often for social reasons

⚠ very informal (double negative), used mainly by the younger generations

"You **can't not** come to the party, it's the biggest bash of the season! Everyone will be there!"

catch [kætʃ]

1. verb, T **** to watch a movie or TV program

⚠ used mainly by the younger generations

🌐 always used in the active voice

"Hey Andi, what do you say we **catch** a flick this weekend?"

2. verb, T to hear a conversation

"Did you **catch** what Jill said to her boyfriend?"

catch up on [kætʃ ʌp ɑːn] 3 word verb *** to become current; to get up-to-date

"If it rains this weekend I'm going to stay home and **catch up on** some reading."

catch up to [kætʃ ʌp tuː] 3 word verb **** to come from behind and overtake

🌐 the object is usually a person or a means of transportation

"Look, isn't that Leonardo up there? Let's walk faster and try to **catch up to** him."

catch you later [kætʃ juː lætɚ] exp *****"good bye"

🔺 used mostly with the younger generation

"Good talking to you. **Catch you later**!"

charge up [tʃɑːrdʒ ʌp] 2 word sep verb, I *** to become excited

🔺 usually used by guys about sporting events

"Your speech before the game **charged** the team **up**!"

🔘 often used in the adjective form

"Greg is really **charged up** about tonight's game!"

check out [tʃek aʊt] 2 word sep verb, T ***** look at, listen to, investigate

"This music video is amazing! **Check** this **out** dude!"

    See: GET A LOAD OF

cheesy [tʃiːzi] adj **** in bad taste, tacky, gaudy

"You're going to wear those tight black leather pants? How **cheesy**!"

chew out [tʃuː aʊt] 2 word sep verb, T *** to angrily criticize someone

🔘 used in both the passive and active voice

"My girlfriend **chewed** me **out** for staying out late and drinking with my buddies."

"I got **chewed out** by my girlfriend for staying out late and drinking with my buddies."

    See: READ THE RIOT ACT

chick [tʃɪk] count noun ***** a woman, usually young

🔺 primarily used by males; some women find this term derogatory

"You know who I mean, that blond **chick** from our history class."

    See: BABE, BROAD, DAME

chicken [tʃɪkɪn] count noun *** a coward

"Larry is such a **chicken**! How did you ever talk him into getting into that race car with you?"

    See: SCAREDY-CAT, WIMP

chicken out [tʃɪkɪn aʊt] 2 word insep verb, I **** to lose one's nerve, to lose one's courage

"When Dave finds out how tough it is in the Marines, he'll **chicken out** of enlisting."

🔘 if the object is stated it will usually be a gerund and will be preceded by **of**; if the object is **it** or is a person, it is preceded by **on**.

"I see you **chickened out** of telling your dad about the damage you did to his car."

"You said you were going to do it! Don't **chicken out** (on me)!"

    See: GET COLD FEET, WIMP OUT, WIMP OUT OF/ON

chill out [tʃɪl aʊt] 2 word insep verb, I/exp *** to relax, calm down from an angry state; "relax" or "calm down"

🔘 often used as an imperative; sometimes **out** is dropped

"You're getting yourself all worked up over nothing. Just **chill out**, would you?"

"Let's just **chill** for a while at your place."

    See: HANG OUT, KICK BACK, KICK IT, TAKE IT EASY

chip in on [tʃɪp ɪn ɑːn] 3 word verb *** to contribute, to share the cost of something

"Ask Charlie if he would like to **chip in on** a retirement gift for our bookkeeper."

🔘 **on** and the object may be dropped

"You must have paid a lot for this party. Are you sure you don't want me to **chip in**?"

    See: GO IN ON

choice [tʃɔɪs] adj *** perfect, of high quality

"That ahi salad we had the other night was **choice**."

chow down [tʃaʊ daʊn] verb, I ** to eat ravenously

🔺 very casual, used by the younger generations

🔘 if the object is stated it is preceded by **on**

"'How about some dinner?' 'Thanks, but we just **chowed down** on some burgers before we got here.'"

chug [tʃʌg] verb, T ** to drink quickly and thirstily

🔺 used primarily by guys

"Come on dude, we gotta go! Quit nursing that beer and **chug** it!"

    See: DOWN, GUZZLE

chum [tʃʌm] count noun *** a friend or companion

"Bill and some of his school **chums** are coming by this weekend."

    See: BUDDY, PAL

clam [klæm] *count noun* ** *one US dollar*

⚠ *dated; used only in the plural form and for whole dollar amounts*

"That watch cost Yousef a hundred **clams**."

See: BUCK, SMACKAROO

clam up [klæm ʌp] *2 word insep verb, I* ** *to become silent, often from embarrassment or nervousness*

🔞 *the subject is always a person*

"Before class, Nadia was chattering about how good her book report was, but she really **clammed up** when the teacher asked her about it."

clunker [klʌŋkɚ] *count noun* *** *an old, unreliable car that is in poor condition*

"My car won't start in the morning when it's cold. It's time to get rid of that old **clunker**."

See: HEAP

cockamamie [kɑːkəmeɪmi] *adj* ** *crazy, stupid, foolish*

⚠ *slightly dated, used occasionally by the older generations when speaking about plans or ideas*

"'So Grandpa, what do you think of my invention?' 'Why it's the most **cockamamie** thing I've ever heard of!'"

See: CRACKPOT, CUCKOO, LOONY, NUTTY, WACKY

cold one [koʊld wʌn] *count noun phrase* ** *a beer*

"Come over to my place Friday and we'll put back a few **cold ones**."

come apart at the seams [kʌm əpɑːrt æt ðe siːmz] *verb phrase* *** *to break down or disintegrate; to lose control of one's emotions*

"I'll be needing a new briefcase soon. This old one is **coming apart at the seams**."

🔞 *dropping* **at the seams** *is common*

"Mindy **came apart** when she was fired."

See: FALL TO PIECES

come clean [kʌm kliːn] *verb phrase* *** *to confess, to stop lying*

"OK, it's time for you to **come clean**. You're the one who's been secretly helping me out all these years, aren't you?"

come down to [kʌm daʊn tuː] *3 word verb* **** *to simplify to, to reduce to*

"Honey, I know you are going to try and talk your way out of this, but what it **comes down to** is that you blew me off!"

See: BOIL DOWN TO

come off it [kʌm aːf ɪt] *exp* **** *"stop acting or speaking pretentiously or foolishly"*

⚠ *usually used when there is a disagreement or argument*

"Oh, **come off it**! You know Lucy didn't serve you spoiled food on purpose! Don't be so angry at her!"

come on [kʌm aːn] *exp* **** *expression used to plead or challenge*

"**Come on** now, I said stop tickling me!"

"You're dating a movie star? Oh, **come on**!"

come on to [kʌm aːn tuː] *3 word verb* **** *to make sexual advances*

🔞 *the object is always a person*

"Did you see Stan? He was **coming on to** Gina at the party last night!"

See: MAKE A MOVE ON

come up to [kʌm ʌp tuː] *3 word verb* ***** *to approach, go towards someone or something*

"So this girl **comes up to** me on the street and goes…"

come up with [kʌm ʌp wɪθ] *3 word verb* ***** *to produce or make up an idea, plan, or excuse*

"Your dog ate your homework again? You'd better **come up with** a better excuse than that or your grade is going to go down."

con [kɑːn] *verb, T* ** *to swindle, persuade, or cajole*

"I can't believe you let him **con** you into lending him money again."

conk out [kɑːŋk aʊt] *2 word insep verb, I* **** *to fall asleep from physical or mental exhaustion*

"I had such a rough day at work! I got home and **conked out** on the sofa in front of the TV until midnight."

See: CRASH

cool [kuːl] *adj* *****

1. *very good, stylish*

"Check out Eric's new car! It's way **cool**!"

See: BADASS, HOT, KILLER, RAD, THE BOMB

⚠ often used by the younger generations as a response meaning "OK" or "that's acceptable"

"'What do you feel like eating?' 'Anything is **cool** with me.'"

2. adj/noun *** poised; self-control, composure

"Vic kept his **cool** after Mona totaled his new Vette."

cornerstone [kɔːrnɚstoʊn] count noun **
foundation, basis

🆎 usually preceded by **the**

"Hamburgers are the **cornerstone** of the American diet!"

corny [kɔːrni] adj ** silly, tiresomely, or childishly sentimental (often used in reference to jokes)

"Mark thinks his jokes are funny but they are always so **corny**."

count one's chickens before they hatch
[kaʊnt wʌnz tʃɪkɪnz bɪfɔːr ðeɪ hætʃ] verb phrase ***
to make plans based on events that may not occur

⚠ this phrase is sometimes shortened to **counting chickens** or **count your chickens**

🆎 usually used in the negative imperative form

"'The word is that I'm up for a raise! I think I'll go buy that car I've had my eye on.' 'Now, don't go **counting your chickens before they hatch**! Wait until you actually get the raise.'"

crack [kræk] verb, I **** to go crazy, loose one's mind, break down

"For fifteen years she had never told anyone that she had murdered her mother. When the cops reopened the case she finally **cracked** and confessed."

See: GO OFF THE DEEP END, LOSE ONE'S MARBLES

cracked up to be [krækd ʌp tu: bi:] adj phrase
**** reputed or claimed to be

"That movie wasn't all it's **cracked up to be**."

"We've heard so much about your new invention. Let's see if it's all it's **cracked up to be**."

crackpot [krækpɑːt] adj/count noun ** eccentric, deviating from convention; a crazy person (often used when referring to professionals such as doctors or scientists)

"That **crackpot** astronomer claims he was abducted by aliens."

"You went to Dr. Jones for a second opinion? Everyone in town knows he's a **crackpot**!"

See: NUTCASE, WACKO

crack up [kræk ʌp] 2 word sep verb *** to laugh uproariously

"Satoko began to **crack up** for no reason and that made everyone else in the class crack up too."

cram for [kræm fɔːr] 2 word insep verb, T **** to study intensely shortly before an exam

🆎 if the object is dropped, **for** is also dropped

"'I haven't studied anything since the last history exam. I really have to **cram for** the test tomorrow.' 'I'm in the same boat. I have to **cram** too.'"

cranky [kræŋki] adj *** in a bad mood, grouchy

"What's eating you? You sure are **cranky** today!"

See: GRUMPY

crap [kræp]
1. non-count noun ***** stuff, things, junk

⚠ crap is vulgar as it refers to excrement. It is sometimes used as a euphemism for **shit**

"I've got so much **crap** to do this weekend."

2. non-count noun ***** something that is worthless or bad

"My car breaks down constantly. It's a real piece of **crap**."

crappy [kræpi] adj ***** bad, foul, worthless

⚠ crappy is vulgar as it describes something as having the qualities of excrement. It is sometimes used as a euphemism for **shitty**. Should be used only in very informal situations with close friends

"You sure are in a **crappy** mood today!"

"That was a **crappy** thing to do to him."

crash [kræʃ] verb, I ***** to fall asleep or go to bed, often after being extremely exhausted

⚠ used mostly by the younger generations

🆎 sometimes the word **out** follows crash

"'What time did you **crash out** last night?' 'I **crashed** as soon as I got home!'"

See: CONK OUT, HIT THE HAY, HIT THE SACK, HIT THE SHEETS

creep [kriːp] count noun *** an unpleasant, distasteful, ill-mannered, or unkind person

⚠ used mainly to describe guys

"You are better off without that **creep**! I don't know how you put up with him for as long as you did!"

See: JERK, SCHMUCK

creep up on [kriːp ʌp ɑːn] 3 word verb *** to advance slowly or stealthily

"You scared me to death! Don't ever **creep up on** me again in a dark room when I'm alone!"

"This deadline really **crept up on** us. We'll have to get this resolved quickly."

See: SNEAK UP ON

creepy [kriːpi] adj *** strange, weird, scary

"This ghost town is giving me the creeps! Did you see that **creepy** old guy back there eyeing us? Let's get out of here!"

crummy [krʌmi] adj *** unpleasant, cheap, bad

"I had a really **crummy** day at work today."

See: LOUSY

cuckoo [kuːkuː] adj *** crazy

⚠ often used by children

"Don't pay attention to that guy. He stands there every morning talking to himself. He's a little **cuckoo**!"

See: BANANAS, BONKERS, LOONY, NUTS, NUTTY, OUT OF ONE'S MIND, OUT TO LUNCH, WACKO, WACKY

cut [kʌt]

1. verb, T **** to be effective, to make the grade

"Tim had to be fired. He just wasn't **cutting** it as a manager."

2. verb, T *** to intentionally miss class

"'Did you get the homework for yesterday's physics class?' 'Nope, I **cut** class.'"

See: BLOW OFF, DITCH

3. adj ** having a very well defined and muscular body

⚠ used mainly by the younger generation

"Check out that guy – he's **cut**! He must work out at least once everyday, if not twice!"

See: BUFF, FIT

cut-and-dried [kʌt ən draɪd] adj *** simple, readymade, predetermined

"I wrote down what you have to do. It's pretty **cut-and-dried**, but if you have any questions give me a ring."

cut in [kʌt ɪn] 2 word insep verb **** to interrupt something, often a conversation, a queue, or a dance

"Hey, that guy **cut in** line!"

See: BUTT IN

cut it out [kʌt ɪt aʊt] exp ***** "stop it!" or "cease an activity"

🔘 generally used in the imperative form; **that** may replace **it**

"You're driving me crazy with that pencil tapping. **Cut that out**, would you!"

🔘 the object may follow **cut out**

"**Cut out** the complaining! We're all in the same boat here."

See: KNOCK IT OFF

cut out for [kʌt aʊt fɔːr] 3 word verb *** to be suited for a task or profession

"Jack just wasn't **cut out for** the Marines."

🔘 the object can be a gerund, or **this**, **that**, or **it**

"If you don't like the sight of blood, then you're not **cut out for** being a surgeon."

cut someone slack [kʌt sʌmwʌn slæk] verb phrase ** to be flexible or lenient with someone

"Aww Mom, come on! Do I have to do all of those things today? I'll never finish! **Cut me** some **slack**. At least don't make me baby-sit tonight!"

cut the crap [kʌt ðe kræp] exp **** "stop talking nonsense!"

⚠ discourteous; level of rudeness depends on the speaker's tone of voice

🔘 used mainly in the imperative form

"You've been beating around the bush for the past ten minutes. **Cut the crap**! I want to know why you didn't come home last night."

cutthroat [kʌtθroʊt] adj *** competitive, vicious

"This business is very **cutthroat** so watch your back at all times and never trust anyone."

cut to the chase [kʌt tu: ðe tʃeɪs] verb phrase ** to get to the main point, to summarize

"This lecturer is putting me to sleep with his anecdotes. I wish he'd **cut to the chase**."

🔄 also used commonly in the imperative form

"I don't have all day so **cut to the chase**."

D

dame [deɪm] count noun * woman

⚠ dated term, used only by older generations

"Look at that **dame** in the red dress next to the piano."

See: BABE, BROAD, CHICK

damn straight [dæm streɪt] exp *** "absolutely right!"

⚠ spoken in anger, frustration, or sarcasm to emphasize agreement or confirmation

"'Did you ask him for your money?' '**Damn straight**! It's been over three months since he bummed it off me.'"

dead [ded]

1. adj ***** exhausted

"I can't believe we moved all of your stuff in one day! I'm **dead**!"

See: BEAT, POOPED, WIPED OUT, WORN OUT

2. adj **** in severe trouble

"You broke the vase Donna bought in Italy? Oh man, you are **dead**!"

dead ahead [ded əhed] adj phrase ** directly or straight in front of one

"Keep going straight, it's **dead ahead**."

dead drunk [ded drʌŋk] adj phrase ** intoxicated to the point of unconsciousness

"How's your brother feeling this morning? I saw him at the party last night and he was **dead drunk**."

dead giveaway [ded gɪvəweɪ] count noun phrase * an obvious sign or indication of an activity

"That pile of beer cans in the trash is a **dead giveaway** that there was a big party here last night."

dead-on [ded ɑːn] adj phrase * perfectly aligned, correct

"OK, the window frame is **dead-on**. I'll hold it while you install the screws."

dead ringer [ded rɪŋɚ] count noun phrase ** a thing or person that closely resembles another

"Check out that guy over there! He's a **dead ringer** for your brother."

dead serious [ded sɪriəs] adj phrase * very solemn, being in earnest

"I'm **dead serious** about this Jack. If you don't improve your grades, I'm not going to pay anymore of your college tuition."

dead set against [ded set əgenst] adj phrase ** adamantly opposed

🔄 sometimes **set** is dropped

"Your father and I are **dead (set) against** your plans to take a year off from college."

dead tired [ded taɪɚd] adj phrase * extremely weary

"We were **dead tired** after hiking ten miles into camp."

dead to rights [ded tu: raɪts] adj phrase * red-handed, caught in the act

"David's business partner caught him **dead to rights** with his hand in the till."

dead wrong [ded rɑːŋ] adj phrase * utterly incorrect

"You're **dead wrong** if you think I've cheated my employees. I've always treated them fairly."

decked out [dekt aʊt] adj phrase ** dressed up, wearing nice clothes

🔄 usually preceded by **all** (meaning **really**)

"Wow, you're all **decked out**! Where are you headed?"

die [daɪ] verb, I ***** to have a very strong desire to do or have something

🔄 **die to** used with the base verb expresses a strong desire for a particular action. **Die for** and a noun indicates a desire to have something

"Emi was **dying** to smoke a cigarette."

"Fumiko was **dying** for a cigarette."

different strokes for different folks
[dɪfərənt stroʊks fɔːr dɪfərənt foʊks] exp ** "every person has different tastes and preferences"

⚠ usually used to register surprise or shock at someone's taste or decisions

"You're going to Alaska for a vacation? Well, you know what they say, '**different strokes for different folks!**'"

See: WHATEVER GETS YOU GOING

dig [dɪg] verb, T *** to enjoy, like

⚠ used mostly by the younger generations

"Dude, the chicks really **dig** my short hair! I'm never growing it long again!"

dig in [dɪg ɪn] exp *** "eat heartily!" or "start to eat!"

🔟 usually used in the imperative form

"Everything is on the table! **Dig in!**"

dillydally [dɪlidæli] verb, I ** to dawdle, delay, or procrastinate

"Come on, we're late! Stop **dillydallying!**"

dimwit [dɪmwɪt] count noun ** a stupid or foolish person

⚠ slightly rude

"Can you believe she bombed that test? It was a piece of cake! She must be a real **dimwit.**"

See: BEANBRAIN, BIRDBRAIN, DOPE, DOOFUS, DUMMY, NINCOMPOOP, PEABRAIN

dingbat [dɪŋbæt] count noun ** a stupid or foolish person, usually used for girls or women

⚠ generally used in a casual manner

"She locked the keys in the car again? How can she be such a **dingbat?**"

See: AIRHEAD, DITZ, DUMMY, SPACE CADET

dirt [dɜːrt] non-count noun *** sensational information or gossip

🔟 usually preceded with **the**

"So, how was your meeting with the boss? Give me the **dirt!**"

See: LOWDOWN, SCOOP, SKINNY

ditch [dɪtʃ]

1. verb, T **** to abandon or discard

"Cathy is a real drag tonight. Let's **ditch** her before we go to the next place."

2. verb, T *** to skip class

"It's a beautiful day so let's **ditch** class and go to the beach instead."

See: BLOW OFF, CUT

ditz [dɪtz] count noun ** stupid or silly girl

⚠ mild insult; often used in jest to describe one's self or friends

"I can't believe I locked my keys in my car. I'm such a **ditz** sometimes!"

See: AIRHEAD, DINGBAT, DUMMY, SPACE CADET

do [duː] count noun *** hairstyle, hairdo

⚠ often used when the style is strange or inappropriate

"Did you see Barbara's new **do**? What was she thinking? It looks terrible!"

do battle [duː bætl] verb phrase * to engage in a contest, struggle, or fight

⚠ dated, generally used in jest

"Vic is about to **do battle** with his new boss."

Docs [dɑːks] non-count noun *** Dr. Martin® brand shoes and boots

⚠ always stated as **Doc Martins** or just **Docs**

"He never wears anything but **Docs**."

dog-eat-dog [dɑːg iːt dɑːg] adj ** vicious, mean, ruthless

"Be careful whom you trust. It's a **dog-eat-dog** world out there."

do it [duː ɪt] verb phrase **** euphemistic for having sexual intercourse

⚠ used by the younger generations

"Jack wants us to **do it**, but I think we should wait. I'm still too young."

See: JUMP SOMEONE'S BONES, SLEEP WITH

doll up [dɑːl ʌp] 2 word sep verb ** to dress smartly or attractively, usually for a special occasion

⚠ used only to refer to women or occasionally drag queens

🔟 usually seen in its adjective form **dolled up**

"Check out Rebecca! She's got herself all **dolled up** tonight."

doofus [duːfʊs] *count noun* *** *a stupid or foolish person, usually used to describe guys*

"Don't worry about what he says, he's just a big **doofus** anyway!"

> See: BEANBRAIN, BIRDBRAIN, DIMWIT, DOPE, DUMMY, NINCOMPOOP, PEABRAIN

dope [doʊp]
1. *count noun* *** *a stupid person*

⚠ *insulting when used to a person's face*

"How could she possibly date him? He's such a **dope**!"

> See: BEANBRAIN, BIRDBRAIN, DIMWIT, DOOFUS, DUMMY, NINCOMPOOP, PEABRAIN

2. *non-count noun* *** *illegal drugs, usually narcotics*

"Hey man, you got any **dope**?"

dork [dɔːrk]
1. *count noun* *** *a socially or physically awkward person, a nerd*

"He was a **dork** in high school. He belonged to the chess club and the science club."

> See: GEEK, NERD

2. *count noun* *** *a physically uncoordinated person, one who is clumsy*

"Don't pick Sally for our volleyball team. She's a **dork**! We'll never win with her on our team."

> See: KLUTZ

dough [doʊ] *non-count noun* *** *money*

"Could you lend me some **dough**? I just need a couple of bucks."

> See: BREAD

down [daʊn]
1. *adj* **** *depressed, sad, blue*

"What's up with Jenny? I saw her yesterday and she seemed really **down**."

> See: BUMMED, IN THE DUMPS

2. *verb, T* *** *to drink or eat quickly*

"Chuck **downed** two sandwiches and a beer before I had finished half of mine."

> See: GULP

down-and-out [daʊn æn aʊt] *adj phrase* *** *penniless, having no prospects for the future*

"The latest drop in the stock market hit him pretty hard. He's pretty **down-and-out**. I heard he might declare bankruptcy."

> See: BROKE, HARD UP

down the drain [daʊn ðe dreɪn] *prep phrase* *** *wasted, ruined, destroyed*

"It's raining? I guess our plans to go to the beach are **down the drain**."

🔊 *often used with* **go**

"Keiko's worked so hard to get this promotion. I hope all of her efforts don't go **down the drain**."

drag [dræg]
1. *count noun* *** *an event or activity that is boring or tedious*

⚠ *usually used by the younger generations*

🔊 *most commonly used in the singular form preceded by* **a**

"This party is really a **drag**. Let's bail!"

2. *count noun* *** *a draw on a cigarette, pipe, or cigar*

"I know I'm supposed to stop smoking, but just let me have a **drag** off of your cigarette."

drag one's feet [dræg wʌnz fiːt] *verb phrase* **** *to deliberately hold back or delay*

"I've called his attorney five times to get a copy of that report, and we still haven't received it. I think they're **dragging their feet**."

draw a blank [drɑː ə blæŋk] *verb phrase* *** *to fail to remember or find something*

"I studied my butt off for the exam but when I got the test in front of me I **drew a blank** on everything!"

> See: SPACE OUT

drive at [draɪv æt] *2 word insep verb, T* *** *to intend to express, to mean to say or do*

🔊 *often used in question form*

"What are you **driving at**?"

"He was talking in circles. I couldn't figure out what he was **driving at**."

drive someone up a/the wall [drɑɪv sʌmwʌn ʌp ə/ðe wɔːl] verb phrase ***** to greatly annoy or bother someone, to make someone crazy

"I wish the neighbors would turn down their music! It's **driving me up the wall**!"

See: BUG

drop by [drɑːp baɪ] 2 word insep verb, T **** to visit somewhere briefly, usually unannounced

"Why don't we **drop by** Leslie's house on the way home?"

See: RUN BY, SHOOT BY, SWING BY

drop it [drɑːp ɪt] exp ***** "stop talking about that" or "forget it"

⚠ can be rude, depending on the intonation

🅟 used in the imperative form

"'I want to know why you owe that guy so much money.' '**Drop it**, would you! I don't want to talk about it!'"

See: GIVE IT A REST, LET UP

drop out of [drɑːp aʊt əv] 3 word verb *** to withdraw from school, competition, or from society because of disillusionment

🅟 the object and **of** are sometimes dropped when they are understood

"Shige tried to run a marathon but he **dropped out (of** it) half way through."

dude [duːd]

1. count noun ***** guy, man

⚠ used mainly by guys

"That **dude** bummed a cigarette off of me."

2. exp ***** a term of address for male friend(s)

⚠ used mainly by guys

"**Dude** I'm telling you, this chick was hot!"

See: BUDDY, PAL

duh [dʊh] exp ***** sarcastic response to the obvious

⚠ sarcastic and has childish undertones, yet it is still used by all age groups

"'Did you hear that the President might be impeached?' '**Duh**! Only everyone in the US knows!'"

dummy [dʌmi] count noun **** a stupid or foolish person

⚠ mild insult, often used in a joking manner to refer to one's self

"I'm such a **dummy** when it comes to math."

See: BEANBRAIN, BIRDBRAIN, DIMWIT, DOOFUS, PEABRAIN, NINCOMPOOP

dump [dʌmp] verb, T ***** to leave a boyfriend, girlfriend, or a situation that is no longer desirable

🅟 used in the active and passive voice

"I heard that Mike **dumped** Jennifer!"

"Mike said he **dumped** me? Nuh-uh. I **dumped** him!"

E

ear-to-ear grin [ɪr tuː ɪr grɪn] count noun ** a very big smile

"I saw Vanessa walking out of class with an **ear-to-ear grin**. She must've done well on her test."

eat [iːt] verb, T *** to fall or fail spectacularly, to take a loss on something

⚠ used by the younger generations

🅟 object is usually **it**, meaning dirt, pavement, financial loss, etc

"Whoa, dude, you were tearing down that hill so fast on your skateboard I thought you were going to **eat** it!"

"There goes our last chance for a loan from the bank. Looks like the company is going to **eat** it!"

"We undercharged this client on parts and materials, but we're going to have to **eat** the loss if we want to keep that customer."

See: WIPE OUT

eat like a bird [iːt laɪk ə bɜːrd] verb phrase *** to eat in small portions; to eat very little

"No wonder you're so thin. You **eat like a bird**!"

eat one's heart out [iːt wʌnz hɑːrt aʊt] verb phrase ** to feel bitter anguish, to be jealous or envious of someone

"Wait until they hear we got front row tickets to the Willy Smith concert! They're going to **eat their hearts out**!"

eat one's words [iːt wʌnz wɜːrdz] *verb phrase* ** to be forced to retract something one has said

"I told him he'd never make it as a lawyer, but when he passed the bar exam, I had to **eat my words**."

edgy [edʒi] *adj* **** *nervous, tense*

"Linda must have had too much caffeine today! She's really **edgy**!"

See: ANTSY, ON EDGE

end up [end ʌp] *2 word insep verb, T* ***** to result in; to reach an outcome

the object is usually a gerund or the words **here** or **there**

"'Hey Jenny, what did you do this weekend?' 'Well, I was supposed to go to the movies with my friend, but we **ended up** renting videos and staying home.'"

See: WIND UP

end up at [end ʌp æt] *3 word verb* **** to arrive at an unexpected destination

object is always a specific place

"'Where did you guys have dinner?' 'We wanted to go to that new Thai place but it was packed! We **ended up at** that burger joint down the street.'"

end up in [end ʌp ɪn] *3 word verb* ***** to arrive at an unexpected destination

object is always a place

"I got off at the wrong freeway exit and **ended up in** Mexico instead of LA!"

See: WIND UP IN

end up with [end ʌp wɪθ] *3 word verb* *** to find oneself in an unexpected or unplanned situation, to reach an outcome

⚠ can apply to desirable or undesirable situations

object is often a person

"I'm so lucky to have **ended up with** someone as nice as you!"

"I was voted most likely to succeed in my high school class, so how did I **end up with** this lousy job?"

See: WIND UP

eye [aɪ] *non-count noun/verb, T* **** *intense scrutiny; to observe intently*

"The teacher's been giving me the **eye** since class started."

often used in the continuous tense

"That guy is giving me the creeps. He's been **eyeing** us ever since we came in here."

See: HAVE ONE'S EYE ON

ex [eks] *count noun* *** a person who no longer holds a position, in particular a former lover, spouse, employee, etc.

"I saw my **ex** (boyfriend, husband, wife, etc.) in line at the restaurant so I went to a different place for lunch."

F

fair and square [fer ænd skwer] *adv phrase* **** fairly, honestly

"I didn't cheat. I won the game **fair and square**!"

fall for [fɔl fɔːr]

1. *2 word insep verb, T* ** to be strongly attracted to someone

"Bob **fell for** Lori the first time he saw her."

2. *2 word insep verb, T* ** to be swindled or deceived

"Cindy **fell for** his phony line and let him move back in with her."

falling-out [fɔlɪŋ aʊt] *count noun* *** an argument or disagreement

"Marcia and Greg made up some time ago, but things just haven't been the same since they had that **falling-out**."

fall to pieces [fɔl tu piːsəs] *verb phrase* ** to lose control of one's emotions

"Melanie **fell to pieces** when she found out she was pregnant."

See: COME APART AT THE SEAMS

far-fetched [fɑːrfetʃt] *adj* **** improbable, unlikely

used when talking about plans, ideas, or schemes

"So you want to build a car that runs on grass? Seems pretty **far-fetched** to me!"

fat chance [fæt tʃænts] *exp* **** "highly unlikely" or "there is little possibility"

often used interjectionally

"'Do you think Barbara will be here on time?' '**Fat chance**. She's always late.'"

> *See:* IT'LL BE A COLD DAY IN HELL, NOT IN A MILLION YEARS, WHEN HELL FREEZES OVER, WHEN PIGS FLY

fed up [fed ʌp] *adj phrase* ***** *sick and tired, frustrated*

🔊 use **with** when specifying the cause of one's frustration

"I'm really **fed up** with the system here at this school! I wish they would change it!"

figure out [fɪgjʊr aʊt] *2 word sep verb* ***** *to solve a problem of any kind, to understand*

"Can you give Jamal a hand? He can't **figure out** the answer to problem number two."

"Carol just burst into tears for no reason. I can't **figure out** what's wrong with her."

> *See:* MAKE OUT

fired up [faɪəd ʌp] *adj phrase* **** *excited, enthusiastic*

"Everyone in the city is all **fired up** about tonight's football game."

> *See:* STOKED

fishy [fɪʃi] *adj* **** *abnormal, unusual*

"Bobby got an 'A' on the test? He's never done that well before. Something's **fishy**."

> *See:* SCREWY

fit [fɪt]

1. *count noun* **** *a tantrum, an emotional reaction*

🔊 often used with **have** or **throw**; most commonly used in the singular form preceded by **a**

"When Mom comes home and sees what you did to this carpet she's going to have a **fit**!"

2. *adj* **** *in good physical condition*

"Of course Janice is **fit**! She goes to the gym five times a week."

> *See:* BUFF, CUT

fix up with [fɪks ʌp wɪθ] *3 word verb* *** *to arrange a date between two persons who have previously not met*

"Jane **fixed** Dan **up with** Gilda."

"I have this friend I think you would really hit it off with. How about if I **fix** you **up with** him?"

> *See:* HOOK UP WITH, SET UP WITH

flabby [flæbi] *adj* ***** *loose, lacking firmness or tone*

"I have to get back to the gym! My upper arms are starting to get **flabby**."

flake [fleɪk] *count noun* **** *an unreliable person*

"Pedro, I can never count on you for anything! You're such a **flake**!"

flake out [fleɪk aʊt] *2 word insep verb, I* **** *to fail to honor one's commitments or responsibilities*

🔊 if the object is stated it is preceded by **on** or **of**

"Can you believe Pedro **flaked out** of our walk again?"

"I'm counting on you to be there, so don't **flake out** on me!"

flaky [fleɪki] *adj* **** *unreliable, undependable*

"Mark is an hour late? Well, I'm not surprised. He's always been pretty **flaky**."

"My car has gotten pretty **flaky**. I can hardly get it started in the morning."

flame [fleɪm] *count noun* *** *a lover*

⚠ often used to refer to ex-lovers

"You were all goo-goo eyed when you where talking to that guy. He must be that old **flame** you were crazy about!"

flap one's lips/gums [flæp wʌnz lɪps/gʌms] *verb phrase* *** *to talk foolishly or incessantly*

⚠ can be insulting

"Stop **flapping your lips** and get to work!"

flick [flɪk] *count noun* *** *a movie, motion picture*

⚠ the term comes from the flickering characteristic of early films

"Have you seen that new sci-fi **flick**?"

fling [flɪŋ] *count noun* *** *a short or casual relationship usually involving sex*

"She was having a **fling** with her boss and when she dumped him, he gave her the axe! Now she's suing the company."

flip [flɪp] *verb, I* **** *to become very enthusiastic; lose one's composure*

🔊 often followed by **out** and a time clause

"Rosie **flipped** when she heard the good news!"

"Your mom is going to **flip** out when you tell her you failed the test."

> See: BLOW A FUSE, HIT THE CEILING, LOSE IT

floor [flɔːr]

1. verb, T *** to shock, to stun

🔊 used in both its adjective and verb form

"The news **floored** Keiko!"

"Keiko was **floored** when she heard the news."

2. verb, T ** to quickly press the accelerator pedal of a car to the floor

"OK, the light turned green; **floor** it!"

flop [flɑːp] count noun/verb, I **** a failure, to fail completely

"That new action flick was a real **flop**!"

"That new action flick **flopped** big-time!"

> See: BOMB

fly [flaɪ] verb, I **** to work properly or successfully

"We put a lot of time and money into this advertising campaign. It had better **fly**!"

fly *off the handle* [flaɪ aːf ðe hændl] verb phrase *** to lose one's temper and loudly express anger

🔊 object is always a person preceded by **at**

"Janice is always **flying off the handle** at Max for the smallest things. I don't know how he puts up with it."

> See: BLOW A FUSE, BLOW ONE'S TOP, HIT THE CEILING, LOSE IT

fly *over one's head* [flaɪ oʊvɚ wʌnz hed] verb phrase *** to be beyond one's understanding or competence

"I explained how to surf the Internet to him three times, but it still **flew over his head**. Why don't you give it a shot?"

> See: GO OVER ONE'S HEAD

folks [foʊks]

1. non-count noun ***** one's parents

🔊 always used in the plural form

"My **folks** are coming in from Bangkok tonight."

2. non-count noun ***** general term for people, sometimes as a term of address

🔊 always used in the plural form

"OK **folks** we have a really big show lined up for you tonight!"

> See: GUYS

fool around [fuːl əraʊnd]

1. 2 word insep verb, I ***** to engage in casual sexual activity

"Gina and Tom were **fooling around** in the back of his car again."

2. 2 word insep verb, I **** to joke with, deceive, engage in horseplay

"Come on, quit **fooling around**. We have work to do."

> See: GOOF AROUND, MESS AROUND, SCREW AROUND

fool with [fuːl wɪθ] 2 word insep verb ***** to deceive, engage in horseplay

"You got the promotion and the raise? You're not **fooling with** me are you?"

> See: GOOF WITH, MESS WITH, SCREW WITH

foot the bill [fʊt ðe bɪl] verb phrase ** to pay expenses, settle an account

"I didn't go to the conference because my company wanted me to **foot the bill**! Can you believe that?"

for crying out loud [fɔːr kraɪŋ aʊt laʊd] exp *** "I'm frustrated" or "I'm angry!"

⚠️ used to express exasperation

"**For crying out loud**, will you cut out that tapping?"

> See: FOR PETE'S SAKE, OH BROTHER

forever and a day [fɔːr evɚ ænd ə deɪ] adv phrase **** a long time

"I wonder what's up? It's taking them **forever and a day** to fill my prescription!"

fork [fɔːrk] verb, T ** to pay or contribute

🔊 often followed by **out**, **over**, or **up**

"I had to **fork** out a bundle to get my car fixed!"

> See: PAY THROUGH THE NOSE

for Pete's sake [fɔːr piːts seɪk] exp ** "I'm angry!" or "my patience has been exhausted!"

⚠️ slightly dated, used more by the older generations and used to express exasperation

"**For Pete's sake**! You've been gabbing on the phone for over an hour!"

> See: FOR CRYING OUT LOUD, OH BROTHER

frazzled [fræzld] adj *** frayed, upset or nervous

"I'm so **frazzled**! That's the last time I offer to baby-sit those kids!"

   See: ONE'S NERVES ARE SHOT

freak [friːk] verb, I **** to become greatly distressed, upset, or astonished

🔘 usually followed by a time clause

"Kazumi is going to **freak** when she hears the news about Vincent!"

fridge [frɪdʒ] count noun ***** refrigerator

⚠ this term is used more frequently than the actual word refrigerator

"While you're up would you grab me a soda from the **fridge**?"

full of it [fʊl əv ɪt] adj phrase/exp ***** full of nonsense, deceitful; "I don't believe you"

⚠ can be insulting, as it replaces the word **crap** (or worse!)

🔘 always used with the verb **be**

"He said that hot chick is his girlfriend? He's **full of it**!"

"She said she'd go to the dance with you? You're **full of it**!"

   See: GET OUT OF HERE, GET OUT OF TOWN, NUH-UH

G

game [geɪm] adj ** ready, willing to proceed

"Are you **game** for a round of tennis?"

geek [giːk] count noun *** an unpopular or unfashionable person

"You're joining the chess club? It's full of **geeks**!"

   See: DORK, NERD

get a grip [get ə grɪp] verb phrase *** "regain your composure" or "take control of your emotions"

🔘 often used as an imperative

"**Get a grip**! So you lost your job. It's a blessing in disguise because you can do a lot better than working for that creep."

   See: PULL ONE'S SELF TOGETHER, SNAP OUT OF IF

get a kick out of [get ə kɪk aʊt əv] verb phrase **** to get a feeling of excitement or a thrill

"Aya **gets a kick out of** watching those blooper shows on TV."

get a load of... [get ə loʊd əv] exp **** "look at that!"

🔘 used in the imperative form or in the question form **would you get a load of this**? Sometimes followed by the tag question **would you**? An object must always be used

"**Get a load of** that!"

"Would you **get a load of** this article: Woman Gives Birth to an Alien Baby!"

"**Get a load of** her, would you?"

   See: CHECK OUT

get away with [get əweɪ wɪθ] 3 word verb ***** to avoid detection or punishment

⚠ to get away with murder is often used as a figure of speech when referring to someone who is able to escape the consequences of his actions

🔘 object is always a thing

"When we were kids, we really raised hell. Our parents let us **get away with** murder!"

"Mary is going to try and cheat on the exam but I don't think she'll **get away with** it (cheating)."

get back at [get bæk æt] 3 word verb *** to get revenge

🔘 object is always a person

"You stole my boyfriend! I'll **get back at** you for this some day!"

get back on one's feet [get bæk ɑːn wʌnz fiːt] verb phrase *** to recover one's physical or mental health, or regain one's financial solvency

"Marge had a tough time after the divorce but she's finally **getting back on her feet** again."

get bent out of shape [get bent aʊt əv ʃeɪp] verb phrase *** to become annoyed or upset

🔘 sometimes **all** comes between **get** and **bent** for emphasis. The object is a thing or a person's actions

"He's really uptight. He **got** all **bent out of shape** because they were five minutes late."

get carried away [kærɪd əweɪ] verb phrase **** to lose one's perspective or self-control

"I know you're angry, but don't **get carried away** with the accusations."

"Don't you think you're **getting** a little **carried away** with the candles? You must have over twenty of them in your room now!"

> See: GO OVERBOARD

get cold feet [get koʊld fiːt] verb phrase ** to lose one's nerve

"Julie wants the wedding to be as soon as possible because she's concerned about Lou **getting cold feet**!"

> See: CHICKEN OUT, WIMP OUT OF/ON

get cracking [get krækɪŋ] verb phrase ** to get going, to make a start

"We'd better **get cracking** if we want to get to the show on time."

> See: GET GOING

get down [get daʊn] 2 word sep verb **** to understand, commit to memory

"'Should I explain it to you again?' 'Nah, I think I've **got it down**.'"

get going [get goʊɪŋ] verb phrase ***** to prepare to leave

🔊 often used with **have to**, **have got to**, **should**, or **had better**

"It's getting late. We really have to **get going**."

> See: GET CRACKING

get hitched [get hɪtʃd] verb phrase *** to get married

⚠ used more commonly by men

"Did you hear the news? Margaret and Tom are **getting hitched**!"

> See: TIE THE KNOT

get it in gear [get sʌmθɪŋ in gɪr] verb phrase *** to get one's affairs organized; to get started

🔊 **it** can be replaced with one's **brain**, one's **act**, etc.

"We're going to have to **get it in gear** if we want to meet our printing deadline."

"I've got to **get my act in gear** and get these college applications out in time for next session."

get off one's case [get ɑːf wʌnz keɪs] verb phrase *** to stop criticizing or nagging

⚠ rude undertones

🔊 often used in the imperative form followed by the tag question **would you**? The question form is also common: **would you get off my case**? Case is sometimes replaced with **back**

"You've been bitching at him all day long! **Get off his case (back)**, would you?"

get one's feet wet [get wʌnz fiːt wet] verb phrase *** to start to gain experience

🔊 often used in the continuous tenses with **just** or **still**, sometimes both

"Don't worry if he makes a mistake. He's still just **getting his feet wet**."

get one's foot in the door [get wʌnz fʊt in ðe dɔːr] verb phrase *** take the first step towards a goal

"I know I'm just an intern, but at least I **got my foot in the door**."

get on one's nerves [get ɑːn wʌnz nɜːrvz] verb phrase ***** to annoy or bother someone

"That guy keeps looking at me out of the corner of his eye and it's really **getting on my nerves**!"

> See: BUG, RUB ONE THE WRONG WAY

get out of [get aʊt əv] 3 word verb ***** to avoid a responsibility or obligation

🔊 the object is always a thing

"I really want to help you out, but I've got a meeting at work and I can't **get out of** it."

"I'm supposed to help my friend move this weekend, but maybe I can **get out of** it."

> See: WEASEL OUT OF, WORM OUT OF

get out of here [get aʊt əv hɪr] exp ***** "you're kidding" or "I don't believe you!"

⚠ used to express shock, surprise, or to challenge a statement; sometimes shortened to **get out**!

🔊 always used in the imperative form

"He popped the question? **Get out of here**! You must be on cloud nine!"

> See: GET OUT OF TOWN, NUH-UH, SHUT UP

get out of town [get aʊt əv taʊn] exp *** "you're kidding" or "I don't believe you!"

⚠ used to express shock, surprise or to challenge a statement; sometimes shortened to **get out**!

"'I landed that new job!' '**Get out of town**! That's great!'"

See: GET OUT OF HERE, NUH-UH, SHUT UP

get real [get riːl] exp ***** "be serious!" or "no way would that happen!"

"Why even bother asking about the price! **Get real**! You know there's no way you can afford a house like that!"

See: AS IF

get rid of [get rɪd əv]

1. 3 word verb ***** to dispose of or throw away

"Those sneakers are thrashed! Why don't you **get rid of** them and buy yourself a new pair?"

See: TOSS

2. 3 word verb ** to kill a person and dispose of the body

⚠ hopefully only heard in this context in the movies!

"'Hey boss, what should we do with these guys?' '**Get rid of** 'em.'"

See: BUMP OFF, KNOCK OFF, TAKE CARE OF

get riled up [get raɪld ʌp] verb phrase ** to become agitated or upset

🔊 if the object is stated, it is preceded by **about** or **over**. Sometimes **all** is used after **get** to emphasize the extent of one's feelings

"Don't let the boss get to you. He **gets** all **riled up** over the smallest mistakes."

See: GET WORKED UP

get something off one's chest [get sʌmθɪn ɑːf wʌnz tʃest] verb phrase **** to speak of something that has been repressed, or to relieve one's guilt

"There's **something** I really need to **get off my chest**. You're constantly borrowing money from me, but you never pay it back. This is putting a real strain on our friendship."

"I've got to **get this off my chest**. I'm the one who broke the window."

get stuck with [get stʌk wɪθ] 3 word verb *** to be handed or left with a predicament or an undesirable situation

"My friends ran out of the bar when I was in the can and I **got stuck with** whole tab."

get stuck with the short end of the stick [get stʌk wɪθ ðə ʃɔːrt end əv ðə stɪk] verb phrase ** to receive the less desirable part of a deal

🔊 occasionally, **get stuck with** is replaced by **end up with**. This expression can also be shortened to **get the short end of the stick**

"We really **got stuck (ended up) with the short end of the stick** on this business deal!"

"Seems like Melanie always **gets the short end of the stick**."

get the ball rolling [get ðə bɔːl roʊlɪŋ] verb phrase *** to get things started

"It's already noon. We've gotta **get the ball rolling**."

get the hang of [get ðə hæŋ əv] verb phrase *** to become familiar with, become accustomed to

🔊 the object is always a thing or activity, often replaced by **it**

"Living in the US must be really strange for you, but you'll **get the hang of it** soon. When you go back home you'll find yourself missing your American life!"

get the picture [get ðə pɪktʃɚ] verb phrase **** to understand

"Maybe I'm dense, but I just can't seem to **get the picture**."

⚠ can be sarcastic or rude in certain situations

"Give it a rest! I **get the picture**! I'll be more considerate of your feelings next time."

get up on the wrong side of the bed [get ʌp ɑːn ðə rɑːŋ saɪd əv ðə bed] verb phrase **** to be in a bad mood for no particular reason

"I'm sorry I snapped at you like that. I think I just **got up on the wrong side of the bed** today."

get with it [get wɪθ ɪt] 3 word verb ** to become alert or informed, bring oneself up to date

"Jack has been goofing off lately. He needs to **get with it** if he wants to keep his job."

🔊 often used as an imperative

"I think your disco shoes are just a little out of style; you need to **get with it**."

See: GET WITH THE PROGRAM, WAKE UP AND SMELL THE COFFEE

get with the program [get wɪθ ðe proʊ grəm] exp ** "become informed!" or "wake up and realize what's going on."

"You didn't know we had a test today? It's in the syllabus. **Get with the program!**"

See: GET WITH IT, WAKE UP AND SMELL THE COFFEE

get worked up [get wɜːrkt ʌp] verb phrase **** to become agitated or angry about something

🔃 if an object is stated, it is preceded by **over**

"It's OK if you didn't get an 'A' on this test; you'll do better next time. Don't **get** all **worked up** over it."

See: GET RILED UP, WIND UP OVER

give it a rest [gɪv ɪt ə rest] exp **** "please stop talking about the subject!" or "I've heard enough!"

⚠ sometimes used with rude undertones

🔃 often used in the imperative form with the adverb **already** and the tag question **would you?**

"OK, OK, you've told me a hundred times! **Give it a rest** already, would you?"

See: DROP IT, LET UP

give out on [gɪv aʊt ɑːn] 3 word verb *** to fail, stop functioning

⚠ often used in reference to one's legs or arms

"This is the last box I can carry. My arms are about to **give out on** me."

See: GO OUT ON

give someone a piece of one's mind [gɪv sʌmwʌn ə piːs əv wʌnz maɪnd] verb phrase **** to defiantly state one's position or opinion

⚠ often said out of anger or frustration

"I can't believe Jennifer said that about me! I'm going to really **give her a piece of my mind** the next time I see her!"

give someone the ax [gɪv sʌmwʌn ðe æks] verb phrase ** to dismiss or fire someone from their job

"Lewis just isn't cutting it. We're going to have to **give him the ax**."

See: CAN, GIVE SOMEONE THEIR PINK SLIP, LET SOMEONE GO, SACK

give someone the cold shoulder [gɪv sʌmwʌn ðe koʊld ʃoʊldɚ] verb phrase ** to ignore, to slight

"Keiko has been **giving me the cold shoulder** all night! I can't figure out what I did wrong!"

give someone the creeps [gɪv sʌmwʌn ðe kriːps] verb phrase *** to cause one to feel a sensation of repugnance or horror

"I don't want to go in that shop. The storekeeper **gives me the creeps**. He looks like a character out of a horror flick."

give someone the finger [gɪv sʌmwʌn ðe fɪŋgɚ] verb phrase *** to make an obscene gesture by sticking up one's middle finger

⚠ very insulting and dangerous; use of this gesture is not recommended

"Whoops! I think I must have cut that guy off. I can see him in my rearview mirror **giving me the finger**."

give someone their pink slip [gɪv sʌmwʌn ðer pɪŋk slɪp] verb phrase ** to fire or lay off someone from their job

🔃 used mainly in the passive voice

"Lori is getting a little nervous about her job 'cause ten people at her company **got their pink slips**."

See: CAN, GIVE SOMEONE THE AX, LET SOMEONE GO, SACK

give someone the third degree [gɪv sʌmwʌn ðe θɜːrd dɪgriː] verb phrase *** to question or interrogate someone intensely

"Chill out! I was a little late 'cause I got tied up at the office! There's no need to **give me the third degree!**"

See: GRILL

give something a shot [gɪv sʌmθɪŋ ə ʃɔːt] verb phrase *** to make an attempt or try

🔃 **it**, **this**, or **these** will replace **something** in actual use

"I probably won't pass the test, but I'm going to **give it a shot** anyway."

go [goʊ] verb, T ***** to say

🔃 usually used in the present tense regardless of the actual time

"I told Hak Kyung I never wanted to see him again and he **goes** 'That's fine with me, I was about to dump you!'"

See: BE ALL LIKE

go all out [goʊ ɔːl aʊt] verb phrase *** to spare no expense or effort

⊕ when the object is stated, it is preceded by **on** if it is a thing, or **for** when it is a person

"This is a great wedding! They really **went all out** (on the food)."

go belly up [goʊ beli ʌp] verb phrase ** to go bankrupt

"That new restaurant has lousy service and the food sucks. They'll **go belly up** before the end of the year if they don't clean up their act."

go down [goʊ daʊn] 2 word verb, I *** to happen or occur

⚠ more commonly used by guys as it stems from police lingo

"What's **going down** this weekend?"

"What **went down** at the game?"

go in on [goʊ ɪn aːn] 3 word verb **** to contribute money to a group purchase

⊕ always used as follows: **go in on something with someone**

"We're thinking of getting Mom a diamond necklace for her birthday. Do you want to **go in on** it with us?"

See: CHIP IN ON

gone [gaːn]

1. adj ***** extremely drunk or intoxicated

"Did you see Marco last night? He was so **gone** I'll bet he doesn't even remember half of what happened!"

See: BOMBED, HAMMERED, LOADED, MESSED UP, RIPPED, SLOSHED, TOASTED, TRASHED, WASTED

2. adj ** involved or infatuated

"Vic was **gone** the first time he met Mona."

goof around [guːf əraʊnd] 2 word insep verb, I **** to joke, engage in horseplay or frivolity

⊕ if the object is stated, it is preceded by **with**

"Look, I didn't mean to hurt your feelings. I was just **goofing around** (with you)."

"Stop **goofing around**! We've got to finish this in half an hour!"

See: FOOL AROUND, MESS AROUND, SCREW AROUND

go off on [goʊ aːf aːn] 3 word verb *** to angrily criticize someone

⊕ the object is always a person. If the object is not stated, **on** is dropped

"'Why are you crying, Lucinda?' 'Our boss is crazy! She called me into the office and **went off** (on me) for something I didn't even do!'"

See: BE ALL OVER, JUMP DOWN SOMEONE'S THROAT

go off the deep end [goʊ aːf ðe diːp end] verb phrase ** to go crazy, lose one's mind

⚠ often used in jest

"You're going to cheat on the final? What if you get caught? Have you **gone off the deep end**?"

See: BE MISSING SOMETHING UPSTAIRS, CRACK, LOSE ONE'S MARBLES, LOSE IT, LOSE ONE'S MIND

goof up [guːf ʌp] 2 word insep verb, I **** to make a mistake, blunder

⊕ if the object is stated, it is preceded by **on**

"We were supposed to be here at eight? I guess we **goofed up** (on the time)."

See: BOTCH UP, MESS UP, SCREW UP ON

goof with [guːf wɪθ] 2 word verb, T *** to deceive, joke with, or engage in horseplay

"Don't blow a fuse. I was only **goofing with** you!"

See: FOOL WITH, SCREW WITH

goo-goo eyes [guː guː aɪz] count noun phrase ** flirtatious eye movements, loving or enticing eyes

⚠ used generally to describe women

⊕ always used in the plural form

"Any time I'm angry at my girlfriend, she gives me these big **goo-goo eyes** and has me wrapped around her finger in no time flat!"

goon [guːn] count noun ** a stupid person; a physically intimidating person used as an enforcer

⚠ goons were hired to break strikes in the early days of organized labor. Sometimes used to refer to bodyguards

"Check out his bodyguards. Those **goons** look like they're right out of the penitentiary!"

go on about [goʊ aːn əbaʊt] 3 word verb ***** to chatter incessantly and tiresomely, often in an annoying or nagging tone

⚠ this expressions has very negative undertones

"He's always **going on about** how much money he makes. It drives me up the wall!"

go out on [goʊ aʊt ɑːn] 3 word verb *** to stop functioning, collapse

"I don't think I can do one more squat. My legs are about to **go out on** me."

> See: GIVE OUT ON

go out on a limb [goʊ aʊt ɑːn ə lɪm] verb phrase *** to put oneself in a vulnerable position, to take a risk

"I **went out on a limb** for you when I got you this job, so you'd better start to pull your weight!"

go out with [goʊ aʊt wɪθ] 3 word verb ***** to date or have a romantic relationship with someone

🔟 the object is always a person. If the subject is plural, **with** and the object are dropped

"'Kevin is **going out with** Elaine?' 'Yeah, they've been **going out** for about two months now.'"

> See: SEE SOMEONE

go overboard [goʊ oʊvɚbɔːrd] verb phrase **** to be excessively enthusiastic or extravagant

⚠ has negative connotations

"He always **goes overboard** on his gifts to his girlfriends."

> See: GET CARRIED AWAY

go over one's head [goʊ oʊvɚ wʌnz hed]

1. verb phrase *** to be beyond one's comprehension

⚠ sometimes used in a negative way. Rather than using the spoken phrase, a gesture of one's hand going over the top of the head is sometimes used to indicate that a person did not understand or realize what has happened

"I know you told him, but I think it **went** right **over his head**. You have to bring your explanation down to his level."

> See: FLY OVER ONE'S HEAD

2. verb phrase ** to go to one's superior

"I turned down Joe's request for more vacation, so he **went over my head** and got permission from my boss."

go through with [goʊ θruː wɪθ] 3 word verb *** to carry out, to complete

🔟 object is always something, usually **it**

"I heard Rob was going to quit his job and start his own business! Do you think he'll **go through with** it?"

go way back [goʊ weɪ bæk] verb phrase **** to have a long-term acquaintance or friendship

🔟 usually used in simple present tense

"I've known Janice since high school. We **go way back**."

grand [grænd] count noun ***** one thousand US dollars

🔟 grand has no plural form: **a grand**, **five grand**, **a hundred grand**, etc. Sometimes shortened to **G**, which has no singular form: **ten G's**, **a hundred G's**, etc.

"It cost Greg a **grand** to fix his car."

"Jenny is loaded: she's pulling in over a hundred **grand** (**G's**) a year!"

grill [grɪl] verb, T *** to interrogate, to question intently

"I don't know why you're **grilling** me like I was some kind of criminal! I'm telling you the truth!"

> See: GIVE SOMEONE THE THIRD DEGREE

grounded [graʊndəd] verb, T *** to limit or restrict one's social activities

"Bill's father **grounded** him for a week because he came home drunk again."

grub [grʌb] non-count noun * food

⚠ unsophisticated

"I'm starving! Got any **grub** in this house?"

grubby [grʌbi] adj *** dirty

"I'm pretty **grubby** after spending the day at the beach. Let me jump in the shower before we go."

grumpy [grʌmpi] adj *** in a bad mood

"What's up with you? Why are you so **grumpy** today?"

> See: CRANKY

gulp [gʌlp] verb, T/count noun ** to drink thirstily and noisily; a single swallow of a large amount of drink or food

"Guido was so thirsty, he **gulped** down the whole glass of water."

"He swallowed the whole sandwich in one **gulp**!"

> See: DOWN, GUZZLE

gung ho [gʌŋ hoʊ] adj ** excited, enthusiastic

"Jack didn't want to go on the trip, but when he heard that Melissa was coming, he was suddenly all **gung ho** about it!"

guns [gʌnz] non-count noun * upper arm or chest muscles

⚠ used mainly by guys

🔟 always used in the plural form

"Get a load of the **guns** on that guy! They're massive!"

gut [gʌt] count noun *** a protruding belly

"I've got to cut down on the junk food! I'm starting to get a **gut**!"

See: BEER BELLY, POTBELLY

gut reaction [gʌt riækʃən] count noun phrase *** a visceral or emotional response

"I know I shouldn't have sounded so shocked when she said they were tying the knot, but that was my **gut reaction**!"

guts [gʌts] non-count noun ***** courage, determination

⚠ somewhat coarse, generally used informally

🔟 often preceded by **the**

"I can't believe Yoshi went deep-sea diving in those shark-infested waters! I don't think I'd ever have the **guts** to pull off something like that!"

See: BALLS

guys [gaɪz] exp/count noun ***** men, people in general

⚠ can refer to men, women, or mixed company depending on context; also a term of address

"Hey **guys**, what are you up to tonight?"

"See those **guys** over there? The girl in the black was my roommate in college."

See: FOLKS

guzzle [gʌzl] verb, T *** to drink thirstily

"You must have been really thirsty! You **guzzled** down that beer in no time flat!"

"My car really **guzzles** gas."

See: GULP

H

hammered [hæməd] adj **** extremely drunk, highly intoxicated

"Don't give him anymore to drink. He's already **hammered**!"

See: BOMBED, GONE, LOADED, MESSED UP, RIPPED, SLOSHED, TOASTED, TRASHED, WASTED

hand [hænd] count noun ***** assistance, help

🔟 always used in the singular form preceded by **a**

"Honey, could you give me a **hand** with dinner?"

handful [hændfʊl] count noun **** all one can manage; a person who is difficult to control or take care of

"My new job is a real **handful**."

"That's the last time I baby-sit Gwenyth's kids! They're a real **handful**."

hand it to someone [hænd ɪt tuː sʌmwʌn] verb phrase **** to congratulate, to give credit to

🔟 often used with **have to**

"I have to **hand it to you**. You handled that situation very professionally."

"You have to **hand it to Joe**. He had the guts to stick it out."

See: TAKE ONE'S HAT OFF TO

hand over [hænd oʊvə] 2 word sep verb **** to release something to another's control

"The boss wants us to **hand over** the keys to the supply room."

🔟 can be used in the imperative form

"OK, **hand over** your weapons!"

hang in there [hæŋ ɪn ðer] verb phrase/exp **** to persevere; "don't give up" or "keep trying"

"**Hang in there**. Nobody said that getting your masters degree would be a piece of cake."

hang on [hæŋ ɑːn] 2 word insep verb, I **** to wait or stay on the line; "wait" or "hold the phone"

"Could you **hang on** a minute? I'll be right with you."

hang out [hæŋ aʊt] 2 word verb, I ***** to spend leisure time, loiter, pass time idly

🔟 sometimes takes objects like **downtown**, **here**, or **there**

"'Let's **hang out** downtown this weekend.' 'Ok, sounds great.'"

"It's been a long time since we **hung out**."

See: CHILL OUT, KICK BACK, KICK IT

hang out at [hæŋ aʊt æt] 3 word verb ***** to spend free time somewhere

🔟 object is always a specific place

"They always **hang out at** (his place, the mall, that club, the beach) on the weekends."

hang out in [hæŋ aʊt ɪn] 3 word verb ***** to spend free time somewhere

🔟 object is always a country, city, area or terrain

"We **hung out in** (the woods, LA, France) all last month."

hang out with [hæŋ aʊt wɪθ] 3 word verb ***** to spend free or leisure time with someone

🔟 object is always a person

"Why don't you come over to my place and **hang out with** me?"

"I didn't do anything this weekend. I just **hung out with** myself."

hang up on [hæŋ ʌp ɑːn] 3 word verb **** to end a telephone conversation abruptly

⚠ to hang up on someone is very insulting, even when as a result of anger or frustration

🔟 the object is always a person

"Hello? Hello? I can't believe it! Kristine **hung up on** me! She must be really pissed!"

hardheaded [hɑːrdheded] adj *** stubborn, obstinate

"You're always so **hardheaded**. Why don't give in just this once?"

See: BULLHEADED

hard up [hɑːrd ʌp] adj phrase ** short of money, in need of something

🔟 if an object is stated, it is preceded by **for**

"I wish I could lend you a couple of bucks, but I'm pretty **hard up** myself."

See: BROKE, BUSTED

haul out of [hɑːl aʊt əv] 3 word verb *** to move quickly, leave a place quickly

🔟 object is always a place; the verb can be shortened to **haul** when a location is not stated

"Let's **haul out of** here before someone comes!"

"We're going to have to **haul** to get to the airport on time."

See: BOOK, MOTOR

have a bun in the oven [hæv ə bʌn ɪn ðe ʌvən] verb phrase ** to be pregnant

"Amy's **got a bun in the oven**!"

See: KNOCK UP

have a crush on [hæv ə krʌʃ ɑːn] verb phrase **** to be infatuated with someone

⚠ often used by younger generations

🔟 object is always a person

"I think Lars **has a crush on** Michiko. He always gets nervous when he talks to her!"

have a field day [hæv ə fiːld deɪ] verb phrase *** to experience a time of great opportunity, enjoyment, or pleasure

"I just got a five grand bonus! I'm going to **have a field day** shopping this weekend!"

have a heart-to-heart [hæv ə hɑːrt tuː hɑːrt] verb phrase *** to have a sincere or candid conversation

"I know you don't want to talk about this, but we need to **have a heart-to-heart** about your college plans."

have a skeleton in one's closet [hæv ə skelɪtən ɪn wʌnz klɑːzɪt] verb phrase ** to have a shameful secret, usually from the distant past

"He won't answer any questions about his military service. I think he may **have a skeleton in his closet**."

have butterflies in one's stomach [hæv bʌtɚflaɪz ɪn wʌnz stʌmek] verb phrase *** to have a feeling of nervous anticipation

⚠ sometimes shortened to **butterflies**

"I have to do my speech in class tomorrow. **I've got butterflies (in my stomach)**!"

See: LEGS LIKE JELL-O

have got it going on [hæv gɑːt ɪt goʊɪŋ ɑːn] verb phrase *** to be dressed in a stylish or elegant manner

"Peggy and Joe are a stylish couple. They really **have got it going on**."

See: LOOK SHARP

have it in for someone [hæv ɪt ɪn fɔːr sʌmwʌn] verb phrase *** to intend to harm, particularly as a result of a grudge

"The boss has **had it in for Peggy** ever since she stood up to him. He criticizes everything she does."

have one's eye on [hæv wʌnz aɪ ɑːn] verb phrase ***** to watch intently, to have as one's objective

"The teacher **has her eye on** the girls in the middle row. She thinks they cheat on her tests."

"**I've had my eye on** that ring for quite a while. Now I finally have enough money to buy it."

See: EYE

have one's face on [hæv wʌnz feɪs ɑːn] verb phrase ** to have applied one's makeup

⚠ usually used only to refer to females!

"Give me a few minutes. I don't **have my face on** yet!"

See: PUT ONE'S FACE ON

have one's head on right [hæv wʌnz hed ɑːn raɪt] verb phrase ** to have clear goals and objectives

"Helen's son Dan really **has his head on right**. He's entered college, decided on a major, and works part-time to support himself. I wish my son could get his act together like that!"

See: TOGETHER

have one's heart set on [hæv wʌnz hɑːrt set ɑːn] verb phrase **** to establish a goal or desire

⚠ implies emotional importance to achieving a goal

🔄 often used in the past tense

"I really **had my heart set on** going to Hawaii, but I just can't afford to take a vacation right now."

"He **has his heart set on** an Ivy League school, but I don't think his grades are going to cut it."

have someone going [hæv sʌmwʌn goʊɪŋ] verb phrase **** to lead on, to deceive or fool someone

"I thought you'd won the lottery. You really **had me going** there for a minute!"

have someone wrapped around one's finger [hæv sʌmwʌn ræpt əraʊnd wʌnz fɪŋgɚ] verb phrase *** to have complete control over another person

"Liz can get Louis to do anything she wants. She's **got him wrapped around her finger**."

have something covered [hæv sʌmwʌn kʌvɚd] verb phrase **** to assume a responsibility, to anticipate a need

🔄 almost always used in the present tense

"'Oh no! My credit card is expired!' 'No sweat, **I've got this one covered**.'"

"'How about security over on that side of the auditorium?' 'No problem, sir; **we've got it covered**.'"

have something up one's sleeve [hæv sʌmθɪŋ ʌp wʌnz sliːv] verb phrase *** to conceal a surprise or secret

"Kris has been pretty quiet about her wedding date. I wonder if she **has something up her sleeve**?"

have the nerve [hæv ðe nɜːrv] verb phrase **** to have the audacity or courage to act

⚠ negative undertones

"I never thought that Billy would **have the nerve** to ask her out again after the way he treated her."

🔄 the expression is sometimes shortened to **the nerve!** as a response to one's behavior

"Jack's been bragging all week about asking Alicia to the big party. Then he waits until the last minute and asks me instead! **The nerve!**"

See: BALLS, GUTS

have two left feet [hæv tuː left fiːt] verb phrase ** to be a poor dancer, to be clumsy

"Are you sure you want to get out on the dance floor with me? When it comes to dancing **I've got two left feet**."

head [hed] verb, I ***** to move or travel

🔄 commonly followed by **up**, **down**, **over**, or these words preceded by **on** when no destination is specified

"Let's **head up** to the mountains this weekend."

"Peggy and Joe are **heading down** to the beach."

"Let's **head over** to Pam's place."

"Pam's having a party! Let's **head on over!**"

headache [hedeik] count noun ***** a problem or difficulty

"That client is always giving me a hard time. He's such a **headache**!"

"I've got so many **headaches** to deal with today!"

head honcho [hed hɑːntʃoʊ] count noun phrase ** the boss, person in charge

⚠ mostly used in jest or in light situations

🔘 usually preceded by **the**

"I need to speak to the **head honcho**."

See: MAIN MAN

head over heels [hed oʊvɚ hiːlz] adj phrase *** infatuated with, crazy about

⚠ usually refers to romantic interests

🔘 when stating the object, it is preceded by **for** or **about**

"Ahmed has stars in his eyes. He's really **head over heels** about Donna!"

heap [hiːp] count noun * an unreliable car that is in poor condition

"Sorry, but I'm not going anywhere in that old **heap**."

See: CLUNKER

hear out [hɪr aʊt] 2 word sep verb **** to allow someone to speak without interruption

🔘 usually used in the imperative form with an object pronoun

"I know you folks don't like the idea, but **hear** me **out**."

hell breaks loose [hel breɪks luːs] verb phrase ** to develop a state of chaos or intense rage

⚠ can refer to desirable or undesirable events

🔘 **all** usually precedes the phrase

"All **hell broke loose** when we scored the winning touchdown!"

"If my mom ever catches me skipping school, all **hell** will **break loose**."

hello [heloʊ] exp **** a playful response to a foolish question or observation; "be more observant!"

⚠ used in jest with close friends

"'Have you seen how much weight Kelly has put on?' '**Hello**! She's pregnant you dummy!'"

See: DUH, GET WITH IT, GET WITH THE PROGRAM, WAKE UP AND SMELL THE COFFEE

henpecked husband [henpekt hʌzbənd] count noun phrase * a weak husband who is dominated by his wife

⚠ slightly outdated term, but sometimes used to tease a man about to be married

"So, you're tying the knot? We'll never see you again. You're going to turn into one of those **henpecked husbands**!"

here's the deal [hɪrz ðe diːl] exp **** "here are the details" or "this is the way things are"

"**Here's the deal**. They want you to help out with the new project, but they won't put you in charge."

hip [hɪp] adj *** cool, stylish

"That girl Yuko, the artist, is a real **hip** chick."

See: WITH IT

history [hɪstəri] non count noun **** the past; a person or thing that is used up or done for

⚠ commonly used to describe a career or personal relationship

"He lost that big account so he's **history**! The boss is going to fire him tomorrow."

"I don't think Fred and Maya will make up. They're **history**."

"You can have those old jeans. They're **history**."

See: OUT OF THE PICTURE

hit [hɪt] verb, T **** to realize, to become aware of

🔘 object is always a person

"I was at the store and it **hit** me that you don't have a warm blanket, so I bought one for you."

hit it off [hɪt ɪt ɑːf] verb phrase ***** to get along well with someone from the outset

"When Shiro and Miho first met they didn't really **hit it off**, but by the end of the term they were best pals."

hit rock bottom [hɪt rɑːk bɑːtəm] *verb phrase* *** *to reach the lowest or worst point*

⚠ *also used when business is bad or personal finances are bad*

"His girlfriend dumped him last week, this week his boss gave him the ax and his cat died today. He's really **hit rock bottom**!"

hit the books [hɪt ðe bʊks] *verb phrase* **** *to study intensely*

"I've got a big test tomorrow so I've got to **hit the books** tonight."

hit the ceiling [hɪt ðe siːlɪŋ] *verb phrase* *** *to explode in anger*

⚠ *slightly dated*

"My dad **hit the ceiling** when I told him I wrecked his new car."

See: BLOW A FUSE, BLOW ONE'S TOP, FLY OFF THE HANDLE, LOSE IT

hit the court [hɪt ðe kɔːrt] *verb phrase* **** *start to play a game of tennis, basketball, or any other game that is played on a court*

"I'm ready to shoot some hoops! Let's **hit the court**!"

hit the hay [hɪt ðe heɪ] *verb phrase* ** *to go to bed or sleep*

"Time for me to **hit the hay**. I've got to be up at the crack of dawn tomorrow."

See: CONK OUT, CRASH, HIT THE SACK, HIT THE SHEETS

hit the nail on the head [hɪt ðe neɪl ɑːn ðe hed] *verb phrase* *** *to be precisely correct, exactly right*

⚠ *often refers to a situation where a person has correctly identified the most significant of a series of issues*

"We had several problems in our sales department, but you really **hit the nail on the head** when you pointed out the unfair commission structure."

See: BINGO

hit the road [hɪt ðe roʊd] *verb phrase* **** *to begin a trip, to leave*

"What do you say we **hit the road** at eleven?"

See: GET GOING

hit the sack [hɪt ðe sæk] *verb phrase* **** *to go to bed or sleep*

"It's almost midnight! Time to **hit the sack**!"

See: CONK OUT, CRASH, HIT THE HAY, HIT THE SHEETS

hit the sheets [hɪt ðe ʃiːts] *verb phrase* *** *to go to bed or sleep*

"OK kids, it's ten. Time to **hit the sheets**!"

See: CONK OUT, CRASH, HIT THE HAY, HIT THE SACK

hit the spot [hɪt ðe spɑːt] *verb phrase* **** *to satisfy one's hunger or thirst*

"It's so hot out! A nice tall glass of lemonade would really **hit the spot**!"

hit the weights [hɪt ðe weɪts] *verb phrase* ** *to lift weights with intensity*

"Man, I'm out of shape. I need to **hit the weights**!"

hit up for [hɪt ʌp fɔːr] *3 word verb* ** *to impose on someone for something, usually money*

⚠ *often a negative sentiment*

🔟 *correct use of the expression is* **hit someone up for something**

"Can you believe my ex called and **hit** me **up for** a hundred bucks?"

"The secretary caught me at the door and **hit** me **up for** the office party."

See: BUM OFF OF, SPONGE OFF OF

hog [hɔːg] *verb, T/count noun* ** *to take more than one's share, one who is greedy*

⚠ *often used by or with children*

"Don't **hog** all of the ice cream! Leave some for me!"

"Don't be such a **hog**! I'd like to use the computer for a while."

holdup [hoʊldʌp] *count noun* ** *an act of armed robbery*

"OK everyone, just be cool. This is a **holdup**, so give me all your money and nobody gets hurt!"

hold up [hoʊld ʌp] *2 word insep verb, I* **** *to survive, endure, persevere*

⚠ *can be used for either people or objects*

"Lucy is pregnant and we've been shopping all day. I don't think she can **hold up** much longer without a food break."

"My car is old but it's still **holding up**. Why should I shell out tons of dough for a new one?"

hold up [hoʊld ʌp] 2 word sep verb, T * to overcharge

"Oh, I wouldn't go to that restaurant. They'll **hold** you **up** at that place."

hold water [hoʊld wɔːtɚ] verb phrase *** to be believable, to be valid

⚠ usually used in reference to excuses or explanations

"You're not off the hook yet. I'm not so sure that your story **holds water**."

hold your horses [hoʊld jʊr hɔːrsɪz] exp ***
"wait" or "be patient"

"'Come on Masaki, hurry up! We don't have all day!' 'OK, just **hold your horses**! I'll be ready in a sec.'"

hole-in-the-wall [hoʊl ɪn ðe wɔːl] count noun phrase **** a small, out-of-the-way place

⚠ often used to refer to a small store, restaurant, bar, apartment, etc.

"Have you been to The Alibi? It's a **hole-in-the-wall**, but it's always packed!"

honey [hʌni]
1. exp ** a general term of address for one's sweetheart, spouse, or occasionally a female friend

"Hi **honey**, I'm home!"

2. count noun ** an attractive girl or woman.

"That Kelly is a real **honey**!"

"Come on Eric, let's go to the party. There'll be a lot of **honeys** there!"

See: BABE

hooked [hʊkt] adj ***** addicted to a substance; fascinated or devoted to something

🔟 if the object is identified, it is preceded by **on**

"Nick is **hooked** on chocolate. He has to eat some everyday!"

"Amy is **hooked** on TV talk shows."

hook up with [hʊk ʌp wɪθ]
1. 3 word verb ***** to meet someone at a predetermined time and/or location

"I'll **hook up with** you tomorrow."

🔟 the object is always a person. When the subject is plural, **with** and the object are sometimes dropped

"We'll/Let's **hook up** tonight."

2. 3 word verb ***** to introduce one person to another

"I know this guy who can help you out. I'll **hook** you **up with** him."

see: FIX UP WITH, SET UP WITH

3. 3 word verb ***** to supply with

"If you answer the question correctly, I'll **hook** you **up with** two tickets for tonight's Big Bad Voodoo Daddy show."

hoot [huːt] count noun *** something amusing or funny

"The play was a real **hoot**. I laughed 'till I cried."

See: RIOT, SCREAM

hop in [haːp ɪn] verb phrase/exp **** to enter a vehicle; "get in the car"

🔟 generally used in the imperative form

"**Hop in** and I'll give you a lift home."

hot [haːt]
1. adj ***** attractive, popular, good

⚠ can refer to people or objects. When applied to people it usually means sexy

"Those male dancers were definitely **hot**!"

"That new band is really **hot**!"

See: KILLER, ROCK, THE BOMB

2. adj ** stolen, illegally obtained

"You bought that entire entertainment system for only three hundred bucks? It must be **hot**!"

huh? [hʌ]
1. exp ***** a substitute for all tag questions; "right?" or "didn't you?"

"Jake is a smart guy, **huh**?"

"You locked the back door, **huh**?"

2. exp ***** "I didn't hear or understand you"

"**Huh?** Were you talking to me? I didn't hear you."

hunk [hʌŋk] count noun **** a good-looking guy

⚠ used primarily by girls

"Did you see Rima's new boyfriend? He's such a **hunk**!"

See: BABE

I

if one's memory serves one right [ɪf wʌnz memrəi sɜːrvz wʌn raɪt] exp **** "assuming one's memory is correct…"

🔄 the expression is sometime simplified to: **if memory serves me**

"This street seems familiar. **If (my) memory serves me (right)**, I'd say we've been here before."

I hear you [aɪ hɪr juː] exp **** "I agree with what you are saying"

"'School is getting so expensive these days!' **I hear you**! I just dropped four hundred clams in the bookstore!'"

See: YOU CAN SAY THAT AGAIN, YOU'RE TELLING ME

I'll give you that [aɪl gɪv juː ðæt] exp **** "I agree with you on a particular point" or "I will concede a particular point"

"Sure, you helped out in the beginning, **I'll give you that**, but you haven't done much since."

I'm all ears [aɪm ɔːl ɪrz] exp **** "I'm listening carefully"

"'Sun Taek, there's something I really need to talk to you about.' **I'm all ears**, shoot.'"

I'm talking… [aɪm tɔːkɪŋ] exp **** adds emphasis to a statement; "I'm emphasizing…"

"This guy was huge! **I'm talking** three hundred pounds!"

in a bind [ɪn ə baɪnd] prep phrase ** to be in trouble or have a problem

"I know you need someone to work this weekend. If you're really **in a bind**, I can help you out."

See: IN A JAM, IN A TIGHT SPOT

in a flash [ɪn ə flæʃ] prep phrase **** fast, quickly

"I'm going to the market to get some coffee. I'll be back **in a flash**."

See: AT THE DROP OF A HAT, IN A HEARTBEAT, IN A JIFFY, IN A NEW YORK SECOND, IN NO TIME FLAT, IN TWO SHAKES OF A LAMB'S TAIL

in a heartbeat [ɪn ə hɑːrtbiːt] prep phrase ***** quickly, without thinking

"If you ever need help with anything, just ask! I'll be there for you **in a heartbeat**!"

See: AT THE DROP OF A HAT, IN A FLASH, IN A JIFFY, IN A NEW YORK SECOND, IN NO TIME FLAT, IN TWO SHAKES OF A LAMB'S TAIL

in a jam [ɪn ə dʒæm] prep phrase **** in a predicament

"Could you help me out? I'm really **in a jam**."

See: IN A BIND, IN A TIGHT SPOT

in a jiffy [ɪn ə dʒɪfi] prep phrase ** fast, quickly

⚠ dated; sometimes shorted to: **in a jif**

"Hold on a minute, don't go. I'll have this ready for you **in a jiffy**."

See: AT THE DROP OF A HAT, IN A FLASH, IN A HEARTBEAT, IN A NEW YORK SECOND, IN NO TIME FLAT, IN TWO SHAKES OF A LAMB'S TAIL

in a New York second [ɪn ə nuː jɔːrk sekənd] prep phrase * fast, quickly

"I'll get you to the hospital **in a New York second**."

See: AT THE DROP OF A HAT, IN A FLASH, IN A HEARTBEAT, IN A JIFFY, IN NO TIME FLAT, IN TWO SHAKES OF A LAMB'S TAIL

in a rut [ɪn ə rʌt] prep phrase **** to be stuck in a boring routine

"I'm really **in a rut**. Everyday it's the same thing: wake up, go to work, come straight home, eat dinner, watch TV, then go to bed."

in a tight spot [ɪn ə taɪt spɑːt] prep phrase **** having a problem, in a difficult situation

"You've got two dates for this Saturday? Sounds like you're **in a tight spot**. If you need some help, I'll be glad to give you a hand!"

See: IN A BIND, IN A JAM

in my book [ɪn maɪ bʊk] exp **** "in my opinion"

⚠ used when stating one's view

"**In my book**, stealing money from someone who trusted you is a horrible thing to do!"

in no time flat [ɪn noʊ taɪm flæt] prep phrase ***** fast, quickly

"I'll have that report ready for you **in no time flat**."

See: AT THE DROP OF A HAT, IN A FLASH, IN A HEARTBEAT, IN A JIFFY, IN A NEW YORK SECOND, IN TWO SHAKES OF A LAMB'S TAIL

in one's dreams [ɪn wʌnz driːmz] *exp* ****
"never!" or "no way!"

🅿 always use the proper possessive adjective

"'Mahmoud wants to know when you'll talk to him again.' '**In his dreams!**'"

"'Will you lend me a hundred bucks until payday?' '**In your dreams!**'"

See: FAT CHANCE, IT'LL BE A COLD DAY IN HELL, NOT IN A MILLION YEARS, WHEN HELL FREEZES OVER, WHEN PIGS FLY

in over one's head [ɪn oʊvɚ wʌnz hed] *prep phrase* *** overwhelmed by obligations; beyond one's understanding or competence

"I charged up a storm on all of these credit cards, and now I'm really **in over my head** with debt. I don't know what to do."

"Scott's not doing too well at his new job. I think he's **in over his head**."

in someone's hair [ɪn sʌmwʌnz her] *prep phrase* ** to be a distraction or annoyance

"Jack, would you take the kids over to the park this afternoon? They've been **in my hair** all morning."

in someone's shoes [ɪn sʌmwʌnz ʃuːz] *prep phrase* ***** in the same situation as another

"If I were **in his shoes**, I'd fire that lazy bum. He hasn't done an honest days work since he was hired."

🅿 used commonly with **wish I were** or **glad I'm not**

"You finished your finals today? I wish I were **in your shoes**. I've still got three more days to go!"

"You have to take physics from Professor Elliot? She's tough! I'm glad I'm not **in your shoes**."

in store [ɪn stɔːr] *prep phrase* ***** planned, in readiness

"What do you have **in store** for Quinci's birthday?"

"I wonder what the future has **in store** for us now that we've graduated?"

in the bag [ɪn ðe bæg] *prep phrase* *** secure, taken care of

"'I keep thinking that something is going to derail this business deal.' 'Don't concern yourself, it's **in the bag**.'"

in the ballpark [ɪn ðe bɔːlpɑːrk] *prep phrase* **** an approximation, a general range

🅿 when a dollar amount is stated, it is preceded by **of**

"I'd like to buy a house, but prices are pretty steep these days. I've been looking **in the ballpark** of two hundred and fifty G's but there's nothing out there!"

in the doghouse [ɪn ðe dɑːghaʊs] *prep phrase* *** in trouble, in disfavor

"You're **in the doghouse** again? What did you do this time?"

"Bill is **in the doghouse** with his girlfriend again."

⚠ when one has been forgiven, he is **out of the doghouse**

in the dumps [ɪn ðe dʌmps] *prep phrase* *** depressed, down, blue

"You've been **in the dumps** for almost a week! Come on, snap out of it!"

🅿 often preceded by **down**

"She was really down **in the dumps** when she got her pink slip."

See: BUMMED, DOWN

in the same boat [ɪn ðe seɪm boʊt] *prep phrase* ***** in a similar predicament as someone else, to be no better off

"I'd like to help the neighbors financially, but with the layoffs at the plant, we're all **in the same boat**."

in the sticks [ɪn ðe stɪks] *prep phrase* ** remote, far away from the city

"If you want to buy an affordable house you've got to live out **in the sticks**!"

into
See: BE INTO

in two shakes of a lamb's tail [ɪn tuː ʃeɪks ʌ ə læmz teɪl] *prep phrase* * fast, quickly

⚠ dated, used mostly by older generations

"Don't worry! I'll be there **in two shakes of a lamb's tail**!"

See: AT THE DROP OF A HAT, IN A FLASH, IN A HEARTBEAT, IN A JIFFY, IN A NEW YORK SECOND, IN NO TIME FLAT

iron out [aɪɚn aʊt] *2 word sep verb* ** to settle, resolve

"Eric and Steven are going to meet and see if they can **iron out** their differences."

See: SMOOTH OVER

I stand corrected [aɪ stænd kərektɪd] *exp* ****
"I acknowledge my error"

⚠ somewhat formal

"'Pardon me, but I graduated from Harvard, not Yale.'
'**I stand corrected**.'"

it goes without saying [ɪt gouz wɪðaut seɪŋ]
exp **** "it is obvious"

"Both of us have a lot riding on this. **It goes without saying** that we can't afford any mistakes."

it'll be cold day in hell [ɪtəl biː ə kould deɪ ɪn hel] *exp* **** "never", "not under any circumstances"

🌐 this expression is usually followed by **before**

"Me skydive? **It'll be a cold day in hell** before you catch me jumping out of a plane!"

"**It'll be cold day in hell** before I get involved in another business partnership."

See: FAT CHANCE, IN ONE'S DREAMS, NOT IN A MILLION YEARS, WHEN HELL FREEZES OVER, WHEN PIGS FLY

it's a long story [ɪts ə lɑːŋ stɔːri] *exp* **** "the details are complicated and lengthy"

⚠ used when the speaker does not wish to tell the entire story

"**It's a long story** but what it boils down to is that he ended up in jail again."

I've had it up to here [aɪv hæd ɪt ʌp tuː hɪr] *exp* **** "my patience has been exhausted"

⚠ this expression is often accompanied by a gesture in which the hand rises to eye level, indicating that the speaker's level of tolerance has been exceeded

🌐 when the object is stated, it is preceded by **with**

"**I've had it up to here** with her constant complaining. If she doesn't like the job, she ought to quit!"

J

Jag [jʒæg] *count noun* *** nickname for any model of the Jaguar automobile

"I just bought a **Jag** from a little old lady who only used it to go grocery shopping."

jerk [dʒɜːrk] *count noun* ***** an obnoxious or contemptible person

"I can't believe you left the party without me! You're such a **jerk**!"

See: CREEP, SCHMUCK

jet [jʒet] *verb*, I ** to leave quickly

"'How about another drink Victor?' 'Sorry, I've got to **jet**. Catch you later.'"

See: BE OFF, BOOK, GET GOING, HIT THE ROAD, SPLIT

john [dʒɑːn] *count noun* *** restroom, toilet

⚠ generally used in male company

🌐 always preceded by **the** and used in the lower case

"Hey dude, if you need me I'll be in the **john**."

See: CAN, LITTLE GIRLS ROOM

joint [dʒɔɪnt]

1. *count noun* *** restaurant or similar establishment

"Let's go check out that new Cajun **joint** downtown."

2. *count noun* ** jail or prison

🌐 always preceded by **the**

"I heard that Nathan is in the **joint** again."

See: BIG HOUSE, CAN, PEN, SLAMMER

jot down [dʒɑːt daun] *2 word sep verb* *** to write briefly or quickly

"Let me **jot down** my number for you."

jump down someone's throat [dʒʌmp daun sʌmwʌnz θrout] *verb phrase* *** to verbally attack someone

"Dude, the coach really **jumped down your throat** when you missed that shot! I thought he was going to kill you!"

See: BE ALL OVER, CHEW OUT, GO OFF ON

jump in the shower [dʒʌmp ɪn ðe ʃauɚ] *verb phrase* *** to take a quick shower

"I'll be ready in a flash. Let me **jump in the shower** before we go."

jump someone's bones [dʒʌmp sʌmwʌnz bounz] *verb phrase* ** to have sexual intercourse with someone

⚠ rude, usually said of a women

"Man, check out the bod on her! I'd like to **jump her bones**!"

"I can't believe he tried to **jump your bones** on the first date!"

See: DO IT, SLEEP WITH

jump the gun [dʒʌmp ðe gʌn] *verb phrase* *** to act or begin before the proper time

"Jason **jumped the gun** when he announced the company merger. The contract hasn't been signed yet."

junior [dʒuːnjɚ] *adj/exp* ** one who is lower in rank than another; a term of address for a young male

"Julie is one of our **junior** executives."

"Hey **Junior**, time to pack up and head home."

K

ka-ching [kaːtʃɪŋ] *exp* *** jocular imitation of the sound of a cash register recording a profitable sale

🄿 can be used in two senses:

"I think we found the lost sunken treasure! **Ka-ching**!"

"Did you see the accident damage to Hania's new car? **Ka-ching**!"

keep a lid on [kiːp ə lɪd aːn] *verb phrase* ** to maintain control or secrecy

🄿 object is always a thing

"They're not announcing the winners until next week, so please **keep a lid on** what I told you here today."

keep a low profile [kiːp ə loʊ proʊfaɪl] *verb phrase* ** to attempt to be inconspicuous, to hide

"I screwed up pretty badly on this business deal, so I need to **keep a low profile** until the boss cools down."

See: LIE LOW

keep an eye on [kiːp æn aɪ aːn] *verb phrase* ***** to observe intently, to watch over someone

"**Keep an eye** on that pressure gauge. If it goes into the red, holler!"

"I'm going to run to the store. Could you **keep an eye on** the kids for me?"

keep down [kiːp daʊn] *2 word sep verb* ** to be able keep food or drink in one's stomach

"I've been feeling queasy all day. I could hardly **keep** my lunch **down**. Maybe I'm coming down with a bug."

keep it down [kiːp ɪt daʊn] *exp* **** "be quiet" or "don't be so noisy"

"It's one AM and people are trying to sleep! **Keep it down**!"

See: PIPE DOWN

keep one's eyes peeled [kiːp wʌnz aɪz piːld] *verb phrase* ** to observe intently, watch carefully

"OK everybody, **keep your eyes peeled**. We want to find these kids before it get dark."

🄿 when the object is stated it is preceded by **for**

"**Keep your eyes peeled** for the teacher. If she catches us stealing answers to the final exam we're dead meat!"

keep one's fingers crossed [kiːp wʌnz fɪŋgɚz kraːst] *verb phrase* *** to wish for good luck

"You're going for your job interview today? I'll **keep my fingers crossed** for you."

keep track of [kiːp træk əv] *3 word verb* *** to stay informed, keep a record of something

"**Keep track of** the time. We don't want to be late."

"I have to **keep track of** my expenses so my company can reimburse me later."

kick-ass/butt [kɪk æs/bʌt] *adj* *** impressive, cool, stylish

⚠ somewhat crude, inappropriate in polite company

"Bill installed this **kick-ass** stereo system in his car."

"Check out this **kick-butt** guitar amp I bought!"

See: BADASS, HOT, RAD

kick back [kɪk bæk] *verb phrase* **** to relax, lay about

"I've had a rough day at work. I think I'll just **kick back** and have a couple of brewskies."

See: CHILL OUT, HANG OUT, KICK IT, TAKE IT EASY

kick it [kɪk ɪt] *verb phrase* **** to relax, lay about

⚠ used mainly by the younger generations

"I don't feel like going out, so why don't we just **kick it** here at home."

See: CHILL OUT, HANG OUT, KICK BACK, TAKE IT EASY

kick off [kɪk aːf] *2 word sep verb* **** to begin, start

"Let's **kick off** our meeting with a funny story about a bear and her cub."

"We're planning a rock concert to **kick off** our fund-raiser."

kick one's self [kɪk wʌnz self] *verb phrase* **** to regret something that one has said or done

🔘 often used in the second conditional **could kick myself**

"I can't believe I said such an idiotic thing! I **could kick myself.**"

kick out of [kɪk aʊt əv] *3 word verb* **** to reject or expel

🔘 object is a place or institution

"Tony was **kicked out of** school because he was always cutting class."

"Jack got **kicked out of** the Marines because he couldn't cut it."

kick someone's butt [kɪk sʌmwʌnz bʌt]

1. *verb phrase* *** to defeat decisively in a game or sport

⚠️ ass can be substituted for butt; both versions are rude

"Let's play another set, I feel like **kicking your butt** one more time."

🔘 frequently used in the passive voice with **get**

"You're playing against the Wildcats this weekend? Your team is going to **get their butts kicked**!"

2. *verb phrase* ** to punish someone severely

"If your father catches you cutting school, he'll **kick your butt**!"

See: WHIP SOMEONE'S BUTT

kill [kɪl]

1. *verb, T* ***** to cause great pain

🔘 the object is always a person, usually used in the continuous tense

"My head is **killing** me. Do you have some aspirin?"

2. *verb, T* **** to have a great desire

🔘 always used in the second conditional

"Those shoes are hot! I would **kill** for a pair of those!"

3. *verb, T* *** to irritate or annoy

⚠️ often used when complaining

"It **kills** me when he breezes in fifteen minutes late and acts as if nothing is wrong!"

killer [kɪlɚ] *adj* **** extremely cool, popular

⚠️ used by the younger generations

"That's a **killer** watch you have on. Where did you get that?"

See: BADASS, HOT, RAD

kiss-ass [kɪs æs] *count noun* ***** one who seeks favor by flattery

⚠️ vulgar term, very rude if said to a person's face

"She's been here for three years and still hasn't learned her job, but she's such a **kiss-ass**, they let her get by with it."

See: BROWNNOSER

kiss up to [kɪs ʌp tuː] *3 word verb* **** to seek favor by flattery

"I can't stand that brownnoser Jeff. He's always **kissing up to** the higher-ups but he treats everyone else like dirt."

🔘 if the object is not stated, **to** is omitted

"Face it. If you want to get anywhere in this company, you'll have to **kiss up**."

See: SUCK UP TO

klutz [klʌts] *count noun* **** an uncoordinated person

"Satoko is coming to your house? Watch out, she's such a **klutz**! She breaks something wherever she goes."

See: DORK

knock it off [naːk ɪt aːf] *exp* ***** "stop!"

🔘 usually used in the imperative form, object is usually **it** or **that**

"**Knock that off**! Your hammering is really getting on my nerves!"

🔘 the object may follow knock off

"**Knock off** the bitching. You all knew there might be layoffs when you came on board."

See: CUT IT OUT

knockoff [naːkaːf] *count noun* *** a copy or fake

"Dina can't afford a real Gucci bag. Her's must be a **knockoff**."

knock off [naːk aːf] *2 word sep verb* **** to kill

🔘 object is always a person. The term can be used in the active and passive voice

"The orders from 'The Boss' are to **knock off** the Coretione family.

See: BLOW AWAY, BUMP OFF, GET RID OF, TAKE CARE OF

knockout [nɑːkaʊt] *count noun* ** a stunningly attractive woman

"You have a date with Bahar? You get all the luck! She's a real **knockout**!"

See: BABE

knock up [nɑːk ʌp] *2 word sep verb* * to impregnate a woman, to become pregnant

⚠ impolite term, often used to refer to unintended pregnancy

"Gino is really in a jam. He **knocked up** his seventeen-year-old girlfriend."

"Betsy got **knocked up** and had to drop out of school."

See: HAVE A BUN IN THE OVEN

know something like the back of one's hand [noʊ sʌmθɪŋ laɪk ðe bæk əv wʌnz hænd] *verb phrase* *** to be thoroughly familiar with something

"We don't need a map. I **know this area like the back of my hand**."

know something right off the bat [noʊ sʌmθɪŋ raɪt ɑːf ðe bæt] *verb phrase* *** to realize something immediately

"I **knew right off the bat** that he wouldn't make the team."

🔄 sometimes **know** is replaced by **could tell**

"I **could tell right off the bat** that they'd hit it off."

knuckle sandwich [nʌkl sændwɪtʃ] *count noun phrase* * a punch in the mouth

⚠ generally used in jest

"You'd better be careful how you use slang. You just might end up with a **knuckle sandwich**!"

L

lame [leɪm] *adj* ***** weak, inadequate

"Jack flaked out again? I wonder what kind of **lame** excuse he'll give you this time."

land [lænd] *verb, T* **** to gain or secure something

⚠ usually used in business related situations: **land a job**, **land an account**, etc.

"Dylan worked on that forever and a day but he finally **landed** the account."

leadfoot [ledfʊt] *count noun* ** a person who drives fast and aggressively

🔄 always preceded by **a**, can be used to describe either the person or the person's foot

"If you care about your car, I wouldn't let Manuel drive it. He's a real **leadfoot**."

left and right [left ænd raɪt] *adv phrase* ***** in every direction, from all directions

"The teacher was getting questions **left and right**."

legs like Jell-O [legz laɪk dʒeloʊ] *adj phrase* ** said of one whose legs are unsteady because of nervousness

🔄 always preceded by a possessive noun or pronoun

"I have to give my speech next! My **legs are like Jell-O**!"

See: HAVE BUTTERFLIES IN ONE'S STOMACH

lemon [lemən] *count noun* *** something that is unsatisfactory or defective, particularly when it is unreliable

⚠ often used **when** talking about cars

"This car is really a lemon. It's always breaking down and I've got to put loads of dough into keeping it running."

let down [let daʊn] *2 word sep verb* **** to disappoint

"I know I said I would be there, but I wasn't able to make it. I'm sorry if I **let** you **down**."

letdown [letdaʊn] *count noun* **** a disappointment

"Everyone said that movie was great, but I thought it was a real **letdown**."

let one's hair down [let wʌnz her daʊn] *verb phrase* ** to behave casually, lose one's inhibitions

"It's very difficult for Yuko to let **her hair down** with new acquaintances."

let someone go [let sʌmwʌn goʊ] *verb phrase* *** *to lay off or fire an employee*

"The economy is not doing well so we'll have to **let** thirty **people go**."

> *See:* CAN, GIVE SOMEONE THE AX, GIVE SOMEONE THEIR PINK SLIP, SACK

let someone have it [let sʌmwʌn hæv ɪt] *verb phrase* **** *to angrily and loudly criticize someone*

"I tried not to say anything, but when she insulted my mother, I really **let her have it**!"

let someone in on something [let sʌmwʌn ɪn ɑːn sʌmθɪŋ] *verb phrase* **** *to inform someone or allow them to participate*

"I know things have been difficult, so I'm going to **let you in on a little secret**. Everybody is getting a substantial bonus next month."

"Nobody was supposed to know about the layoffs. Who **let you in on this**?"

> *See:* SPILL THE BEANS

let someone off the hook [let sʌmwʌn ɑːf ðe hʊk] *verb phrase* ** *to release someone from blame, responsibility, or an obligation*

"I'll **let you off the hook** this time, but don't make that mistake again."

🔵 sometimes shortened to **off the hook**

"The other driver accepted responsibility for the accident, so you're **off the hook**."

> *See:* LET SOMETHING SLIDE

let something go to one's head [let sʌmθɪŋ goʊ tuː wʌnz hed] *verb phrase* **** *to become vain, conceited, or overconfident*

"Jake **let that promotion go to his head**. He won't even talk to us peons anymore."

⚠ often used as a warning in imperative form

"You did well on the test, but don't **let it go to your head**. This class gets a lot tougher from now on."

🔵 sometimes **let it** is omitted

"Akiko told Taro he looked good today and it **went** straight **to his head**. He spent the rest of the day preening himself in front of the mirror."

let something slide [let sʌmθɪŋ slaɪd] *verb phrase* **** *to ignore or be flexible about a problem or difficulty*

🔵 object is usually **it** or **this** and refers to the problem or difficulty. The object may also be specified

"Greg, this is the fifth time you messed up. I can't **let it slide** anymore. I've got to tell the boss."

"We'll **let these software problems slide** for now and fix them later."

> *See:* LET SOMEONE OFF THE HOOK

let up [let ʌp] *2 word verb, I* **** *to stop or cease*

⚠ can be rude when spoken directly to a person. Sometimes used to talk about the weather

"If the rain **lets up**, we can go to the beach later."

"You have been complaining all morning. Do you ever **let up**?"

> *See:* DROP IT, GIVE IT A REST

lie low [laɪ loʊ] *2 word insep verb, I* *** *to hide, to attempt to be inconspicuous*

"Just **lie low** a minute! My boss is heading this way and I called in sick today!"

> *See:* KEEP A LOW PROFILE

lift [lɪft] *count noun* ***** *transportation to one's destination, a ride*

🔵 usually preceded by **a**

"Your car is in the shop? I can give you a **lift** home."

lightweight [laɪtweɪt] *count noun* *** *a person who is weak, timid, or has little ability*

"Thelma is a real **lightweight** when it comes to drinking. She gets bombed very easily."

"Those two programmers they sent over this morning are **lightweights**. They don't know what's going on."

like pulling teeth [laɪk pʊlɪŋ tiːθ] *prep phrase* *** *very difficult*

"Trying to explain calculus to you is **like pulling teeth**!"

like taking candy from a baby [laɪk teɪkɪŋ kændi frɑːm ə beɪbi] *prep phrase* ** *very simple or easy*

"Don't worry about it! It'll be **like taking candy from a baby**!"

> *See:* CUT-AND-DRIED

line

See: PICK UP LINE

line up for [laɪn ʌp fɔːr] *verb phrase* *** to plan a series of activities or events

"While you're in town I'm going to **line up** some interviews **for** you."

🔊 common usage: **have something lined up for someone**

"We have a really big show **lined up for** you this evening! Let's kick things off with our first act 'The Wildflowers!'"

lip [lɪp] *non-count noun* ** back talk, rude or insolent replies

"Don't give me any **lip** or you'll find yourself grounded."

🔊 often used with **hear**

"I'm your mother and I said you can't go to the party. I don't want to hear any more of your **lip**!"

little girls room [lɪtl gɜːrlz ruːm] *count noun* *
women's restroom, bathroom

⚠ only used by women

"Excuse me for a minute. I've got to go to the **little girls room**."

See: CAN, JOHN

loaded [loʊdɪd]
1. *adj* ***** wealthy, having a large amount of money

"Mohamed wears a different watch everyday. He must really be **loaded**!"

2. *adj* ***** intoxicated with drugs or alcohol

"Those guys at the next table are really **loaded**. They've been doing shots of tequila since they got here."

See: BOMBED, GONE, HAMMERED, MESSED UP, RIPPED, SLOSHED, TOASTED, TRASHED, WASTED

loads [loʊdz] *count noun* ***** a lot, a large amount

"She's got **loads** of time."

See: BUNCH, MOUNDS, PLENTY, TON

long time, no see [lɑːŋ taɪm noʊ siː] *exp* *****
"it's been a long time since I last saw you"

"Hey Jill, what's up? **Long time, no see**!"

See: WHERE HAVE YOU BEEN HIDING/KEEPING YOURSELF

look like a million bucks [lʊk laɪk ə mɪljən bʌks] *verb phrase* *** to look attractive or prosperous

"Did you check out Carrie last night? She **looked like a million bucks**!"

look like one has lost one's best friend [lʊk laɪk wʌn hæz lɑːst wʌnz best frend] *exp* ** to look sad or depressed

"What's up Miho? **You look like you've lost your best friend**."

look like one was born yesterday [lʊk laɪk wʌn wɑːz bɔːrn jestɚdeɪ] *exp* *** "does one appear unsophisticated or inexperienced?"

⚠ often used as a rhetorical question in response to an absurd proposition

"Khalid wants me to invest in some Florida swampland. Oh sure! Do I **look like I was born yesterday**?"

"I'm not going to invest in Florida swampland. **I wasn't born yesterday**, you know!"

See: WHAT DO YOU TAKE ME FOR

look sharp [lʊk ʃɑːrp] *verb phrase* ** to look stylish, fashionable

"You **look sharp** in your new tux."

See: HAVE GOT IT GOING ON

look the other way [lʊk ðe ʌðɚ weɪ] *verb phrase* ** to deliberately overlook a shortcoming or wrongdoing

"You're report is late. I'll **look the other way** this time but don't let it happen again."

look up to [lʊk ʌp tuː] *3 word verb* **** to respect or admire someone

🔊 the object is always a person

"Josh really **looks up to** his older brother."

loony [luːni] *adj* *** crazy or eccentric

⚠ usually used in jest to express one's disbelief at another's actions

"Don't worry about what he said. Everyone around here thinks he's a little **loony** anyway."

See: BANANAS, BONKERS, CUCKOO, NUTS, NUTTY, OUT OF ONE'S MIND, OUT TO LUNCH, WACKO, WACKY

lose it [luːz ɪt]
1. *verb phrase* ***** to be overcome by grief or anger, to lose one's temper or self-control

"I **lost it** when I saw him with another girl."

"When she saw the earthquake damage to her house, she just **lost it**."

"Jack really **lost it** when his lawyer called with the bad news. You could hear the yelling all the way out in the lobby."

🄖 a person can **lose it over something**. Also used in the imperative form

"She's just trying to rattle you. Don't **lose it over her insulting questions**. Keep your cool."

> See: BLOW A FUSE, BLOW ONE'S TOP, FLY OFF THE HANDLE, HIT THE CEILING

2. verb phrase *** to go crazy, to lose one's sanity

🄖 commonly used in present perfect yes/no question form

"You're dropping out of school! Have you **lost it?**"

> See: BE MISSING SOMETHING UPSTAIRS, GO OFF THE DEEP END

lose one's head [luːz wʌnz hed] verb phrase **
to panic, become confused

"You won't make it as a stockbroker if you **lose your head** every time the market drops."

🄖 often used in the imperative form

"Don't **lose your head**! We have plenty of time to hike back to camp before it gets dark."

lose one's lunch [luːz wʌnz lʌntʃ] verb phrase **
to vomit, feel nauseous, or be sick

⚠ used both figuratively and literally

"Hisayoshi almost **lost his lunch** on that roller coaster!"

> See: BARF, PUKE, TOSS ONE'S COOKIES

lose one's marbles [luːz wʌnz mɑːrblz] verb phrase ** to become crazy or insane

"Leon keeps babbling that he's decended from royalty. I think he's **losing his marbles**."

> See: BE MISSING SOMETHING UPSTAIRS, CRACK, GO OFF THE DEEP END, LOSE IT, LOSE ONE'S MIND

lose one's mind [luːz wʌnz maɪnd] verb phrase *** to become crazy or insane

🄖 commonly used in present perfect yes/no questions

"You want me to lie to the police about your car accident? Have you **lost your mind?**"

> See: BE MISSING SOMETHING UPSTAIRS, CRACK, GO OFF THE DEEP END, LOSE IT, LOSE ONE'S MARBLES

loser [luːzɚ] count noun ***** one who is incompetent or unable to succeed

⚠ very rude if said directly to a person's face

"Brandon's thirty and he's still trying to impress high school girls. What a **loser!**"

> See: LOWLIFE

lousy [laʊzi] adj ***** unpleasant, bad

"Biff left Muffy standing at the altar. What a **lousy** thing for him to do!"

"I can't believe they get two G's a month for this **lousy** apartment!"

> See: CRUMMY

lover's spat [lʌvɚz spæt] count noun phrase *** a quarrel or minor disagreement between sweethearts

⚠ **lover's** is dropped if it is a quarrel between two people who are not romantically involved

🄖 generally used with **a** or **another**

"Don't take it so seriously. It was just a **lover's spat**. You two will be back to normal soon."

"You guys had another **lover's spat**? It must be that time of the month again."

> See: FALLING-OUT

lowdown [loʊdoʊn] non-count noun ***
information, gossip

🄖 always preceded by **the**

"So give me the **lowdown** on this new guy you're seeing!"

> See: DIRT, SCOOP, SKINNY

lowlife [loʊlaɪf] count noun **** a degenerate, unsophisticated, or unsuccessful person

⚠ rude, very insulting; not used to someone's face

"I'm concerned about Marta. She spends a lot of time with those **lowlifes** from her old high school."

> See: LOSER

luck out [lʌk aʊt] 2 word insep verb, I *** to have good fortune

"Nanami really **lucked out**! He's got a date with that hot Italian chick from the other class!"

lucky dog [lʌki dɑːg] count noun phrase *** a lucky person

"Alex got an 'A' on the last calculus test so he doesn't have to take the final. He sure is a **lucky dog**!"

M

madhouse [mædhaʊs] *count noun* ***** *a chaotically busy and uproarious place (literally a hospital for the insane)*

"Our home turns into a **madhouse** every summer when the family visits."

See: ZOO

main man [meɪn mæn] *count noun phrase* *** *one's most important male friend*

⚠ *may refer to a male acquaintance in a romantic, platonic, or business relationship*

🔟 *generally used in the singular form*

"I want you to meet Bill, my **main man**. He landed the big computer contract."

"Honey, those other guys don't mean a thing. You'll always be my **main man**."

See: MAIN SQUEEZE

main squeeze [meɪn skwiːz] *count noun phrase* *** *one's most important romantic interest*

"Sure, my boyfriend flirts a bit, but I know I'm his **main squeeze**."

make a killing [meɪk ə kɪlɪŋ] *verb phrase* *** *to make a large profit quickly*

⚠ *used for business deals, not when talking about someone's salary*

"Ata **made a killing** in the stock market last year. Now he's rolling in dough!"

make a mountain out of a molehill [meɪk ə maʊntɪn aʊt əv ə moʊlhɪl] *verb phrase* ** *to exaggerate minor difficulties or obstacles*

"'I just heard from Frank that we won't make our deadline because of several serious problems.' 'He's **making a mountain out of a molehill**. The problems are minor and they'll be corrected in plenty of time to meet the release date.'"

See: BLOW THINGS OUT OF PROPORTION

make a move [meɪk ə muːv] *verb phrase* **** *to make a sexual advance*

"Can you believe her husband tried to **make a move** on her best friend?"

See: COME ON TO

make a stink [meɪk ə stɪŋk] *verb phrase* ** *to complain loudly*

🔟 *if the object is stated it is preceded by **about** or **over***

"Excuse me, waiter, I don't want to **make a stink** about this but there's a fly in my soup!"

make ends meet [meɪk endz miːt] *verb phrase* *** *to have enough money to meet one's needs*

"Chris needs to find a part-time job 'cause he can barely **make ends meet** as a freelance writer."

make headway [meɪk hedweɪ] *verb phrase* *** *to make progress*

"Asuka is really **making headway** in her English classes."

make it snappy [meɪk ɪt snæpi] *exp* *** "hurry up!" or "be quick"

"Come on, **make it snappy**! We've got to be there in half an hour!"

make out [meɪk aʊt]

1. *2 word sep verb* **** *to understand, be able to read or recognize*

"You have to speak up. We have a bad connection and I can't **make out** what you are saying."

"Can you **make** that sign **out** up ahead?"

See: FIGURE OUT

2. *2 word insep verb, I* ** *to manage or perform*

"How did you **make out** on the exam?"

3. *2 word insep verb, I* *** *to engage in passionate kissing or sexual foreplay*

"Frank and Melissa went behind the gym to **make out**."

🔟 *with each other often follows **make out***

"Frank and Melissa went behind the gym to **make out** with each other."

make up for [meɪk ʌp fɔːr] *3 word verb* ** *to compensate for*

"You'll have to do a special project to **make up for** your missing book report."

make up for lost time [meɪk ʌp fɔːr lɑːst taɪm] *verb phrase* *** *to compensate for wasted time or a missed opportunity*

"Amy and John are both home for summer vacation and they've been seeing each other every night. I guess they want to **make up for lost time**."

make up with [meɪk ʌp wɪθ] 3 word verb ***** to settle differences, stop quarreling

"Johnny, you can't go out and play until you **make up with** your sister!"

measly [miːzli] adj **** small or insignificant

"After busting my butt all last year, I only got a **measly** three percent raise!"

mess around [mes əraʊnd] 2 word insep verb, I **** to joke or play around with someone, to meddle or tamper with something

"Don't take Kelly seriously, she was just **messing around**."

🅟 if the object is stated it is preceded by **with**

"Don't **mess around** with the stereo!"

⚠ sometimes this term refers to sexual foreplay

"Why don't we do back to my place and **mess around**?"

See: GOOF AROUND, FOOL AROUND, SCREW AROUND

mess around on [mes əraʊnd ɑːn] 3 word verb **** to be unfaithful to one's boyfriend or girlfriend, husband or wife

"Carol left him after she found out he had been **messing around on** her for six months!"

See: PLAY AROUND ON, SCREW AROUND ON

messed up [mest ʌp] adj **** intoxicated with drugs or alcohol

"Dave's too **messed up** to drive. Who can give him a lift home?"

See: BOMBED, GONE, HAMMERED, LOADED, RIPPED, SLOSHED, TOASTED, TRASHED, WASTED

mess up [mes ʌp] 2 word sep verb ***** to damage, to confuse, to make a mistake

"Did you see Maureen this morning? That new hairdresser really **messed up** her hair."

See: BOTCH UP, GOOF UP

mess up on [mes ʌp ɑːn] 3 word verb ***** to make a mistake

"How could you have **messed up on** the test? It was a piece of cake!"

🅟 the object and **on** can be dropped

"I'm sorry, I really **messed up**."

See: SCREW UP ON

mess with [mes wɪθ]

1. 2 word inset verb, T ***** to joke good-naturedly with someone

"Oh, you didn't really win the lottery; you're just **messing with** me!"

See: TOY WITH

2. 2 word inset verb, T ***** to bother or annoy, to tamper with

"You **mess with** me and there'll be hell to pay!"

"My brother will get pissed off if he sees you **messing with** his stereo!"

See: FOOL WITH, SCREW WITH

mighty [maɪti] adv *** very, really

"That's a **mighty** big gift he bought her! I wonder what it is."

mooch [muːtʃ] verb, T/ count noun ** to live on the hospitality of others; one who begs or sponges

⚠ negative undertones

🅟 often used as **mooch something off of someone**

"Sam is such a **mooch**. When we go out, he's always **mooching** smokes off of me."

See: SPONGE

motor [moʊtɚ] verb, I ** to drive quickly, to travel fast

"We're going to have to **motor** to make it to the show on time."

See: BOOK, GET GOING, HIT THE ROAD, JET

mounds [maʊndz] count noun *** a large quantity

"I wish I could go out with you tonight, but I've got **mounds** of homework to do."

See: BUNCH, LOADS, PLENTY, TONS

mug [mʌg] count noun ** a person's face

"Have you seen Tara's new boyfriend? That guy has got one ugly **mug**."

munchies [mʌntʃiz] non-count noun *** snack foods

"Don't forget the **munchies** when you go shopping later!"

N

nail [neɪl]

1. verb, T **** to catch or trap someone

"She was trying to swipe something, but security **nailed** her."

2. verb, T **** to complete or perform perfectly or impressively

"We **nailed** the Jones contract today!"

"The Chargettes really **nailed** the Bengalis in last week's game!"

3. verb, T * to have sexual intercourse with a woman

⚠ very derogatory! Used only by guys with other guys

"You **nailed** Lisa? Man, how do get all those women?"

need something like one needs a hole in the head [niːd sʌmθɪŋ laɪk wʌn niːdz ə hoʊl ɪn ðe hed] verb phrase *** to have neither a need nor a desire for something

"I'm already putting in twelve-hour days. **I need more work like I need a hole in the head**."

nerd [nɜːrd] count noun *** a person who is unpopular or unfashionable

⚠ often refers to persons who are interested in science or computers

"Sure, William is a computer **nerd**, but he's also rolling in dough!"

See: DORK, GEEK

nightmare [naɪtmer] count noun ** an unpleasant or terrifying experience or situation

"The traffic in the city is always a **nightmare** during the Christmas season."

nincompoop [nɪnkʌmpuːp] count noun ** a stupid or foolish person

⚠ has childish and rude undertones unless used by friends in a joking manner

"That **nincompoop** at the repair shop forgot to reconnect my tail lights. I nearly got rear-ended on the way home!"

See: BEANBRAIN, BIRDBRAIN, DIMWIT, DOPE, DOOFUS, DUMMY, PEABRAIN

nitty-gritty [nɪti grɪti] non-count noun *** specific practical details

"We're going to have to pull an all-nighter and get down to the **nitty-gritty** of this case."

nix [nɪks] verb, T * to veto or reject

"His suggestion was pretty far-fetched, so we **nixed** it."

no biggy [noʊ bɪgi] exp **** "it's not a big problem"

"'I just called to tell you I'm going to be a little late.' '**No biggy**, I'm running a little late myself.'"

noggin [nɑːgɪn] count noun * person's head, brain

"You've got a good **noggin** on your shoulders, so use it!"

no hard feelings [noʊ hɑːrd fiːlɪŋz] count noun phrase **** no resentment or anger

⚠ this expression can be used either by one who is offering an apology, or by the injured party

"I hope there are **no hard feelings** about damaging your car."

"'I'm sorry I failed to notify you about the meeting.' 'I'm sure it was just an oversight; **no hard feelings**.'"

noodle [nuːdl] count noun * person's head, brain

"You'd better learn to use your **noodle** so you can figure out these problems by yourself."

no sweat [noʊ swet] exp ***** "there is no difficulty" or "no problem"

"'Can you help me with my homework?' 'Sure, **no sweat**!'"

nosy [noʊzi] adj **** annoyingly inquisitive

🔄 one of the few adjectives that may be used with the continuous form of **be**. **Being nosy** implies a temporary state, e.g. **Just tell me if I'm being nosy.**

"I'm not being **nosy**. I'm just concerned about you."

not be caught dead [nɑːt biː kɑːt ded] verb phrase *** detest, not have anything to do with

"I **wouldn't be caught dead** in a revealing dress like that!"

not by a long shot [nɑːt baɪ ə lɑːŋ ʃɑːt] exp ** "very unlikely" or "not remotely"

"'Do you think we'll win tonight's game?' '**Not by a long shot**!'"

See: FAT CHANCE, IN ONE'S DREAMS, NOT IN A MILLION YEARS

not in a million years [nɑːt ɪn ə mɪljən jɪrz] *exp*
**** *"never" or "no way"*

"'Hey Steve, we're going out for sushi. Want to come?'
'Not in a million years! I hate that stuff!'"

> See: IT'LL BE A COLD DAY IN HELL, NOT BY A LONG SHOT, WHEN
> HELL FREEZES OVER, WHEN PIGS FLY

now you're talking [naʊ juːr tɔːkɪŋ] *exp* *** *"now you are saying the right thing"*

*"You say I can double my money on this deal? **Now you're talking**!"*

nuh-uh [nʌ ʌ] *exp* **** *"I don't believe you!" , "no way!"*

⚠️ the **nuh** is stressed, **uh** said with a lower intonation

*"'Nick got busted for shoplifting!' **'Nuh-uh**!'"*

> See: GET OUT OF HERE, GET OUT OF TOWN, SHUT UP, YEAH RIGHT

nurse [nɜːrs] *verb, T* *** *to use or consume slowly*

⚠️ often used in reference to an alcoholic beverage

*"Jack is over at the end of the bar **nursing** a beer."*

nut [nʌt]

1. *count noun* **** *a crazy person, an eccentric*

⚠️ generally used lightheartedly

*"Don't go to that shrink, he's a **nut** himself!"*

> See: CRACKPOT, NUTCASE, WACKO

2. *count noun* *** *an enthusiast*

*"James is a real car **nut**."*

nutcase [nʌtkeɪs] *count noun* *** *a crazy or mentally unstable person*

⚠️ Americans sometimes call completely normal people crazy as a way to express surprise or disbelief at a person's behavior. Care should be used since the term can be used jokingly or seriously

*"Watch out for him. He's a **nutcase**!"*

*"You're going skydiving? What kind of **nutcase** are you?"*

> See: CRACKPOT, NUT, WACKO

nuts [nʌts] *adj* ***** *crazy or insane, eccentric*

🔄 Used with **be** or **go**; never followed by a noun

*"Don't tell Omar you scratched his car. He'll go **nuts**!"*

> See: BANANAS, BONKERS, CRACKPOT, CUCKOO, LOONY, NUTTY,
> OFF ONE'S ROCKER, OUT OF ONE'S MIND, WACKO, WACKY

nutty [nʌti] *adj* **** *crazy, foolish*

*"How did you come up with such a **nutty** scheme? We could never pull that off!"*

> See: CUCKOO, LOONY, WACKO, WACKY

O

off [ɑːf] *verb, I* ** *to leave, to depart*

*"Catch you later. I'm **off** to Hawaii for vacation!"*

off again, on again relationship [ɑːf əgen ɑːn əgen rɪleiʃənʃɪp] *count noun phrase* *** *uncertain or intermittent romantic relationship*

🔄 sometimes **again** is dropped

*"Connie has been in an **off and on relationship** for the past year, but I think she's ready to move on."*

off one's rocker [ɑːf wʌnz rɑːkɚ] *prep phrase* * *crazy, eccentric*

*"Katie's company finally offered her the promotion she's wanted for so long, and she turned them down. I think she's **off her rocker**."*

> See: BANANAS, BONKERS, CUCKOO, LOONY, NUTS, NUTTY, OUT
> OF ONE'S MIND, WACKO, WACKY

off the hook [ɑːf ðe hʊk] *prep phrase* **** *to be released from obligation or responsibility*

🔄 generally used in three patterns: **let someone off the hook**, **get someone off the hook**, or **be off the hook**

*"This is the third time she's been late this week! I'm not going to let her **off the hook** this time."*

*"His lawyer got him **off the hook** but everyone knows he was guilty."*

*"I'm **off the hook**! I don't have to take the makeup exam."*

oh brother [oʊ brʌðɚ] *exp* ** *expression of frustration or disbelief*

*"**Oh brother**! They're back together again? This must be the fifth time they've broken up!"*

> See: FOR CRYING OUT LOUD, FOR PETE'S SAKE

old bag [oʊld bæg] *count noun phrase* *** an unattractive elderly woman

⚠ *extremely rude and insulting; the term is sometimes used to refer to a nagging or angry old woman*

"'What took you so long?' 'This **old bag** at the cash register grilled me like I was a criminal for returning the sweater.'"

old lady [oʊld leɪdi] *count noun phrase* *** mother, girlfriend, or wife

⚠ *sometimes has derogatory undertones*

"My **old lady's** always bagging on me about one thing or another."

old man [oʊld mæn] *count noun phrase* *** father, boyfriend, or husband

⚠ *sometimes has derogatory undertones*

"Sherry went home to cook dinner for her **old man**."

Olds [oʊldz] *count noun* *** nickname for any model of automobile manufactured by the Oldsmobile Division of General Motors

"My grandfather still drives the **Olds** he bought in 1959."

on a roll [ɑːn ə roʊl] *prep phrase* **** continuously successful

"I'm **on a roll**! I've already hit triple sevens three times on this slot machine!"

on cloud nine [ɑːn klaʊd naɪn] *prep phrase* **** blissfully happy

"I wonder what's up with Shinichi. He's been **on cloud nine** for the past week!"

on edge [ɑːn edʒ] *prep phrase* *** anxious, irritable

"I've really been **on edge** lately. Look at my nails. I've bitten them down to the skin!"

See: ANTSY, EDGY

one doesn't look so hot [wʌn dʌzənt lʊk soʊ hɑːt] *exp* ** said of one who appears unhealthy, sick, or troubled

"Charlie got pretty hammered last night. **He didn't look so hot** this morning."

one in a million [wʌn ɪn ə mɪljən] *adj phrase* *** extraordinarily rare

"You would do that for me? Thanks Tomomi. You're **one in a million**!"

one's back is to the wall [wʌnz bæk ɪz tuː ðə wɔːl] *exp* ** said of one who has no options, no way to escape

"I'm sorry Eric, but **my back is to the wall**. If you don't get this project finished on time, I'm going to have to let you go."

"Looks like they have **our backs to the wall**. If we don't sign the agreement, they'll take us to court."

one's brain is fried [wʌnz breɪn ɪz fraɪd] *verb phrase* **** said of one who is mentally exhausted

"We've been studying for eight hours and I need a break. **My brain is fried**!"

one's eyes are bigger than one's stomach [wʌnz aɪz ɑːr bɪgɚ ðən wʌnz stʌmek] *exp* *** said of a person who has taken more than he can handle

"Look at all this wasted food on Jake's plate. **His eyes were bigger than his stomach**."

"Randy is not going to be able to meet all of his business contracts. I think **his eyes were bigger than his stomach**."

one's nerves are shot [wʌnz nɜːrvz ɑːr ʃɑːt] *verb phrase* *** said of one who is extremely agitated or worried

"**My nerves are** really **shot** because the hospital won't tell me about my brother's condition."

See: FRAZZLED

on one's case [ɑːn wʌnz keɪs] *prep phrase* *** to be critical of, to nag

"Mayumi's dad was always **on her case** about her grades."

on one's toes [ɑːn wʌnz touz] *prep phrase* *** alert, prepared

"The agency could come in for a surprise inspection, so you need to be **on your toes** at all times."

See: ON THE BALL

on someone
See: BE ON

on the ball [ɑːn ðə bɔːl] *prep phrase* *** to be efficient, particularly capable, or alert

"Take your car to Art's shop. The mechanics down there are really **on the ball**."

See: ON ONE'S TOES

on the blink [ɑːn ðe blɪŋk] *prep phrase* ** inoperative, out of order

⚠ often used in reference to electrical appliances or equipment

"Honey, I think it's time we buy a new TV. Ours is **on the blink** again."

See: BUSTED, SHOT

on the dot [ɑːn ðe dɑːt] *prep phrase* **** exactly, precisely

🔵 used when speaking about the time

"Be here at eight AM **on the dot**!"

See: SHARP

on the line [ɑːn ðe laɪn] *prep phrase* **** at risk, at stake

⚠ often used in business situations

"The boss told Marco that his job is **on the line**. If he doesn't land that new account, he's going to get canned."

on the rocks [ɑːn ðe rɑːks]

1. *prep phrase* *** spoiled or ruined

⚠ often used to describe personal relationships that are failing

"It's no surprise that they broke up. Their relationship has been **on the rocks** for the past two months."

2. *adj phrase* *** a drink served over ice

"Scotch **on the rocks** please."

on the up-and-up [ɑːn ðe ʌp ænd ʌp] *adj phrase* *** genuine, frank, honest

"I wonder if this free software offer is **on the up-and-up**?"

🔵 if an object is needed it is preceded by **with**

"Get out of here! You used to be a woman? Are you being **on the up-and-up** with me?"

out of hand [aʊt əv hænd] *prep phrase* ** out of control, chaotic

"The meeting got **out of hand** when Tom's boss called him a liar."

out of it [aʊt əv ɪt] *prep phrase* **** dazed or bewildered, sometimes from alcohol or drug intoxication

"What's the deal with Nancy? She was really **out of it** in class today. She must have something on her mind."

See: OUT TO LUNCH, SPACY

out of line [aʊt əv laɪn] *prep phrase* *** inappropriate, wrong

"Michael was **out of line** when he blamed you for the low turnout at the reception. It's actually his fault because he didn't get the invitations out in time."

out of one's league [aʊt əv wʌnz liːg] *prep phrase* *** to be in a superior class or category

"You want to date Cindy? Fat chance dude! She's way **out of your league**!"

out of one's mind [aʊt əv wʌnz maɪnd] *prep phrase* **** crazy, foolish

⚠ sometimes used to register disbelief at someone's behavior

"You want to drive home after you've been drinking all night? Are you **out of your mind**?"

See: BANANAS, BONKERS, CUCKOO, LOONY, NUTS, NUTTY, OFF ONE'S ROCKER, WACKO, WACKY

out of the blue [aʊt əv ðe bluː] *prep phrase* *** without warning, suddenly

"We were driving down the road when **out of the blue**, a cat ran out into the street. I had to slam on the brakes to avoid it. We're lucky there was no one behind us!"

See: BOOM

out of the picture [aʊt əv ðe pɪktʃɚ] *prep phrase* **** to be uninformed or ignorant, to be uninvolved

"The local cops always seemed to be **out of the picture** when it comes to illegal guns."

⚠ can be used to refer to any type of relationship that has ended. Sometimes changed to **out of the story**

"Her husband has been out **of the story** for a long time."

See: HISTORY

out of the question [aʊt əv ðe kwestʃən] prep phrase ***** impossible, not worth considering

"'Hey Mom, can I go to that party at Linda's tonight?' 'Sorry, it's **out of the question**. Tonight's a school night.'"

out of this world [aʊt əv ðis wɜːrld] prep phrase **** exceptional, marvelous

"You made this delicious cake? It's **out of this world**!"

"That movie was **out of this world**!"

out of whack [aʊt əv hwæk] prep phrase *** broken, improperly adjusted

⚠ rude when used to refer to people; more commonly used for appliances or machines that are not in proper order

"Martha is always making the same mistake over and over. Her brain must be **out of whack**."

"Let's watch the game at your place. My TV is a little **out of whack** and the picture isn't very clear."

out to lunch [aʊt tu: lʌntʃ] prep phrase *** inattentive, unaware

"My secretary has been **out to lunch** lately. This is the third time she's mixed up my plane reservations."

⚠ always used to describe people

See: OUT OF IT, SPACEY

P

packed [pækt] adj ***** crowded

"This place has great food at reasonable prices. That's why it's always **packed**!"

pad [pæd] count noun ** apartment, living quarters

⚠ slightly dated

"Let's go kick it at my **pad**."

See: PLACE

pain [peɪn] count noun ***** an annoyance or difficulty

⚠ shortened form of a **pain in the neck** or a **pain in the butt**. Slightly rude when used in reference to a person who is annoying or difficult

🌐 generally used in the singular form preceded by **a**

"I hate taking the bus to school. It's such a **pain**!"

"You're really getting on my nerves with your complaining! Stop being such a **pain**!"

pal [pæl]

1. count noun **** a close friend

"There's nothing going on between Hee Young and Tae Young. They're just **pals**."

See: BUDDY, CHUM

2. exp *** a male term of address for a male stranger

"Hey **pal**, could you give me a hand with these bags?"

⚠ occasionally has rude undertones

"Hey **pal**, why don't 'cha watch where yer goin'?"

See: BUDDY, DUDE

party pooper [pɑːrti puːpɚ] count noun phrase ** one who ruins the fun of others

"Come on, we're all going to down to Mexico this weekend. Don't be such a **party pooper**!"

See: STICK-IN-THE-MUD

pass [pæs] verb, I ***** to decline an offer

⚠ used in informal situations

"'Care for another beer?' 'Thanks, but I'll **pass**. Two beers is my limit.'"

🌐 if an object is stated it is preceded by **on**

"It's kind of late so I think I'll **pass** on coffee."

pass out [pæs aʊt] 2 word insep verb, I *** to faint, to lose consciousness

⚠ used commonly in a figurative manner to demonstrate one's shock or surprise

"Anna almost **passed out** when she heard the news."

patch up [pætʃ ʌp] 2 word sep verb *** to repair, to set right

🌐 the object is usually things or **it**

"Sure, we had an argument, but we **patched** things **up**."

pay through the nose [peɪ θruː ðe noʊz] verb phrase ** to pay an excessive amount of money

"You still haven't fixed the brakes on your car? You're going to have to **pay through the nose** now!"

See: FORK

peabrain [piːbreɪn] count noun ** a stupid or foolish person (literally, one's brain is the size of a pea)

⚠ can be rude, but is commonly used in jest

"Don't be such a **peabrain**! Of course I was messing with you when I said you can't come with us!"

See: BEANBRAIN, BIRDBRAIN, DIMWIT, DOPE, DOOFUS, DUMMY, NINCOMPOOP

peanuts [piːnʌts] non-count noun ** a small or insignificant amount of money

"They're paying me **peanuts** at this job, but at least I got my foot in the door."

peg for [peg fɔːr] 2 word verb, T ** to classify or place in a category

"Lars is pretty embarrassed because he had Julie **pegged for** a bimbo. Turns out she has a PhD in engineering."

pen [pen] count noun ** penitentiary, prison

⚠ slightly dated, often heard in movies

🅖 preceded by **the** when used in the singular form

"Craig has been in and out of the **pen** for most of his adult life."

See: BIG HOUSE, CAN, JOINT, SLAMMER

pick-me-up [pɪk miː ʌp] count noun *** something that refreshes or stimulates

"Man, my brain is fried! I could use a little **pick-me-up**. Why don't we go outside and get some fresh air?"

pick on [pɪk ɑːn] 2 word insep verb, T *** to single out for criticism, bullying, or teasing

🅖 the term is used mainly in the active voice; the object is always a person or an animal

"Benny, stop **picking on** your brother and give him back the remote control!"

See: BUG

pick up [pɪk ʌp] verb, T *** to make a casual acquaintance, particularly in anticipation of sex

"Jeff cruises the bars hoping to **pick up** chicks."

pick up line [pɪk ʌp laɪn] count noun phrase **** persuasive words used to attract a potential lover

⚠ usually spoken by guys to women; sometimes just referred to as **a line**

"'What did that guy say to you?' 'He used some lame **pick up line** like "You've got the most beautiful eyes I've ever seen" I mean, come on! Do I look like I was born yesterday?'"

picture [pɪktʃɚ] verb, T ***** to imagine, to form a mental image

"**Picture** this: you, me, the beach, a couple of cold beers? What do you say?"

piece of cake [piːs əv keɪk] count noun phrase ***** something easily accomplished

🅖 sometimes the word **of** is dropped and replaced with **a**, or just the term **cake** is used

"'How was the test?' '**Piece a cake**!'"

"The test was **cake**!"

See: BREEZE, SNAP

pig out [pɪg aʊt] 2 word insep verb, I **** to eat hungrily

⚠ used mainly by girls with other girls

🅖 if the object (always a food item) is stated, it is preceded by **on**

"I'm going to get fat if I don't stop **pigging** out on ice cream."

See: POLISH OFF, PUT AWAY, STUFF ONE'S FACE, WOLF DOWN

pipe down [paɪp daʊn] exp ** "be quiet"

⚠ slightly rude; said out of annoyance, frustration or anger

"**Pipe down**! You guys are too loud!"

See: KEEP IT DOWN

piss off [pɪs ɑːf]
1. 2 word sep verb ***** to make angry

⚠ somewhat coarse, inappropriate in polite company

"Could you stop talking about that? You're really starting to **piss** me **off**!"

🅖 used frequently in the passive voice, **off** is sometimes dropped

"The teacher is really **pissed (off)** at the students because all of them blew the exam."

See: SORE

2. exp ** "stop bothering me!" or "leave me alone!"

⚠ very rude! On the same level as "**Go to hell!**"

"You're really getting on my nerves! **Piss off**!"

place [pleɪs] count noun ***** an apartment or living quarters

"Why don't you come by my **place** this afternoon?"

See: PAD

plastic [plæstɪk] non-count noun *** any credit card

"I don't have any cash on me. What kind of **plastic** do you guys take?"

play around on [pleɪ ə raʊnd ɑːn] 3 word verb *** to cheat on a boyfriend, girlfriend, husband, or wife

🔄 the object is always a person

"Rick left his wife after he found out she was **playing around** on him."

See: MESS AROUND ON, SCREW AROUND ON

play hardball [pleɪ hɑːrdbɔːl] verb phrase **** to act aggressively and ruthlessly

⚠ often used in business dealings

"The other side wanted a lot of concessions, but we **played hardball** and got a deal that was good for us."

See: PLAY HARD TO GET

play hard to get [pleɪ hɑːrd tuː get] verb phrase *** to act coyly, to pretend to be uninterested

⚠ can apply to personal or business relationships

"Don't go out with him at the drop of a hat or he'll think you're desperate. **Play** a little **hard to get**!"

"I think we'll improve our negotiating position on this contract if we **play hard to get**."

See: PLAY HARDBALL

play it by ear [pleɪ ɪt baɪ ɪr] verb phrase **** to improvise, to proceed gradually, to make plans as time progresses

"'So what are our plans for the weekend?' 'Nothing in particular. I may have to work, so why don't we just **play it by ear**.'"

See: WING

play it cool [pleɪ ɪt kuːl] verb phrase ***** to act cautiously, to remain calm and collected

"I think Mary may suspect that we are throwing her a surprise party, so if you happen to run into her just **play it cool**, OK?"

See: BE COOL

play one's cards right [pleɪ wʌnz kɑːrdz raɪt] verb phrase ** to make good use of one's resources, to have a good strategy

🔄 often used with **if**

"If I had **played my cards right**, I would be sitting in the bosses' chair right now!"

play with [pleɪ wɪθ] 2 word insep verb ***** to joke or kid with someone

🔄 usually used in the continuous tense

"Hey, don't get all bent out of shape, I am/was/have been **playing with** you. I didn't really break your favorite vase."

See: MESS WITH, SCREW WITH, TOY WITH

plenty [plenti] non-count noun ***** a large amount, more than adequate

"There's no rush, we've got **plenty** of time."

See: BUNCH, LOADS, MOUNDS, TON

PMS [piː em es] non-count noun/verb, I ***** abbreviation for premenstrual syndrome

⚠ term for the condition characterized by bloating, fatigue, depression, and irritability experienced by many women before a menstrual cycle. While women in the US are more open about discussing their monthly cycle or period, this term should be used with care, particularly by men

🔄 used in the continuous tenses as a verb. When used as a noun, proceed with have

"She's got a bad case of **PMS**. If I were you, I'd stay away from her!"

"She always loses it when she is **PMSing**."

See: THAT TIME OF THE MONTH

polish off [pɑːlɪʃ ɑːf] 2 word sep verb *** to dispose of or finish quickly and easily

"That guy **polished off** an entire blueberry pie by himself!"

See: PIG OUT, PUT AWAY, STUFF ONE'S FACE, WOLF DOWN

pooped [puːpt] adj *** exhausted, very tired

"I'm so **pooped**, I can't take another step. Let's stop and sit for a while."

See: BEAT, DEAD, WIPED OUT, WORN OUT

pop [pɑːp] verb, I *** to occur suddenly or unexpectedly

"He **popped** in to see how I was doing."

"As I show you these drawings, tell me whatever **pops** into your mind."

pop the question [pɑːp ðe kwestʃən] verb phrase *** to propose marriage

🌐 used in the active voice

"I remember when my husband **popped the question**! He was so nervous he could barely speak!"

potbelly [pɑːt beli] count noun **** an enlarged or protruding abdomen

"Susan had better start watching what she eats. She's starting to get a **potbelly**!"

> See: BEER BELLY, GUT

pour one's heart out [pɔːr wʌnz hɑːrt aʊt] verb phrase *** to express one's innermost thoughts and feelings to another

"Ellen really **poured her heart out**. I didn't realize she felt so strongly."

🌐 a person often **pours his heart out to someone**

"Jake **poured his heart out to me** last night. He sounds serious about going to art school."

pretty penny [prɪti peni] count noun phrase *** a lot of money

"Bill bought a Beemer? It must've cost him a **pretty penny**!"

> See: AN ARM AND A LEG, BUNDLE

pricey [praɪsi] adj *** expensive

"Wow, these restaurants are **pricey**. How about going someplace cheaper?"

> See: STEEP

psyche out [saɪk aʊt] 2 word sep verb *** to undermine the confidence of or intimidate a competitor

"'Look at the sized of their football players! We're going to get our butts kicked!' 'They're just trying to **psyche** you **out**. Those guys aren't even on the team!'"

> See: HAVE SOMEONE GOING

psyche up [saɪk ʌp] 2 word insep verb, I **** to become excited or enthusiastic

⚠️ generally used by younger generations

🌐 often used in adjective form. If a reason for excitement is stated, it is preceded by **about** or **for**

"Cathy is really **psyched up**."

"Cathy is really **psyched up** about the party."

"Nathan is **psyched up** for the 10K this afternoon."

> See: CHARGE UP

puke [pjuːk] verb, T ** to vomit

⚠️ somewhat crude, used by the younger generations

🌐 the object is frequently dropped

"Rafael drank one too many shots of tequila. He's in the bathroom **puking** his guts out."

> See: BARF, LOSE ONE'S LUNCH, TOSS ONE'S COOKIES

pull [pʊl] verb, T ***** to attempt

🌐 often used with the verb **try**

"I don't know what you're trying to **pull**, but you're not going to get away with it!"

pull a fast one [pʊl ə fæst wʌn] verb phrase *** to engage in deceitful practice or play an unfair trick

🌐 if the object is stated, it is preceded by **on**

"Hold on a second, I gave you a hundred and you only gave me change for a twenty! Are you trying to **pull a fast one** (on me)?"

> See: PULL SOMEONE'S LEG, PUT ON

pull a few strings [pʊl ə fjuː strɪŋz] verb phrase *** to use one's influence

"You want a job as a journalist? My dad's in the newspaper business so maybe he can **pull a few strings** for you."

pull an all-nighter [pʊl æn ɔːl naɪtɚ] verb phrase *** to stay up the entire night and study or work

"There's so much material on tomorrow's exam! Looks like I'm going to be **pulling an all-nighter**."

pull off [pʊl ɑːf] 2 word sep verb **** to succeed at doing something difficult

"I know it'll be tough, but if we work hard, we can **pull off** this deal."

pull one's self together [pʊl wʌnz self təgeðɚ] verb phrase **** to regain one's composure or self-control

"I know you're still upset about being fired, but you need to **pull yourself together** and go find another job."

"It's been over three months since he walked out on you and you're still falling apart! You need to **pull yourself together.**"

See: GET A GRIP, SNAP OUT OF IT

pull one's weight [pʊl wʌnz weɪt] *verb phrase* *** to do one's proper share of the work

"John, if you don't start **pulling your weight** around here, I'm going to can you."

pull over [pʊl oʊvɚ] *2 word sep verb/ insep verb, I* **** to drive one's car to the side of the road and slow down or stop

"I just heard the police over the loud speaker telling me to **pull over.** I never even saw them flashing their lights behind me."

pull someone's leg [pʊl sʌmwʌnz leg] *verb phrase* ** to deceive or fool someone

"Mark was just **pulling your leg.** He never served in the Navy."

See: PULL A FAST ONE, PUT ON

pull up to [pʊl ʌp tuː] *3 word verb* **** to drive one's car to a certain point and stop

"Please **pull up to** the window, sir."

"I was waiting for my ride when this hot chick **pulled up** and asked for directions."

pump someone for information [pʌmp sʌmwʌn fɔːr ɪnfɚmeɪʃən] *verb phrase* *** to persistently question someone for news, data, or facts

"Mark, I wish you would stop trying to **pump me for information.** You know I can't tell you about the project."

punch the clock [pʌntʃ ðe klɑːk] *verb phrase* ** to work at a job that pays hourly wages; to start working or go to work

"I'm off. Time for me to **punch the clock.**"

See: BRING HOME THE BACON

puny [pjuːni] *adj* ** small in size or importance

"You're pulling my leg! That **puny** guy whipped your butt?"

put a dent in one's wallet [pʌt ə dent ɪn wʌnz wɑːlɪt] *verb phrase* ** to cost a lot of money

"I'll bet that new Benz really **put a dent in his wallet.**"

put away [pʌt əweɪ] *2 word sep verb* *** to eat a lot

"Miki's as thin as a rail but she can really **put** it **away!**"

See: PIG OUT, POLISH OFF, STUFF ONE'S FACE, WOLF DOWN

put back [pʌt bæk] *2 word sep verb* *** to drink a beverage, usually alcoholic

"What do you say we stop in Jorge's and **put back** a few cold ones before heading home?"

See: DOWN, GUZZLE

put it that way [pʌt ɪt ðæt weɪ]

1. *verb phrase* ***** to express one's position in a convincing or threatening way

"'If you don't cooperate, I'll have you arrested.' 'Well, when you **put it that way,** I guess I'd better cooperate.'"

2. *verb phrase* ** to express one's position in an annoying or irritation fashion

"I realize he's correct, it's just the **way he put it** that got under my skin."

put on [pʌt ɑːn] *2 word sep verb* *** to deceive or mislead, often for amusement

ⓖⓟ the object is always a person

"Meg and Tom are seeing each other? You're **putting** me **on!**"

See: PULL SOMEONE'S LEG, PULL A FAST ONE

put-on [pʌt ɑːn] *count noun* *** a spoof

"It turns out that the newspaper article Tom was so upset about was just a **put-on.**"

put one's cards on the table [pʌt wʌnz kɑːrdz ɑːn ðe teɪbl] *verb phrase* *** to be candid about one's position or situation

ⓖⓟ often used with **let's**

"**Let's put our cards on the table** here. None of us has the resources to do the job alone, so we'll have to put aside our differences and join forces to be successful."

put one's face on [pʌt wʌnz feɪs ɑːn] *verb phrase* ** to apply one's make-up

⚠ usually used in reference to females

"I can't answer the door, I haven't **put my face on yet!**"

See: HAVE ONE'S FACE ON

put one's finger on something [pʌt wʌnz fɪŋgɚ ɑːn sʌmθɪŋ] verb phrase *** to identify the cause or source of a problem

"I can't quite **put my finger on what's wrong** with your CD player. I think you'd better take it in to the shop."

put one's foot down [pʌt wʌnz fʊt daʊn] verb phrase *** to take a firm stand or establish a definite position

"Your boss is walking all over you when she asks you to work overtime every night. You've got to **put your foot down** and not let her take advantage of you."

put one's foot in one's mouth [pʌt wʌnz fʊt ɪn wʌnz maʊθ] verb phrase *** to inadvertently say something tactless or embarrassing

🔊 **put** may be replaced by **stick** with no change in meaning

"When Tom said he was no longer dating that girl, I interrupted him and said it was a good thing 'cause she was always cheating on him anyway. Then he finished his sentence and said that she was now his wife! Boy, did I **put my foot in my mouth!**"

put one's nose where it doesn't belong [pʌt wʌnz noʊz wer ɪt dʌzənt bɪlɑːŋ] verb phrase *** to interfere in another person's affairs, or to offer unsolicited advice

"I wish Sally would stop **putting her nose where it doesn't belong.**"

🔊 **put** is sometimes replace with **stick**

"I don't want to **stick my nose where it doesn't belong**, but shouldn't you be a little suspicious about Bob working late every night?"

put up [pʌt ʌp] 2 word sep verb *** to accommodate visitors at one's house; or to pay for someone's accommodations

"I've got a big house so I can **put** your sister **up** for a few days when she comes to town."

"My company **put** me **up** in this beautiful five-star hotel when I went to Hawaii on business."

put up to [pʌt ʌp tuː] 3 word verb *** to incite or instigate; encourage one to do something

"Gary, it's not like you to do something so mean and thoughtless! Who **put you up** to this? Was it that low-life friend of yours?"

put up with [pʌt ʌp wɪθ] 3 word verb ***** to tolerate, bear

"'I won't **put up with** your smoking in this house! Either you call it quits or you'll have to move out!"
See: TAKE

put your money where your mouth is [pʌt jʊr mʌni hwer jʊr maʊθ ɪz] exp *** "back up your position by risking your money"

"So, you think England is going to beat Germany in tonight's soccer match? OK, **put your money where your mouth is.**"

R

rack one's brain [ræk wʌnz breɪn] verb phrase ** to exert great effort to remember or to find a solution

"I really had to **rack my brain** during the calculus test this morning."

rad [ræd] adj ** awesome, great, cool (shortened form of radical)

⚠ dated, but making a comeback

"Dude, your new hair style is totally **rad!**"

rake in the dough [reɪk ɪn ðe doʊ] verb phrase **** to make a lot of money, to be well paid

🔊 generally used in the continuous tenses; sometimes **the dough** is replaced by **it**

"She's **raking in the dough!**"

"She opened up her own software company. I hear she's **raking it in!**"

ramble on [ræmbl ɑːn] 2 word insep verb ** to talk incessantly or tiresomely

"What an awful evening. My date **rambled on** all night about his boring job."

raring to go [rerɪŋ tu: goʊ] adj phrase ** eager to begin

"Let's get the show on the road! I'm **raring to go!**"

read [riːd] verb, T/count noun ***** to understand or interpret one's thoughts or intentions

"Your boyfriend always has such a blank expression. How can you **read** him?"

"She's never said much about her feelings. I just can't get a **read** on her."

read into [riːd ɪntuː] 2 word sep verb, T **** to find an unintended meaning in something someone has said or done

"You're **reading** too much **into** Marcos' comments. He doesn't have a very good command of English yet."

read the riot act [riːd ðe raɪət ækt] verb phrase ** to angrily criticize or complain

"Damn, I was only ten minutes late, but she really **read** me **the riot act!**"

See: CHEW OUT

ride [raɪd] count noun *** a means of transportation such as a car, cab, train, etc.

⚠ often refers to the person providing the transportation

"I'd like to stay and party, but Kim's leaving and she's my **ride**."

ride shotgun [raɪd ʃɔtgʌn] verb phrase ** to ride in the front passenger seat of a vehicle

"I'll drive. You **ride shotgun** and be the navigator."

ring [rɪŋ] count noun **** a telephone call

🔘 generally used in the singular form with **a**

"I'll give you a **ring** later on tonight."

ring a bell [rɪŋ ə bel] verb phrase **** to sound familiar, to remind one of something

🔘 the subject is always a thing

"His name **rings a bell**, but I don't remember meeting him."

riot [raɪət] count noun ** a good time, a person who is very entertaining or funny

🔘 always used in the singular form preceded by **a**

"You should've come to the party. It was a **riot!**"

"Did you catch that new comic down at the club? He's a **riot!**"

See: BALL, BLAST, HOOT, SCREAM

rip off [rɪp ɑːf] 2 word sep verb **** to steal, to swindle

🔘 used in the passive and active voices

"Hey, that's my bike! That's the one that was **ripped** off last week. That guy **ripped off** my bike!"

"You paid five grand for that old heap? Dude, you got **ripped off** big-time!"

See: SWIPE

rip-off [rɪp ɑːf] count noun **** a swindle, an act of stealing

"Those credit card protection schemes are nothing but a **rip-off**."

See: SCAM

ripped [rɪpt] adj ** drunk

"We went out last night to celebrate Melissa's birthday and got **ripped**."

See: BOMBED, GONE, HAMMERED, LOADED, MESSED UP, SLOSHED, TOASTED, TRASHED, WASTED

rock [rɑːk]

1. count noun *** a large gemstone, usually a diamond

"Did you see the size of that **rock** on her finger?"

2. verb, I *** to be good, cool

"Have you heard that new tune by the Wallflowers? It **rocks!**"

See: BE ALL THE RAGE

rock bottom [rɑːk bɑːtəm] adj **** the very lowest

⚠ often used to describe a price

"If you need car insurance why don't you call AA Insurance. They advertise that they've got **rock bottom** prices, even for lousy drivers."

rolling in dough [roʊlɪŋ ɪn doʊ] adj phrase **** wealthy, very rich

🔘 always used with the verb **be**. The word **dough** is sometimes replaced with **it**

"She got a Porsche for her sixteenth birthday? Her parents must be **rolling in dough/it!**"

roomie [ruː mi] count noun * a roommate, a person who shares a room, house, or apartment

"My old roommate Michiko moved out, so I need to find a new **roomie** ASAP."

rubber check [rʌbɚ tʃek] count noun phrase ** a check returned to the maker for insufficient funds

⚠ also referred to as a bounced check

"He's broke! He's been writing **rubber checks** all over town."

rub one the wrong way [rʌb wʌn ðe rɑːŋ weɪ]
verb phrase *** to irritate or annoy someone,
usually unintentionally

"I don't know what it is about Jim. He just **rubs me
the wrong way.**"

See: BUG, GET ON ONE'S NERVES

run [rʌn]

1. verb, T *** to cost

🔘 the object is usually a person, sometimes
followed by an amount of money

"I wonder how much these car repairs are going to
run me?"

"A house in this neighborhood will **run** you about half a
million."

2. verb, I ***** to travel somewhere quickly

🔘 always use **run to** with the exception of
downtown and **home**

"Could you **run** to the store and pick up some milk?"

"I'm just going to **run** home and change my clothes
before we go."

run a tab [rʌn ə tæb] verb phrase **** to keep a
record of expenses to be paid at the end of the
evening

⚠ often used in bars and restaurants

"We'll be drinking all night, so could you **run** us **a tab?**"

run by [rʌn baɪ]

1. 2 word sep verb **** to solicit one's advice or
opinion

⚠ common in business settings

🔘 always used as: **run something by someone**

"Hector, you'd better **run** these figures **by** the boss
before you send them out to the client."

2. 2 word insep verb, T *** to visit somewhere quickly,
sometimes unexpectedly

"I'll **run by** the store on my way home from work."

See: DROP BY, SHOOT BY, SWING BY

run into [rʌn ɪntuː] 2 word insep verb, T ***** to
meet by chance

"I **ran into** Mikki while I was at the supermarket
today."

See: BUMP INTO

run-of-the-mill [rʌn əv ðe mɪl] adj **** average,
ordinary

"'What happened while I was on vacation?' 'Not much,
it was a pretty **run-of-the-mill** week.'"

run out of [rʌn aʊt əv] 3 word verb ***** to
exhaust one's supply of something

🔘 used in present continuous when something is
almost used up

"We are **running out of** tea. Would you get some when
you go to the store?"

🔘 used in the simple past when the supply is
exhausted

"We **ran out** of tea. Would you go to the store and
pick some up?"

See: BE OUT OF

RV [ɑːr viː] count noun *** abbreviation for
Recreational Vehicle

"The traffic heading out of town the Friday before
the holiday weekend was a steady stream of **RV's.**"

S

sack [sæk]

1. count noun *** one's bed

🔘 **sack** is always preceded by **the**

"OK kids, time to hit the **sack.**"

2. verb, T ** to fire someone from a job

🔘 frequently used in the passive voice

"Greta got **sacked** last week 'cause she was always
late."

See: CAN, GIVE SOMEONE THEIR PINK SLIP, GIVE SOMEONE THE
AX, LET SOMEONE GO

same old, same old [seim oʊld, seim oʊld] exp
** "the same old thing"; a boring routine

"'How's your job been lately?' 'Oh, **same old, same old.**'"

save one's skin [seɪv wʌnz skɪn] verb phrase ***
to rescue oneself or another person from harm

"Hey buddy, if you hadn't come along those guys
would've had me for lunch! Thanks for **saving my skin.**"

scam [skæm]

1. count noun *** a swindle, a fraudulent operation

"All of those fast weight-loss diets are **scams**."

2. verb, T *** to cheat, to swindle

"Don't listen to him. He's **scamming** you."

> *See:* RIP-OFF

scammer [skæmɚ] *count noun* ** a person who lies, cheats, or swindles

"He's such a **scammer** that he actually got those people to believe his story!"

scaredy-cat [skerdi kæt] *count noun* ** a person who is easily frightened

⚠ childish undertones

"Come on, you can jump off the high dive. Don't be such a **scaredy-cat**!"

> *See:* CHICKEN, WIMP

scare the living daylights out of someone
[sker ðe lɪvɪŋ deɪlaɪts aʊt əv sʌmwʌn]
verb phrase *** to frighten severely

⚠ somewhat dated

"Don't sneak up on me like that! You **scared the living daylights out of me**!"

schmuck [ʃmʌk] *count noun* ** a jerk, a despicable person

"That **schmuck** at the repair shop tried to charge me for an estimate even though their advertisement said it was free."

> *See:* CREEP, JERK

scoop [skuːp] *count noun* ***** current information, late breaking news, gossip

"How was your date? Give me the **scoop**!"

"Check it out, there's Megan and Tom! I'd heard they'd broke up. What's the **scoop**?"

> *See:* DIRT, LOWDOWN, SKINNY

score [skɔːr] *verb, T* ***** to accomplish a goal, to obtain a quantity of something, often drugs

"You got that deal with JBC corporation? You **scored** big-time!"

"David keeps bragging about how he **scored** some really good grass downtown."

scout out [skaʊt aʊt] *2 word sep verb* ** to evaluate, to explore or observe an area

"Why don't you **scout out** the park and see if there are any good campsites left."

scouts honor [skaʊts ɑːnɚ] *exp* ** "I promise" or "I swear"

⚠ refers to Boy Scouts or Girl Scouts who are taught the importance of honesty and integrity

"I'll be there at eight AM, **scouts honor**."

scram [skræm] *exp* *** "leave" or "disperse quickly"

⚠ often used when speaking to kids or animals; can be rude

ⓟ used mainly in the imperative

"Get out of the room, I'm trying to wrap your Christmas gifts. Now **scram**!"

> *See:* BEAT IT, TAKE A HIKE

scratch [skrætʃ]
1. verb, T *** to call off, cancel

"Look at this rain. I guess we'll have to **scratch** the picnic."

ⓟ sometimes used in the imperative form

"'Why don't we take Jake's set of wheels?' '**Scratch** that! His car's still in the shop!'"

2. non-count noun *** basic ingredients

"No, I didn't use a cake mix! I made this cake from **scratch**."

scrawny [skrɑːri] *adj* **** very small and thin, appearing powerless or unhealthy

"Get out of here! That giant cat is the same **scrawny** kitten you found a few months ago?"

scream [skriːm] *count noun* ** a good time, a person who is very entertaining or funny

ⓟ always preceded by **a**

"Have you seen that new Jim Tarey movie? It was a **scream**!"

"I met your mother last night. She's a **scream**."

> *See:* BALL, BLAST, HOOT, RIOT

screw [skruː] *verb, T* ** to have sexual intercourse

⚠ very rude and disrespectful

"He **screwed** Lonni? He'd better hope her boyfriend doesn't find out!"

> *See:* DO IT, JUMP SOMEONE'S BONES, NAIL

screw around [skru: əraʊnd] 2 word insep verb
**** to joke with, deceive, engage in horseplay

"The reason for your poor grades is that you constantly **screw around** in class."

See: FOOL AROUND, GOOF AROUND, MESS AROUND

screw around on [skru: əraʊnd ɑ:n] 3 word verb
**** to be promiscuous, cheat on one's significant other

Ⓟ if the object is not stated, **on** is dropped

"Hillary dumped Sebastian after she caught him **screwing around on** her."

See: FOOL AROUND, MESS AROUND ON, PLAY AROUND ON

screwed [skru:d] adj ***** in serious trouble or difficulty

"I forgot to deposit my paycheck last week and I wrote a ton of checks yesterday. I'm **screwed!**"

screw it [skru: ɪt] exp ***** "forget it"

⚠ **screw** is also a rude term for sexual intercourse

Ⓟ generally used in the imperative form

"You didn't tell them we were leaving? Well, it's too late now. **Screw it!**"

screw over [skru: wʌn oʊvɚ] 2 word sep verb **
to exploit or victimize someone

Ⓟ **over** may be dropped

"He **screwed over** his friend rather than keep his promise."

screw up on [skru: ʌp ɑ:n] 3 word verb ***** to make a mistake

"Paul **screwed up on** the test big-time. He thinks he might have failed."

Ⓟ the object is always a thing; **on** is dropped when the object is not stated

"He's really **screwing up** this semester."

screw with [skru: wɪθ]
1. 2 word insep verb, T ***** to joke with, to deceive

⚠ considered rude by many people

"You got the contract? You're not **screwing with** me, are you?"

See: FOOL WITH, MESS WITH

2. 2 word insep verb **** to bother or annoy

⚠ rude undertones

"I'm not in the mood so don't **screw with** me."

See: FOOL WITH, MESS WITH

3. 2 word insep verb **** to tamper or meddle with something

"Stop **screwing with** the TV. The repair person is coming to fix it soon."

See: FOOL WITH, MESS WITH

screwy [skru:i] adj **** strange or unusual

"Anita got an 'A' on the test? She never even opens up a book! There's something **screwy** going on here."

See: FISHY

sec [sek] count noun ***** a brief period (literally, one second of time)

Ⓟ always used in the singular preceded by **a**

"Hang on, I'll be with you in a **sec**."

see eye-to-eye [si: aɪ tu: aɪ] verb phrase **** to agree, to have similar views

"When I was a teenager I hardly ever **saw eye-to-eye** on anything with my parents."

see red [si: red] verb phrase *** to be furious, to be indignant

"Mitch **saw red** when his girlfriend agreed to dance with Jack."

see someone [si: sʌmwʌn] verb phrase ***** to be involved in a romantic relationship with someone

"Marie and Don have been **seeing each other** for about three months now."

See: GO OUT WITH

see something coming a mile away [si: sʌmθɪŋ kʌmɪŋ ə maɪl əweɪ] verb phrase *** to recognize that something is bound to occur

"Ed got canned, huh? Well, you could **see that coming a mile away**. He was always slacking off, late almost every day, and he gave the boss a lot of lip."

see straight through [si: streɪt θru:] verb phrase *** to recognize deception

"I **saw straight through** David's phony act."

Ⓟ sometimes preceded by **can**. **Straight** may be replaced with **right**

"When I was a kid I could never get away with lying. My folks could always **see right through** me."

set back [set bæk] 2 word sep verb ** to cost

🔵 the object is the person who paid

"Harry just bought a rock for Sally and it **set** him **back** five grand!"

"Nice Benz! How much did that **set** you **back**?"

set of wheels [set əv hwiːlz] count noun phrase *** an automobile

"Justine just bought herself a new **set of wheels**."

⚠ sometimes shortened to **wheels**

"I can't get a date 'cause I don't have any **wheels**!"

set someone straight [set sʌmwʌn streɪt] verb phrase *** to correct someone using accurate information

"Jack did not have the authority to assign that job to you. Looks like I need to **set him straight**."

⚠ can be rude when spoke directly to a person

"We have a chain of command around here, so I'm going to **set you straight**. The next time you go over my head, you'll be looking for a new job."

set up with [set ʌp wɪθ]

1. 3 word verb *** to introduce two people to each other for a specific purpose

🔵 always: **set someone up with someone**

"My doctor is great. I'll **set** you **up with** her if you like."

See: FIX UP WITH, HOOK UP WITH

2. 3 word verb *** to give away a prize, often heard on the radio

🔵 always: **set someone up with something**

"We'll **set** you **up with** front row tickets to tonight's Rolling Pebbles concert."

See: FIX UP WITH, HOOK UP WITH

shack up [ʃæk ʌp wɪθ] 2 word verb ** living with a boyfriend or girlfriend before marriage; to live with someone out of wedlock

⚠ often used when the speaker has negative feelings about the relationship

"Craig left his wife and now he's **shacking up** with some girl he met at a bar!"

shades [ʃeɪdz] non-count noun ***** sunglasses

🔵 always used in the plural form

"Check out my new **shades**! Pretty cool, huh?"

shady [ʃeɪdi] adj *** dishonest, disreputable

"I want you to stay away from those **shady** characters down by the pool hall."

shake [ʃeɪk] verb, T *** get rid of or get away from

"I've tried, but I just can't **shake** this feeling that something is going to go wrong."

See: GET RID OF

sharp [ʃɑːrp] adv ***** exactly

🔵 only used with time phrases and is always preceded by the time

"I'll be there at ten PM **sharp**."

See: ON THE DOT

shell out [ʃel aʊt] 2 word sep verb ** to pay, use money

"Hiroshi **shelled out** a ton of dough on his last vacation."

shoot [ʃuːt]

1. exp ***** "begin to speak"

🔵 always used in the imperative form

⚠ used more by males

"'Bart, can I talk with you?' '**Shoot**, what's on your mind?' It's about that dog of yours, Alpha Vox.'"

2. exp **** an expression of surprise, frustration, or anger

⚠ sometimes used as a euphemism for **shit**

"**Shoot**, I forgot to tell your father to pick up Lucy from school."

shoot by [ʃuːt baɪ] 2 word insep verb, T *** to visit somewhere quickly, sometimes unexpectedly

"Frankie got a new computer, so let's **shoot by** his place on the way home and check it out."

See: DROP BY, RUN BY, SWING BY

shoot the breeze [ʃuːt ðe briːz] verb phrase *** to talk or converse idly

"We were too beat to go to the party last night so we just stayed home and **shot the breeze**."

shot [ʃɑːt]

1. count noun ***** an attempt or try

"This computer is really screwed up. I don't know if I can fix it, but I'll give it a **shot**."

2. adj *** worn out, no longer usable

⚠ usually used to describe things

"I just got bad news from the mechanic. Our car needs a new engine; the old one's completely **shot**."

See: BUSTED

show up [ʃoʊ ʌp] 2 word insep verb, I ***** to arrive, to appear

🔵 if the object is stated it is preceded by **at** or **in**

"Michelle finally **showed up** at ten in some cheesy outfit."

shrink [ʃrɪŋk] count noun ***** clinical psychiatrist or psychologist

⚠ somewhat disrespectful term (It is common for Americans living in larger cities to visit a psychologist on a regular basis, although they have no serious problems)

"I can't have lunch with you today. I've got an appointment with my **shrink**."

shuteye [ʃʌtaɪ] non-count noun *** sleep

"I've got to go home and get some **shuteye**. I hardly slept a wink last night."

shut up [ʃʌt ʌp] exp ***** "you're kidding!" or "no way!"

⚠ used mainly by the younger generation

"I told her that Charlie popped the question and she was all like '**Shut up**, get out of here! It's about time!'"

See: GET OUT OF HERE, GET OUT OF TOWN, NUH-UH

significant other [sɪɡnɪfɪkənt ʌðɚ] count noun phrase *** one's spouse or girlfriend/boyfriend

"You're invited to my party Friday night, and bring your **significant other**."

since I don't know when [sɪnts aɪ doʊnt noʊ wen] exp ** "for longer than I can remember"

"We haven't had a thunderstorm like this **since I don't know when**!"

sink one's teeth into something [sɪŋk wʌnz ti:θ ɪntu: sʌmθɪŋ] verb phrase *** to become fully involved

"Here's a book you can really **sink your teeth into**. It's about the hot new scene in Hollywood."

six-pack [sɪks pæk] count noun *** a very well-defined muscular stomach

"Dude, you must be working out hard! You're starting to get a **six-pack**!"

skinny [skɪni] non-count noun ***** current information, late breaking news

"What's the **skinny** on the Bonnie and Clyde situation?"

See: DIRT, LOWDOWN, SCOOP

slack off [slæk ɑ:f] 2 word insep verb, I *** to decrease in activity or intensity

"I've been **slacking off** for the past month and I'm starting to get a gut! I've really got to go to the gym!"

slammer [slæmɚ] count noun * jail, prison

⚠ sometimes heard in movies

🔵 always used in the singular form preceded by **the**

"Jeremy got busted trying to score some weed downtown, and they threw him in the **slammer**."

See: BIG HOUSE, CAN, JOINT, PEN

sleep with [sli:p wɪθ] 2 word insep verb, T *** euphemistic for sexual intercourse with someone

🔵 object is (hopefully) always a person

"Can you believe he **slept with** Monica?"

See: DO IT, JUMP ONE'S BONES

slip one's mind [slɪp wʌnz maɪnd] verb phrase ***** to forget, to overlook

"Bill was supposed to hook up with Jackie last night but it totally **slipped his mind** and Jackie is really pissed!"

See: SPACE OUT ON

sloshed [slɑ:ʃt] adj * drunk, inebriated

"They got **sloshed** at the New Years party."

See: BOMBED, GONE, HAMMERED, LOADED, MESSED UP, RIPPED, TOASTED, TRASHED, WASTED

smackaroo [smækəru:] count noun * one US dollar

⚠ dated, used in jest

"Five **smackaroos** for one ice cream? Man, this place is expensive."

See: BUCK, CLAM

small potatoes [smɔ:l pəteɪtoʊz] count noun ** something of little importance or worth

🔵 always used in the plural form

"The sales commission is **small potatoes**. The bonus for making quota is where you make the real money."

small talk [smɔːl tɔːk] *non-count noun* ***
unimportant or idle conversation

🔟 *often used with* **make**

"I don't want to go to the party. I'm just not in the
mood for making **small talk**."

smooth over [smuːð oʊvɚ] *2 word sep verb* *** *to
correct problems or eliminate difficulties*

🔟 *the object is usually things*

"Hopefully these roses will help me **smooth** things
over with my wife."

See: IRON OUT

snap [snæp] *count noun* *** *something easily
accomplished*

🔟 *always preceded by* **a**

"I hooked up my new computer in just ten minutes
last night. It was a **snap**."

See: BREEZE, PIECE OF CAKE

snap at [snæp æt] *2 word insep verb, T* **** *to
speak irritably or abruptly at someone*

🔟 *the object is always a person, usually used in the
active voice*

"I'm pissed at her because she **snapped at** my mom
for no reason at all!"

snap out of it [snæp aʊt əv ɪt] *verb phrase* **** *to
return to one's normal state of mind*

"I know he's had a rough time, but he's just going to
have to **snap out of it**."

🔟 *often used in the imperative form*

"Hey Joey, you've been bummed all week. **Snap out of
it** buddy!"

See: GET A GRIP, PULL ONE'S SELF TOGETHER

snazzy [snæzi] *adj* ** *flashily attractive, fancy*

"That red Vette is pretty **snazzy**!"

sneak up on [sniːk ʌp ɑːn] *3 word verb* *** *to
approach someone stealthily or inconspicuously*

"Gerry, you scared the living daylights out of me!
Don't you ever **sneak up on** me like that again!"

"Tax time always **sneaks up on** me."

See: CREEP UP ON

sore [sɔːr] *adj* ** *upset, angry*

⚠ *slightly dated but still heard on occasion*

"Joe is still **sore** about losing that game last week."

🔟 *a person as an object is preceded by* **at**

"I'm still **sore** at him for blowing me off last week."

See: PISS OFF

sore loser [sɔːr luːzɚ] *count noun phrase* ** *poor
sport*

"I won't be playing anymore poker with Joe. He's a
sore loser."

sour [saʊɚ] *adj* *** *bad, unpleasant; used for
business or personal situations or relationships*

🔟 *usually used with the verb* **go**

"It was about 1995 when the real estate business
went **sour** and we had to declare bankruptcy."

space cadet [speɪs kədet] *count noun* *** *a flaky
or forgetful person*

"You are such a **space cadet**! This is the fifth time
you've locked your keys in your car!"

See: AIRHEAD, DINGBAT, DITZ, DUMMY

space out [speɪs aʊt] *2 word verb, I* **** *to
daydream or allow one's mind to wander*

🔟 *most commonly used in the continuous tenses*

"Your teacher says your grades are bad because you
are always **spacing out** in class."

"'What are you thinking about?' 'Nothing in particular;
I was just **spacing out**.'"

See: VEG

space out on [speɪs aʊt ɑːn]

1. *3 word verb* ***** *to miss an appointment or forget
a responsibility or duty*

"I know I was supposed to bring the book today, but I
spaced out on it. I'll make sure to bring it tomorrow."

🔟 *sometimes shortened to* **spaced on**

"Oh no! I **spaced on** my dentist appointment again."

See: SLIP ONE'S MIND

2. *3 word verb* ***** *to lose track of*

"Sorry I'm late. I started doing things around the
house and I **spaced out on** the time."

spacey [speɪsi] *adj* **** *strange, distant, or
stupefied*

"It's impossible to hold a conversation with Jay. He's
so **spacey**."

See: OUT OF IT

spic and span [spɪk ænd spæn] adj *** spotlessly clean, fresh and new

I spent all day cleaning up the kitchen, and now it's **spic and span.**

spill the beans [spɪl ðe biːnz] verb phrase * to reveal a secret

⚠ dated and slightly childish

"Someone must've **spilled the beans** about the surprise party 'cause Billy didn't look too surprised!"

See: LET SOMEONE IN ON SOMETHING

spin [spɪn] count noun *** a short drive

🔄 usually used in the singular, preceded by **a**

"What do you say you take me out for a **spin** in your new set of wheels?"

split [splɪt] verb, I **** to leave

"I've got to **split** after the next song."

See: BAIL, BE OFF, BOOK, GET GOING, HIT THE ROAD, JET

split up [splɪt ʌp] 2 word verb, I ***** to break up a romantic relationship, to divorce

"I didn't hear that Marisa and Jon **split up**! Who's going to take the kids?"

See: BREAK UP, CALL IT QUITS

sponge [spʌndʒ] count noun ** one who lives at the expense of others

🔄 usually preceded by **a**

"Darren hit you up for gas money again? What a **sponge**!"

See: MOOCH

sponge off of [spʌndʒ aːf əv] 3 word verb *** to borrow, to live at the expense of others

🔄 usage is always: **sponge something off of someone**; often, **of** is dropped

"Don't look now, but here comes Darren. He's been **sponging money off (of)** everybody left and right!"

See: BUM OFF OF, HIT UP FOR

sport [spɔːrt] verb, T ** to display or wear in a showy manner

"How did you score that new watch you're **sporting**? You've been telling me you're broke."

spot [spɑːt] verb, T **** to locate or identify

"See if you can **spot** John in this crowd. I'll keep my eyes open for Lisa."

spread [spred] count noun ** a ranch, a large house

"Gary bought a big **spread** up in the mountains."

spring for [sprɪŋ fɔːr] 2 word insep verb, T *** to pay for something

"You got the movie tickets, so I'll **spring for** the munchies."

stack up to [stæk ʌp tuː] 3 word verb **** to compare

"I know that company makes great cars, but how do they **stack up to** the car I drive now?"

stall [stɔːl]

1. verb, I *** to delay

"Come on, quit **stalling**, and let's get this show on the road."

See: BEAT AROUND THE BUSH

2. count noun *** a small compartment with a toilet in a public restroom

⚠ used mainly by men

"Steve got caught smoking in a **stall** in the high school restroom!"

stand up [stænd ʌp] 2 word sep verb *** to intentionally fail to keep an appointment

🔄 used in both the passive and active voices

"I can't believe he **stood** me **up**! I'll never talk to him again!"

See: BLOW OFF, CUT, DITCH

stand up for [stænd ʌp fɔːr] 3 word verb **** to speak or act in defense of

"If you don't **stand up for** yourself, no one else will."

See: STICK UP FOR

steal [stiːl] count noun ***** a bargain

🔄 always preceded by **a**

"She got that blue and green glass table for only twenty bucks? What a **steal**!"

steep [stiːp] adj *** overpriced

"The rental car is a hundred bucks a day? That's pretty **steep**."

See: PRICEY

stick around [stɪk ə raʊnd] 2 word insep verb, T **** to remain, stay, or linger

"You should **stick around** because there's a hot new band coming on after these guys."

"**Stick around** and we'll talk after the show."

stick-in-the-mud [stɪk ɪn ðe mʌd] count noun ** a boring person, one who is old fashioned or unprogressive

"Come snowboarding with us! Don't be such a **stick-in-the-mud**. It'll be fun!"

See: PARTY POOPER

stick up for [stɪk ʌp fɔːr] 3 word verb **** to speak or act in defense of

"Don't let them intimidate you! You have to **stick up for** yourself!"

See: STAND UP FOR

stiff [stɪf]

1. count noun *** a dead body

⚠ disrespectful to the deceased, often heard in movies and TV shows

"Let's get this **stiff** over to the city morgue."

2. count noun *** a boring or excessively formal person

⚠ slightly dated

"Who's the **stiff** standing next to Richard?"

3. verb, T ** to refuse to pay a bill or leave a tip

⏱ the object is always a person, used in the active and passive voice

"Mr. C's is supposed to be a five-star restaurant, but the service was so lousy that we ended up **stiffing** the waiter."

"Can you believe that guy? I bust my butt repairing his car and he **stiffs** me on the bill!"

stink [stɪŋk] verb, I /count noun **** to be offensive or bad; a public outcry

"You can't come on vacation with us? That **stinks**!"

"Tom's ideas always **stink**."

"Jonathan raised a **stink** when David stiffed him on the phone bill."

See: SUCK

stoked [stoʊkt] adj ***** excited or enthusiastic

⚠ used mainly by the younger generations, especially teenagers

"Bob is gonna be **stoked** when he see how big the surf is today."

⏱ if the object is stated, it is preceded by **about**

"The football team is really **stoked** about the game this weekend."

See: FIRED UP, PSYCHE UP

storm into [stɔːrm ɪntuː] 2 word verb *** to enter suddenly and forcefully, often because of anger or frustration

"Judging from the way she **stormed into** the house and headed straight up to her room, I'd say things didn't work out the way she had planned."

storm out of [stɔːrm aʊt əv] 3 word verb *** to leave suddenly and forcefully because of anger or frustration

"Did you see the way Inga **stormed out of** here? Henrich must have really insulted her!"

strapped for cash [stræpt fɔːr kæʃ] adj phrase ** to be short of money

"Sorry I can't lend you any dough, but I'm a little **strapped for cash** myself."

strip down to [strɪp daʊn tuː] 3 word verb ** to partially remove one's clothing

⏱ the object is a particular piece of clothing remaining

"Jake and Tom **stripped down to** their shorts and went swimming."

stuck with [stʌk] adj ** to be saddled with a burden or disagreeable responsibilty

"Her boyfriend ditched her at the restaurant, so she got **stuck** with the entire bill."

stuff one's face [stʌf wʌnz feis] verb phrase *** to eat a lot

"There is so much food on those ocean cruises! I spent the whole time **stuffing my face**!"

See: PIG OUT, POLISH OFF, PUT AWAY, WOLF DOWN

stump [stʌmp] verb ** to baffle or confuse

"Math test questions always **stump** me."

⏱ often used in the adjective form **stumped**

"Question four has me completely **stumped**."

suck [sʌk] verb, I ***** to be objectionable or unacceptable

⚠ many people find this word rude, but it is very common with younger generations

"That movie **sucked**! I can't believe I wasted my money and my time to see it."

⚠ this term can also have the following meanings: "that's too bad" or "I'm sorry to hear that"

"You got a 'C' on the test? That **sucks**! You really studied hard for it."

    See: STINK

sucker into [sʌkɚ ɪntuː] 2 word sep verb *** to fool, deceive, or hoodwink someone

⚠ the term **sucker** is considered rude by some people

🔊 always say: **sucker someone into something**

"I can't believe Phil **suckered** you **into** paying ten grand for that car! It's a piece of junk!"

suck up to [sʌk ʌp tuː] 3 word verb *** to seek favor by attention or flattery

"Of course Mandy got an 'A' on her paper. She's always **sucking up to** the teacher."

    See: KISS UP TO

sugarcoat [ʃʊgɚkoʊt] verb, T ** to make something that is unpleasant or unattractive sound better than it really is

"I'm a big girl and I can handle the gory details so please don't try to **sugarcoat** them."

sugar daddy [ʃʊgɚ dædí] count noun *** a rich older man who takes care of a young girl financially in exchange for companionship

"Get a load of that couple! He's old enough to be her grandfather. We're talking big-time **sugar daddy**!"

suit [suːt] count noun *** a businessperson, a professional

"You're going to work downtown? You're going to be with all the **suits**!"

suss out [sʌs] 2 word sep verb * to investigate, to inspect

"Let's **suss out** these files. I'm sure we'll find evidence of Leon's embezzling."

SUV [es juː viː] count noun **** abbreviation for Sports Utility Vehicle

"I'm planning to sell my **SUV** and buy something that gets better gas mileage."

swallow [swɑːloʊ] verb, T **** to accept without resentment, question, or protest

"Did you hear what he said about her? I just don't think I can **swallow** that."

sweat [swet] verb, T ***** to worry about, to exert oneself

⚠ used mainly by the younger generations

"That's OK if you forgot to bring my book today. Don't **sweat** it. Just bring it tomorrow."

"'I can't get these darn lug nuts loose!' 'Don't **sweat** it, we'll call a tow truck.'"

swing by [swɪŋ baɪ] 2 word insep verb, T **** stop somewhere briefly

"Could you **swing by** the store on your way home and pick up some ice cream?"

    See: DROP BY, RUN BY, SHOOT BY

swipe [swaɪp] verb, T *** to steal

⚠ sometimes followed by from right under one's nose, suggesting a blatant act of theft

"He swiped my idea from right under my nose."

    See: RIP OFF

T

tad [tæd] count noun *** a small amount, a little bit

🔊 always preceded by **a**

"Your sauce is almost perfect! It just needs a **tad** more salt."

"'How about a refill on your coffee?' 'OK, but just a **tad**, please.'"

tag along with [tæg əlɑŋ wɪθ] 3 word verb ** to go along with someone

"I was going to go home but if you guys are going shopping, I'll **tag along with** you."

take [teɪk]
   1. verb, T ***** to tolerate, put up with

℗ always used in the active voice

"Larisa is not going to **take** any more of Dimitri's abuse. I think she's about to walk."

   See: PUT UP WITH

2. count noun *** one's impression or opinion

⚠ used most commonly when asking for someone's opinion

℗ always preceded by a possessive pronoun

"What's your **take** on this matter?"

take a hike [teɪk ə haɪk] exp ** "get lost" or "go away"

⚠ very rude when used as an imperative

"**Take a hike**! I said I don't want to contribute."

"You should've told that guy who was bugging you to **take a hike**! Sometimes you are too nice to people."

   See: BEAT IT, SCRAM

take a nosedive [teɪk ə noʊzdaɪv] verb phrase ** to experience a sudden drop

"When we bought that stock it was at 125, but it **took a nosedive** and now it's at 38!"

take a stand [teɪk ə stænd] verb phrase *** to adopt a firm position

℗ if the object is stated, it is preceded by **on**

"It is important that we **take a stand** on this new legislation."

take care of [teɪk ker əv]

1. verb phrase **** to look after, watch

"Could you **take care of** my plants while I'm out of town?"

2. verb phrase *** to dispose of or fix a problem

⚠ occasionally a euphemism for kill

"She knows too much! **Take care of** her, but do it gently."

   See: BLOW AWAY, BUMP OFF, KNOCK OFF

take it easy [teɪk ɪt iːzi] verb phrase ***** to relax

"I'm just going to veg in front of the tube all weekend and **take it easy**."

   See: CHILL OUT, HANG OUT, KICK BACK, KICK IT

℗ in the imperative form means "**calm down**"

"Hey man, **take it easy**! It's nothing to get all bent out of shape over."

take one's hat off to [teɪk wʌnz hæt ɑːf tuː] verb phrase *** to express one's respect or admiration

℗ usually used in the following two patterns: **I've got to take my hat off to you** or **Let me take my hat off to you**

"You got those two brats into bed? **I've got to take my hat off to you**!"

   See: HAND IT TO SOMEONE

take out on [teɪk aʊt ɑːn] 3 word verb ***** to find a release for one's anger or frustration

℗ usage is always: **take something out on someone/ something**

"Every time my roommate has a problem at work he **takes** it **out on** me when he gets home. I'm really getting fed up!"

take the cake [teɪks ðe keɪk] verb phrase **** to be outstanding in some respect, good or bad

"Lucy, you've done a lot of nutty things, but giving all your possessions to some guru **takes the cake**!"

take up on [teɪk ʌp ɑːn] 3 word verb **** to accept an offer

"A drink after work? Sounds great. I think I'll **take** you **up on** that!"

talk into [tɔːk ɪntuː] 2 word sep verb **** to persuade someone to act

℗ in the active voice: **talk someone into something** or **doing something**; passive voice: **I was talked into something**

"If Nancy hadn't **talked** me **into** going out with Eddie, we never would've ended up together."

   See: TWIST SOMEONE'S ARM

talk out of [tɔːk aʊt əv] 3 word verb **** to dissuade someone from a particular course of action

℗ the use is always: **talk someone out of something** or **doing something**

"It's a good thing Joe **talked** me **out of** buying that expensive car or I'd be up to my ears in debt right now."

talk someone's ear off [tɔːk sʌmwʌnz ɪr ɑːf] verb phrase *** to talk incessantly, talk too much

"I hope we don't run into Jackie – she always ends up **talking our ears off**. I just don't have the time to listen to her today."

   See: BABBLE ON

talk through one's nose [tɔːk θruː wʌnz nouz]
verb phrase * to exaggerate or lie

⚠ slightly rude

"Don't pay attention to what Alfonso says about how much money he makes. He's always **talking through his nose**."

T-bird [tiː bɜːrd] count noun *** term for the Ford Thunderbird

"We had fun until her dad took her **T-bird** away."

tear out of [ter aʊt əv] 3 word verb ** to leave somewhere very quickly, usually in a moving vehicle

"Gerald must have been pissed off about something! Did you see the way he **tore out** of here?"

teensy [tiːnsɪ] adj **** small in size or amount

"I'm really full, but it was so yummy, I'll have a **teensy** bit more."

⚠ childish term, often used in jest. Sometimes followed by **weensy** for emphasis

"She was wearing nothing but a **teensy-weensy** bikini!"

tell [tel] verb, T/I ***** to recognize or know by observing

"You were wasted at the party? I couldn't **tell**!"

"You can **tell** Marty likes you by the way he looks at you."

that time of the month [ðæt taɪm əv ðe mʌnθ] count noun phrase ** the time when a woman menstruates

⚠ sometimes used as a disparaging comment about a woman who is in a bad mood

"Alicia just about bit my head off; must be **that time of the month**."

"You sure are in a lousy mood! Is it **that time of the month** again?"

See: PMS

the bomb

See: BOMB

there are a lot of fish in the sea [ðer aːr ə laːt əv fɪʃ ɪn ðe siː] exp *** "there are many prospects to choose from"

"Don't feel badly about Josh dumping you. He wasn't your type anyway. You're young and **there are a lot of fish in the sea**."

thrashed [θræʃt] adj **** worn out, ruined

"I walked all over Asia in these boots. They're totally **thrashed**."

through thick and thin [θruː θɪk ænd θin] adv phrase *** through good and bad times

"Don't worry honey, I'll be with you **through thick and thin**."

throw for a loop [θrou fɔːr ə luːp] verb phrase ** to confuse, surprise, or shock

"I thought he was going to break up with me given the way he's been acting. It totally **threw** me **for a loop** when he popped the question!"

throw in the towel [θrou ɪn ðe taʊəl] verb phrase *** to concede, to acknowledge defeat

"I can't figure out these math problems. I think I'll **throw in the towel**."

ticker [tɪkɚ] count noun *** a persons heart

"'I heard Bill is in the hospital. What's up?' 'It's his **ticker** again. He's having a pacemaker put in.'"

tied up [taɪd ʌp] adj phrase ***** occupied, to have a previous engagement

"I wish I could go to the game with you this weekend, but I'm **tied up**."

tie the knot [taɪ ðe naːt] verb phrase *** to get married

"So, Myrna, I hear you and Jim are thinking about **tying the knot**."

See: GET HITCHED

tight [taɪt] adj *** having a close personal or business relationship

"Michelle and I are **tight**. We've been through thick and thin together."

tightwad [taɪtwaːd] count noun *** a stingy or miserly person

"Don't expect the boss to give you a raise – he's a **tightwad**!"

tipsy [tɪpsi] adj *** slightly drunk

⚠ used commonly by girls

"Shahala is a real lightweight! She gets **tipsy** after drinking just half a beer."

See: BUZZED

TLC [ti: el si:] *count noun* ** abbreviation for **Tender Loving Care**.

"Don't throw that plant out! It's not dead, it just needs a little **TLC**."

toasted [toʊstɪd] *adj* *** drunk, intoxicated

"Don't pay any attention to what he says. He's **toasted**."

> See: BOMBED, GONE, HAMMERED, LOADED, MESSED UP, RIPPED, SLOSHED, TRASHED, WASTED

together [təgeðɚ] *adj* *** well organized with clear priorities

"Unlike her brother, Nancy is really **together**. She worked and saved her money to go to college."

> See: HAVE ONE'S HEAD ON RIGHT

ton [tʌnz] *count noun* ***** a large amount

🔘 sometimes stated as **a ton of**

"The teacher gave us **tons of (a ton of)** homework tonight, huh?"

> See: BUNCH, LOADS, MOUNDS, PLENTY

tongue-tied [tʌŋ taɪd] *adj* *** unable to say anything, usually due to fear, shock, or embarrassment

"Jun was **tongue-tied** his first day in English class, but now you can't shut him up!"

too rich for one's blood [tu: rɪtʃ fɔːr wʌnz blʌd] *adj phrase* ** too expensive

"Look at the prices on the menu! This is definitely **too rich for my blood!**"

toss [tɑːs] *verb, T* **** to throw away, discard

"I don't need those papers. You can **toss** them."

> See: GET RID OF

toss one's cookies [tɑːs wʌnz kʊkiz] *verb phrase* *** to vomit, feel nauseous

"The flight home was really turbulent. I thought I was going to **toss my cookies**."

> See: BARF, LOSE ONE'S LUNCH, PUKE

to top things off... [tu: tɑːp θɪŋz ɑːf] *exp* ***
"and even worse..."

> ⚠ usually used when complaining or criticizing

> 🔘 **and** usually precedes the phrase

"Jackie's roommate is always late with the rent, won't pay her share of the phone bill, and **to top things off**, she borrows her clothes without asking!"

tough cookie [tʌf kʊki] *count noun phrase* ** a determined individual, a person with strong character

> ⚠ positive undertones

"I think Jane can handle this job alone. She's a **tough cookie**."

toy with [tɔɪ wɪθ] *2 word insep verb, T* *** to treat someone in a trifling way, to joke with

"We're going to the Caribbean for our vacation? You're not **toying with** me are you?"

> ⚠ often refers to a person not being taken seriously

"That record company is just **toying with** you. They'll never sign you to a contract."

> See: FOOL WITH, MESS WITH, SCREW WITH

trash [træʃ]
1. *verb, T* **** to speak disparagingly about someone or something

"The critics really **trashed** that new action flick."

2. *verb, T* **** to destroy, vandalize

"They got bombed and **trashed** the hotel room. Now they have to pay through the nose to repair the damage."

trashed [træʃt] *adj* *** extremely intoxicated with drugs or alcohol

"The reason you feel so awful today is because you got **trashed** last night."

> See: BOMBED, GONE, HAMMERED, LOADED, MESSED UP, RIPPED, SLOSHED, TOASTED, WASTED

trip [trip]
1. *verb, I* **** to act crazily or foolishly

> 🔘 generally used in the present continuous tense

"You paid two hundred bucks for that piece of junk? Are you **tripping**?"

"I don't know what got into Irene last night. She was really **tripping**."

2. *count noun* ***** an exceptional, amazing, or entertaining experience or person

> 🔘 always preceded by **a** and generally used in the following two patterns:

"Skydiving was a **trip**!"

"My philosophy prof is a **trip**!"

trippy [tripi] adj *** strange, weird

"That tarot card reader was really **trippy**. She told me the most disturbing things!"

tube [tu:b] count noun *** TV, television

"What's on the **tube** tonight?"

turn the other cheek [tɜːrn ðe ʌðɚ tʃiːk] verb phrase *** to refuse to retaliate to injury or insult

"Be the bigger guy – just **turn the other cheek** and walk away."

twist someone's arm [twɪst sʌmwʌnz ɑːrm] verb phrase ** to persuade someone to do something

"I wanted to leave much earlier, but John **twisted my arm** and I ended up staying longer than I had planned."

See: TALK INTO

U

unwind [ʌnwaɪnd] verb, I ***** to mentally relax, release from tension

"I've had a rough day. I'm going home and taking a long, hot bath to **unwind**."

See: CHILL OUT, KICK BACK

...up a storm [ʌp ə stɔːrm] adv phrase *** in an energetic or extraordinary manner

used as an intensive

"Tom really dances **up a storm** when he goes out to the clubs."

"My girlfriend can really talk **up a storm** when she gets on the phone."

up-front [bi: ʌp frʌnt] adj/adv *** candid, frank

"OK doctor, I want you to be **up-front** with me; don't sugarcoat the facts."

up in the air [ʌp ɪn ðe er] adj phrase **** undecided

"Our plans for the weekend are still **up in the air**, so we're open to suggestions."

up to one's ears [ʌp tu: wʌnz ɪrz] adj phrase **** deeply involved, overwhelmed

"Since we bought this new house we've been **up to our ears** in bills! I haven't been able to buy one thing for myself."

use one's head [juːz wʌnz hed] verb phrase **** to apply one's intellect to solve a problem

"OK class, we don't spoon-feed students in these upper division courses. You're expected to **use your heads**."

 often used to admonish a person to face reality

"That's the fifth message you've left for them. **Use your head**! It's obvious they don't want to talk to us."

See: DUH, GET WITH THE PROGRAM, HELLO, WAKE UP AND SMELL THE COFFEE

V

veg [vedʒ] verb, I **** to relax with an inert or passive mental state (from vegetable)

"I'm beat! The only thing I feel like doing is **veging** in front of the TV all night."

See: SPACE OUT

vent [vent] verb, I *** to complain loudly or expressively

"Why don't you take Donna for a short walk? I think she needs to **vent**."

"I'm all ears if you need to **vent**. You'll feel better if you let it out."

See: BITCH, BLOW OFF SOME STEAM

Vette [vet] count noun *** nickname for the Chevrolet Corvette

"Vic just bought a brand new red **Vette**."

VW [vi: dʌblju:] count noun ** term for any automobile manufactured by Volkswagen

sometimes pronounced: vi: dʌb

"Ricki showed up to school in a brand new **VW**."

W

wacko [wækoʊ] adj/count noun ***** crazy; a crazy or strange person

⚠ usually used in jest but should be used with care as it could be taken the wrong way

"Not again! I have to take physics from that **wacko** professor."

"You should meet my friend Haruna. She's a real **wacko**! One time she…"

See: CRACKPOT, NUT, NUTCASE

wacky [wæki] adj **** crazy, eccentric

⚠ generally used in jest

"That's a **wacky** idea but you know, it just might work."

See: COCKAMAMIE, CRACKPOT, CUCKOO, LOONY, NUTTY, WACKO

wake up and smell the coffee [weɪk ʌp ænd smel ðe kɑːfi] exp **** "become aware" or "face reality"

"She thinks they're going to get married? He's such a playboy! She needs to **wake up and smell the coffee**!"

⚠ often used to admonish

"**Wake up and smell the coffee**, honey. That guy is never gonna marry you."

See: GET WITH IT, GET WITH THE PROGRAM

wake up on the wrong side of the bed [weɪk ʌp ɑːn ðe rɑːŋ saɪd əv ðe bed] verb phrase *** to be in a bad mood for no particular reason

"What's eating you? Did you **wake up on the wrong side of the bed** today?"

walk [wɑːk] verb, I ** to withdraw from a situation, to quit a job

"If the boss gets on my case again, I'm going to **walk**!"

walk all over [wɑːk ɔːl oʊvɚ] 3 word verb *** to treat someone badly or disrespectfully, to take advantage of someone

🅖 the object is always a person

"Don't let your boss **walk all over** you. He has no right to ask you to work overtime without pay."

"I think she's out of her mind. He **walks all over** her and then she brings him breakfast in bed!"

walk in on [wɑːk ɪn ɑːn] 3 word verb *** to surprise someone in an embarrassing situation

🅖 generally used in the simple past tense; the object is usually a person

"The boss **walked in on** her while she was taking money from the register."

⚠ used when catching a lover with another person

"He **walked in on** her while she was with another guy."

walk out on [wɑːk aʊt ɑːn] 3 word verb **** to abandon or desert, to withdraw abruptly

"Don't bring up the subject of kids. He's very sensitive because his wife **walked out on** him and took the kids with her."

🅖 sometimes **out** is dropped to emphasize severity

"I can't believe he **walked on** that business deal! It was the chance of a lifetime!"

wasted [weɪstɪd] adj ***** very intoxicated with drugs or alcohol

"Joe's so **wasted** he didn't even recognize me!"

See: BOMBED, GONE, HAMMERED, LOADED, MESSED UP, RIPPED, SLOSHED, TOASTED, TRASHED

watch one's back [wɑːtʃ wʌnz bæk] verb phrase *** to exercise caution, to be wary

"We'll have to **watch our backs** on this business deal."

⚠ often used as an admonition

"I just don't trust Nicky. You'd better **watch your back**."

way [weɪ] adv ***** much, really

"I don't agree with you. George's fish tacos are **way** better than Alfonso's!"

way to go [weɪ tu goʊ] exp ***** "good job!"

"You aced the test? **Way to go**, dude!"

weasel out of [wiːzəl aʊt əv] 3 word verb *** to back out of a commitment or evade an obligation, particularly when done in a devious manner

🅖 sometimes **one's way** is added after **weasel** for emphasis

"I'm supposed to hook up with Janet later, but I'll see if I can **weasel my way** out of it."

See: GET OUT OF, WORM OUT OF

weed out [wiːd aʊt] 2 word sep verb *** to discard the bad or less desirable things or people

"This course will **weed out** those of you who are not serious about a career in medicine."

"You've got a tough job in front of you. We've got ten good candidates and you have to **weed out** five of them."

weirdo [wɪrdoʊ] count noun **** a strange or odd person

⚠ used both seriously and in jest

"Roll up your windows and lock your doors. That guy heading over here looks like a **weirdo**."

what brings you to this neck of the woods? [hwaːt brɪŋz ju: tu: ðis nek əv ðe wʊdz] exp *** "why are you in this area?"; a general greeting to inquire about one's well being

"Hey Shiro, **what brings you to this neck of the woods?**"

what came over someone? [hwaːt kæm oʊvɚ sʌmwʌn] exp **** acknowledgment that a person's behavior is abnormal; "why is one behaving strangely?"

"I don't know **what came over Brad**. It's not like him to fly off the handle like that."

what do you say? [hwaːt du: ju: seɪ] exp ****
"would you consider?"

ⓟ change the subject pronoun (most commonly **you** or **we**) to reflect to whom the suggestion is being made, the base verb follows

"**What do you say** we/you paint the fence this weekend?"

what do you take me for? [hwaːt du: ju: teɪk mi: fɔːr] exp *** "do you think I'm a fool?"

"You want me to put ten grand into your almost bankrupt business? **What do you take me for?**"

See: LOOK LIKE ONE WAS BORN YESTERDAY

whatever gets you going [hwaːtevɚ gets ju: goʊɪŋ] exp *** "everyone has their own tastes"

⚠ usually said to acknowledge differing tastes

"'Check out that chick over there, she's hot!' 'Her? Uh, well, **whatever gets you going**.'"

See: DIFFERENT STROKES FOR DIFFERENT FOLKS

what gives? [hwaːt gɪvz] exp *** "what is going on?" or "I want an explanation"

"You and Khalid broke up and you haven't told me yet? **What gives?**"

what's eating someone? [hwaːts iːtɪŋ sʌmwʌn] exp **** "what's bothering someone?"

"You haven't been yourself lately. **What's eating you?**"

See: WHAT'S GOTTEN INTO SOMEONE, WHAT'S WITH SOMEONE

what's gotten into someone? [hwaːts gaːtən ɪntu: sʌmwʌn] exp **** acknowledgment that a person's behavior is abnormal; "why is one behaving strangely?"

ⓟ may be used in the 1st, 2nd, or 3rd person

"**What's gotten into you** lately? It's not like you to blow a fuse over getting a 'B' on an exam."

"I wonder **what's gotten into Sam?** He's usually pretty easygoing."

See: WHAT'S EATING SOMEONE, WHAT'S WITH SOMEONE

what's his/her face [hwaːts ɪz/ɚ feɪs] exp **** term used to refer to a person whose name has been forgotten; "I can't remember his/her name"

"You know who I mean, **what's his face**, the cute Japanese guy who's always late to class."

what's up? [hwaːts ʌp]
1. exp ***** "hello"

⚠ used in this manner mainly by the younger generations

"Bob, **what's up?**"

2. exp ***** "what's going on?" or "what's new?"

ⓟ when another greeting precedes **What's up?** (e.g., **hey** or **hi**) the meaning then becomes **What's new?**

⚠ used in this manner by all generations

"'Hey Paul, **what's up?**' 'Hey Richard, nothing much. **What's up** with you?'"

3. exp **** "what can I do for you?", "what do you need?", or "what are the plans?"

"'Amy, you called me earlier, **what's up?**' 'I need a favor. Do you think you could give me a hand with the kids this weekend?'"

what's up with that? [hwaːts ʌp wɪθ ðæt] exp ** "I don't understand" or "I'd like an explanation"

⚠ used to express disbelief or surprise

"Did you hear that Scott got sacked? **What's up with that?** He was one of our best employees."

what's with someone? [hwɑːts wɪθ sʌmwʌn] *exp* ***** *acknowledgment that a person's behavior is abnormal*

"**What's with him?** He's usually so easygoing. I asked him a simple question and he bit my head off!"

> *See:* WHAT'S EATING SOMEONE, WHAT'S GOTTEN INTO SOMEONE

wheel [hwiːl] *count noun* **** *a steering wheel*

🌐 usually preceded by **the**

"I don't want you behind the **wheel** – you've had too much to drink. I'll drive."

when hell freezes over [hwen hel friːzɪz oʊvɚ] *exp* **** *"never"*

"'When are you going to let me drive your new car?' '**When hell freezes over!**'"

> *See:* IN ONE'S DREAMS, IT'LL BE A COLD DAY IN HELL, NOT IN A MILLION YEARS, WHEN PIGS FLY

when pigs fly [hwen pɪgz flaɪ] *exp* * *"never"*

"'When do you think he's going to return the tools he borrowed?' '**When pigs fly.** I'll have to go over to his place and pick them up myself.'"

> *See:* IN ONE'S DREAMS, IT'LL BE A COLD DAY IN HELL, NOT IN A MILLION YEARS, WHEN HELL FREEZES OVER

where have you been hiding/keeping yourself? [hwer hæv juː bɪn haɪdɪŋ/kiːpɪŋ jɜrself] *exp* *** *"it's been a long time since we last met"*

"'How's it going Johnny? **Where have you been hiding yourself?**' 'Anne, long time, no see! How have you been?'"

> *See:* LONG TIME, NO SEE

whip out [hwɪp aʊt] *2 word sep verb* **** *to pull out something quickly*

"That guy just **whipped out** a wad of dough thick enough to choke a horse! He must be loaded."

whip someone's butt [hwɪp sʌmwʌnz bʌt] *verb phrase* ** *punish someone severely; to defeat decisively*

⚠ somewhat coarse

"If you kids don't knock it off, your father is going to **whip your butts** when he gets home!"

🌐 used in the active and passive voice, especially with **get**

"You want to race me? You'd better be ready to get **your butt whipped!**"

> *See:* KICK SOMEONE'S BUTT

whip up [hwɪp ʌp] *2 word sep verb* *** *to produce or assemble something quickly*

"Deedee **whipped up** that chocolate cake from scratch!"

white lie [hwaɪt laɪ] *count noun* **** *a harmless lie told to spare someone's feelings*

"We couldn't tell Vladimir that Anna thought he was a loser, so we made up a **white lie.**"

whole nine yards [hoʊl naɪn jɑːrdz] *count noun phrase* *** *the entire thing, everything that is relevant.*

⚠ positive undertones

🌐 always preceded by **the**

"I went to Amanda's wedding last Saturday. They had a sit-down dinner, open bar, twelve piece band – the **whole nine yards.**"

wimp [wɪmp] *count noun* **** *a weak person, a coward*

"Go ahead, ask her out on a date! Don't be such a **wimp!**"

> *See:* CHICKEN, SCAREDY-CAT

wimp out [wɪmp aʊt] *2 word insep verb, I* **** *to back out, lose one's nerve*

⚠ commonly used by men to describe other men

"Bill was supposed to hit his boss up for a raise, but he **wimped out** at the last minute."

> *See:* CHICKEN OUT, GET COLD FEET, WIMP OUT OF/ON

wimp out of/on [wɪmp aʊt əv/ɑːn] *3 word verb* **** *to back out, lose one's nerve*

🌐 the object is always a thing or an activity

"I can't believe Tom **wimped out** of the game/skydiving/asking for a raise."

> *See:* CHICKEN OUT, GET COLD FEET, WIMP OUT

windbag [wɪndbæg] *count noun* ** *an exhaustively talkative person*

"That **windbag** kept me on the phone for over an hour!"

🌐 often used in the form: **bag of wind**

window shop [wɪndoʊ ʃɑːp] *verb phrase* *** to view goods for sale without the intention of purchasing

"'Do you want to go shopping this weekend?' 'Just **window shopping**, thanks. I'm broke!'"

wind up [waɪnd ʌp]

1. *2 word sep verb* **** to finish, conclude something

"We have one more thing to cover before we **wind up** the meeting."

> *See:* WRAP UP

2. *adj phrase* **** excited, agitated

"It's almost bedtime so don't get the kids all **wound up** or they won't be able to get to sleep."

3. *2 word insep verb, T* ***** to arrive at or result in

"If you don't straighten yourself out, you're going to **wind up** in jail."

Ⓟ often the object is a gerund

"We wanted to see that new movie but the tickets were sold out. We **wound up** renting some videos and eating pizza at home."

> *See:* END UP

wind up in [waɪnd ʌp ɪn] *3 word verb* **** to arrive at an unexpected destination

Ⓟ the object is usually a place

"I thought I was going home but I took the wrong freeway entrance and **wound up in** Carlsbad!"

> *See:* END UP IN

wind up over [waɪnd ʌp oʊvɚ] *3 word verb* ***** to agitate or excite

Ⓟ when used in the active voice it is usually used in the negative imperative form with a reflexive object pronoun

"Don't **wind** yourself **up over** this, it's not worth it."

Ⓟ used frequently in the adjective form wound up

"He's pretty **wound up** after that argument. I'd let him cool down if I were you."

> *See:* GET WORKED UP

wing [wɪŋ] *verb, T* ** to improvise

"I hadn't prepared my speech in time for class and the teacher called on me. I had to **wing** it, but I think I did OK."

> *See:* PLAY IT BY EAR

wiped out [waɪpt aʊt] *adj phrase* *** exhausted, very tired

"We spent all day skiing. I'm really **wiped out**!"

> *See:* BEAT, DEAD, POOPED, WORN OUT

wipe out [waɪp aʊt]

1. *2 word insep verb* *** to fall or crash usually as a result of losing control

"I was skiing down the hill too fast and **wiped out** big-time!"

> *See:* EAT

2. *2 word sep verb* *** to cause to become tired or exhausted

"That run **wiped** me **out**!"

wishy-washy [wɪʃi wɑʃi] *adj* ** indecisive, unable to make up one's mind

"You're always so **wishy-washy**! Please make a decision!"

with it [wɪθ ɪt] *adj phrase* **** up-to-date, cool, fashionable

"I really like our new teacher. He's really **with it**."

> *See:* HIP

wolf down [wʊlf daʊn] *2 word sep verb* *** to eat very quickly

"'Oh man, I have indigestion again.' 'I'm not surprised, given the way you **wolf down** your food.'"

> *See:* PIG OUT, POLISH OFF, PUT AWAY, STUFF ONE'S FACE

wolf in sheep's clothing [wʊlf ɪn ʃiːps kloʊðɪŋ] *count noun phrase* ** a person who conceals a hostile intention with a friendly manner

Ⓟ usually preceded by **a**

"Hiroyuki looks so sweet and innocent, but don't let appearances fool you. He's a **wolf in sheep's clothing**!"

word [wɜːrd] *count noun* ***** a short conversation, often of a serious nature

Ⓟ usually used with **a**

"Jessy, before you head home, I'd like to have a **word** with you."

word is... [wɜːrd ɪz] *exp* ***** "the rumor is..." "the gossip is..."

Ⓟ generally preceded by **the**

"The **word is** that the company is going to can all of the sales managers."

work one's butt/balls off [wɜːrk wʌnz bʌt/bɑːlz ɑːf] *verb phrase* **** to work very hard

⚠ *typically, only males use the coarse term* **balls** *(testicles)*

"She **worked her butt off** for them, but they always snubbed her on the promotion she wanted."

See: BUST ONE'S BALLS/BUTT/HUMP

work out [wɜːrk aʊt] *2 word insep verb, I* ***** to engage in a physical exercise program

"It's been almost 2 months since I've gone to the gym. I really need to **work out** – I'm starting to get a gut!"

work up over [wɜːrk ʌp oʊvɚ] *3 word verb* ** to become agitated and angry, to become upset

"Don't get all **worked up over** this memo. I'm sure it's just a misunderstanding."

worm out of [wɜːrm aʊt əv] *3 word verb* *** to evade responsibility for an obligation or commitment

"David always manages to **worm out of** his obligations."

🔟 *sometimes* **one's way** *follows* **worm** *for emphasis*

"Can you believe Lucy **wormed** her way **out of** another meeting!"

See: GET OUT OF, WEASEL OUT OF

worn out [wɔːrn aʊt]

1. *adj* **** physically tired or exhausted

"I'm **worn out**. Let's call it a day, and start again tomorrow morning."

See: BEAT, DEAD, POOPED, WIPED OUT

2. *2 word sep verb* ** to cause to become extremely tired or exhausted

"Taking care of kids will really **wear** you **out**."

wrap up [ræp ʌp] *2 word sep verb* *** to conclude, to finish; to summarize

"Before we **wrap up** today's class, there is one final point I'd like to go over."

🔟 *the object is often dropped*

"Before we **wrap up**, there is one final point I'd like to go over."

See: WIND UP

wrapped up in [ræp ʌp ɪn] *adj phrase* *** deeply involved

"Don't bother me right now. I'm really **wrapped up in** this book."

wreck [rek] *count noun* ***** something in a state of damage or ruin; a person in poor physical or mental health

 generally used with **a**

"The house was a **wreck** after the party. It took us two days to get it cleaned up."

"He was really a **wreck** after his wife walked out on him."

wrong crowd [rɑːŋ kraʊd] *count noun phrase* *** a group of rebellious young troublemakers, typically of high school age

🔟 *usually preceded by* **the**

"We worried about her because she was always hanging out with the **wrong crowd** in high school."

Y

yeah, right [jæ raɪt] *exp* *** sarcastic response to a question or comment; "unlikely" or "no way!"

"'So, are you going out with Biff again?' **Yeah, right**. It'll be a cold day in hell before I go out with that loser again!'"

See: FAT CHANCE, IN ONE'S DREAMS

yellow [jeloʊ] *adj* * cowardly

"Don't be **yellow**! You can do it!"

you can say that again [ju kæn seɪ ðæt əgen] *exp* ***** "I strongly agree with you"

"'Man, today is a real scorcher!' **You can say that again**! It's hot enough to fry an egg on the sidewalk!'"

See: I HEAR YOU, YOU'RE TELLING ME

you're telling me [juːr telɪŋ miː] *exp* **** "I am well aware of that"

"'That calculus assignment is a real killer!' **You're telling me**! I've been working on it for six hours, and I'm still not finished!'"

See: I HEAR YOU, YOU CAN SAY THAT AGAIN

Z

you've got me [juːv gɑːt miː] *exp* *****
"I don't know"

"'What was the homework assignment for today?'
'**You've got me**! I was spacing out the whole class.'"

See: BEATS ME

zero in on [zɪroʊ ɪn ɑːn] *3 word verb* *** to focus
on, direct one's attention at

"We found the problem and **zeroed in on** it
immediately."

you've got my vote [juːv gɑːt maɪ voʊt] *exp* ***
"I agree with your suggestion"

"'Let's call it a day and head home.' **You've got my
vote**! I'm beat!'"

zoo [zuː] *count noun* **** a chaotically busy place

⏺ always used in the singular

"The DMV was really a **zoo** today!"

See: MADHOUSE

yummy [jʌmi] *adj* ***** delicious

⚠ used in casual situations as it has childish
undertones, but is widely used by all age groups

"These cookies are **yummy**!"

For information about the optional audio tape or CD that accompanies <u>Ya Gotta Know It!</u> or to
inquire about any of our other books and tapes, contact Optima Books at the address below:

Optima Books
2820 Eighth Street
Berkeley, CA 94710

Toll free:

Phone 1-877-710-2196
FAX   1-800-515-8737

Outside US:

Phone 1-510-848-8708
FAX   1-510-848-8737

Order on-line at: optimabooks.com

email: esl@optimabooks.com

If you find any errors in this book, please bring them to our attention so that they can be corrected
for the next printing.

4633